6.95

Children
and Dance
and Music

BY OLGA MAYNARD

The Ballet Companion, a primer on ballet.

The American Ballet, a study of ballet from
Colonial into contemporary times.

Bird of Fire: Story of Maria Tallchief, study of
a 20th century American ballerina in her setting.

American Modern Dancers: The Pioneers, a history of
Modern dance.

Enjoying Opera, a book for the new opera goer.

Children
and Dance
and Music

OLGA MAYNARD

Charles Scribner's Sons, New York

This book is for my daughters-in-law:

SUSAN SWEENEY MAYNARD

PAMELA MAYNARD

POLOTEMI MAYNARD

SUSAN FIELDS MAYNARD

MARTHA COONEY MAYNARD

*and all who, like these, are parents
and teachers of growing children*

Contents

Musical education is of the greatest importance, a more potent instrument than any other, because rhythm and harmony penetrate very deeply to the inward places of the soul, and affect it most powerfully, imparting grace . . . one who has been so trained will commend and enjoy the noble and good, blame and hate the bad . . . with a true taste . . . now in the days of his youth, even before he is able to know the reason why; and when reason comes he will recognise and salute the friend with whom his education has made him long familiar.

PLATO: *The Dialogues,*
Book III of *The Republic.*

Author's Note

IN THE United States today we have more than 1,400 symphony orchestras, over half the orchestras in the world. There are even more chamber music ensembles, professional and amateur, with at least 100 colleges maintaining chamber music ensembles in residence. There are over 750 opera groups, more than 200 dance troupes, about 40,000 theatrical enterprises that include the musical arts.*

Cinema, radio and television, regardless of subject matter, have musical formats; mass media communication about the news and weather is accompanied by music. Science and industry utilize music to stimulate production by animals and increase efficiency in human workers. Medicine is making use of dance and music as physical and mental therapy for the ill.

Music in America is a vast commercialized project as well as art form. Four big record clubs gross approximately $80 billion per annum, from an approximate membership of 2,500,000. Instruments, like guitars, are manufactured wholesale.

Man-made and machine-recorded, music is the most ordinary artistic experience of daily life. In our time and place we Americans hear more music than any other people have heard in the history of mankind. Music is piped like gas and water into our homes, offices and factories, and into restaurants and railroad depots. We work and play to music, most of us worship in church with music, music underlines mundane and significant acts, a palpitating carpet of sound; music stands as the background for every imaginable purpose. In all seriousness, we have already been offered music for every reason, except as "music to listen to music by."

* As determined by the Rockefeller Panel Report on dance, music and theatre in the United States of America, 1965.

Since music is inescapable in contemporary society it is an inevitable experience for the child. It floods the air in the hospital, when he is born, and continues thereafter to permeate life into the grave, in burial services of the church.

The child at home, in school and among his peers, as a social person, hears music almost as continuously as he hears speech. Then, are not children so exposed to musical stimulus as to require nothing save instruction in techniques for performance, and theory for composition? And are not children also sufficiently stimulated through theatre, cinema, and television dance to develop "natural" talents for dancing without further encouragement and aid?

Before we reply to such queries we need to inquire into the musical estate in America, and the attitude towards music in contemporary society. If we approach music from the child's point of view we discover (as he soon does) there are social as well as artistic mores in musical forms and styles. There is not simply good and bad music as degrees of excellence or mediocrity but "good" and "bad" as abstract virtues, in popular ideas.

Music is the voice of protest and evangelism, and agitation, in modern society. There is a *morality in music* whereby music, like hair, is believed to have adverse influences on adolescents. They, in turn, use music as symbol of defiance of authority and also as expressions of their inchoate feelings about growing up.

The criteria of "good" and "bad" music is no longer made only by musicians; social savants and the clergy, parents and educators, take it on themselves to qualify music. Music as a battle for propriety and freedom, between generations, has been fostered as a cult by businessmen acting as music makers and entrepreneurs. Music is being chastized and villified (in "pop" styles and modern "forms") to such extent that we might fear its total ban from America, in the return to a Puritan horror of 'sweet, seductive sounds that steal away the soul' and 'wanton ditties' that enchant—and, with these, 'lascivious dancing . . . especially after feasts.' The shades of John Cotton, William Bradford, John Endecott and their fellows still obscure a great deal of American opinion on the arts of dance and music.

Puritanical laws are unlikely to be passed to control music, but social mores already positively influence attitudes and approaches to music in America.

At the same time that we have entered on a grand musical renaissance, said to exceed that of the Medieval European—and despite the establishment of a mass culture in society—there is not yet a thorough understanding of the character of music, as there is not yet a total concept of the true nature of the arts. When we approach the child in studied attempts to introduce him to dance and music, we must admit that we have so used music for propaganda as to have abused it.

"Piped audio" is the principal and most public abuse of music. Music has become an inescapable experience twenty-four hours of the day—an outrage against privacy, that we accept with incredible fortitude and apathy. Medical science studies the injurious effects of contemporary noise on human beings, and part of that noise is musical. Incessant sound, even when it is from so-called "good" music, stupefies the mind and exacerbates the nerves. Music without stint ruins the musicianly ear and satiates the sense of taste in art.

Children compelled to live in homes and work in schools to persistent music insulate themselves from hearing; they do not listen, in a real sense. In this earliest time a child is powerless to stem or alter the musical flood. Later, when he can assert his independence, he chooses music that he makes his own, and plays it at tremendous volume, obliterating all other sound. Adolescents today are musical bigots, ignorant of almost any musical form except the current popular or faddist music, quick to derogate other music, but unable to qualify, intelligently, the music that they call old, out-worn, and not in style.

On what is considered the credit side of the musical ledger, children are being encouraged to sing, dance and make music in terms human and divine. In work-and-play activities, especially for children of the illiterate and poor, dance and music are now instructional tools. The churches show a surging interest in music, and a nicely balanced choice between the old and the new—some of the new being used in wonderfully inventive ways to relate to ordinary life. More than any other agency, religion has made good use of radio and television for music and dance. Methodists are singing, the Mormons dancing and the Episcopalians commissioning instrumental music (to name only three denominations) with unprecedented energy and enthusiasm. Even the laggard Federal government, the least artistically minded government in any nation today, has bestirred itself to patronize musical arts, and, even, to apportion funds for them.

We balance, therefore, between heights and depths in American music. It is this precarious route that the child travels in an approach to musical arts.

Children and Dance and Music describes a series of approaches to children, and their responses. It is a useful book for parents and teachers by merit of being a true book. It is not written as a theoretical treatise but as the compilation of case histories of work with real children. I have divided the material into parts pertinent to *The Child at Home, The Child in School* and *The Child as a Social Person*. In response to the earnest requests of many parents, I have also written here of *The Child as Artist*.

There are a great number of books on children, and dance, and music. In the wide variety of books on these subjects there is a range between books which promise to teach any kind of child to make music of any kind, generally in a few, easy lessons, and books which quote statistical proof that musical-mindedness and ability are exceedingly rare. These books vary from the euphemistic notion that every infant is a potential virtuoso, to the dismal premise that very few children need or desire music in their lives. *Children and Dance and Music* is wholly unlike books of these conventions.

My work with children and dance and music has been continuous for more than thirty years, but I am not a professional dancer and musician or a dance and music teacher. My work, more precisely, is with the values of theatre arts as applied in practice within education, and in such work I believe dance and music to be the most cogent of the arts, capable of arousing the deepest and most spontaneous responses.

I have no formulas for discovering musical genius or encouraging musical talent. I do not even undertake to offer guides on how to make children "love" music. Scientists have ways of stimulating set responses but the arts must be loved for their own, true sakes.

Children—like adults—grow to like or dislike music from emotions arising out of personal associations with certain forms and styles in music. Such responses are psychological but there is another, much deeper psychical element, whereby all children, because they are sentient beings, respond to music.

In working in musical arts the scope is extraordinarily wide since poetry and drama, as well as dance, have musical properties. To clarify: *all rhyme and rhythm are "musical"* within the ideal of "values" of the arts. My principles of applying these values in education may be said to relate to the Platonic concept of the artistic life, and the gymnastic life integrated into the artistic one—such concept encourages the unity of dance with song and instrumentation, and of poetry and drama with dance and music. It is a concept within lyrical theatre arts, creative and performing.

This concept is the foundation of all my work with children, and the children with whom I have worked include the "average" within the physical and mental norms; and the "exceptional," which in American education categorizes children who are aurally deaf as well as children estimated to have superior intelligence (called "gifted"). I have also worked with children who were considered to be anti-social, in that they would not or could not work, to the accepted norm, in groups of their peers; and children described as delinquent, in that they had no love or respect for persons and property, including themselves as persons. Children of so-called "minority" groups, racial and religious; and children from "deprived" and "underprivileged" societies (social environments and "cultures" far below the economic norm in contemporary urban America) are also among the "types" with whom I have worked. The basics of my pilot programs are in effect in such projects as Head Start and Titles I and III—but also in effect among social strata of "senior citizens" and persons retired from active employment. Although my work is loosely classified as "enrichment resource" and is most often included under Recreation, it is integrated into Education.

While the practice of my work is based on a flexibility of approach to match the variety of response, the principles in which I work are adamant. I do not advocate mass culture by mechanized media, and I believe that commercial use of music has abused music. I believe, too, that if education presumes to make use of music merely as an instructional tool, within techniques or methodologies for indoctrinating students in set curricula, education will eventually misuse music. I feel that the mass culture which Americans are said to be developing must be founded on *ethics in art*, and that we must recognize these, as true moral values.

My premise is that the arts exist of themselves and in the course of history have achieved standards, the *quality of excellence* by which master-works in art are recognized. Therefore we in America, in establishing national arts and national culture, must aspire to artistic standards—we cannot make our standards day to day, and regionally, simply to please and flatter—even, to encourage—American artists and American audiences. The *pursuit of excellence* is an artistic trait, as it is also artistic acumen to differentiate between excellence and mediocrity. Any attempt to approach the arts, especially for children, must be predicated by such knowledge, and the definitions between "creativity" and what is dubbed "creative work-play." In the art world, we need to know and accept the distinctions that qualify art by the professional and by the amateur.

This premise is the very vital basis of my work with children, and it should be known and understood by readers of this book. My principles are controversial within certain aspects of contemporary education, and infuriate and dismay those who advocate a quick, easy and universal "culture" for the masses. The idea of "culture" for some of my contemporaries is a horticultural one: that a layer spread judiciously over a certain social strata will cause an artistic and intellectual apperception to bloom. On the contrary, I tend to treat culture as anthropologists do: a root source more influential than heredity. While philanthropists are congratulating themselves on enriching the lots of "underprivileged" American children, I deplore the rapidly diminishing artistic life in schools for children who are not economically deprived, but are likely to become culturally so.

Art is older than Education, and more universal, as children instinctively know.

Children become educated, whether approached or not—they learn more from choice than through applied techniques and methodologies, and children learn from each other perhaps more and more easily than they learn from adult teachers. To develop American culture, we must all contribute to it; it cannot be cultivated in single homes, and in only a few districts, in a hot-house climate, but must exist and persist in a national standard of education. Education is not merely the concern of many but of all, because, ultimately, the national standard affects the national character.

I believe this, and have therefore written *Children and Dance and Music* for the general reader, not as a text book particular only to some types of readers. The pilot program material can be extracted for use but the book is essentially one about the *personal associations* formed by children with dance and music. Parent and teacher must read the book in entirety, even though the parent will find the first two parts more pertinent; the teacher, the second two. Throughout, the child moves in his total environment, at home, in school; as the artist, as a social person. And parent and teacher, equally, will need to accept my principles of treating the child as a person in his time and place, while approaching the arts in their timeless and incorruptible character.

The book pertains to the infant to age five; the child who, about age six, begins "normal" school; and the adolescent, into the teens.

The programs described here were formulated, conducted and evaluated with the help of several teachers, who put them into practice in a variety of classroom courses; many adolescents, graduates of earlier programs, helped me to evaluate responses. My debt to these teachers and students is, of course, incalculable.

I include material from four sources: the informed approach by a musician and music teacher to *The Child at Home,* by Sara Kreger; insight into the musical mind of *The Child as Artist*, from composer Conrad Susa; experiments in creativity through contemporary music for *The Child in*

School, from *Contemporary Music Project,* Music Educators National Conference, 1966-67; and in *The Child as a Social Person,* demonstration programs by choreographer-dancer-teacher Bruce King on methods of teaching children's creative dance.

Quotations appear by courtesy of the authors' publishers, as follows: Houghton Mifflin Company for Havelock Ellis and Sydney J. Harris; Charles Scribner's Sons for George Santayana; Methuen & Company, England, for Oscar Wilde; and The Museum of Modern Art, New York, for Harold Taylor, excerpt from his lectures for the National Committee on Art Education.

SARA KREGER earned her music degree from University of the Pacific, Stockton; University of California at Berkeley; San Francisco State College; and San Diego State College, California. She studied choral music in workshops taught by Robert Shaw and Julius Herford, at SDSC. As teacher of choral music Mrs. Kreger has worked with mixed (co-educational) and boys' choirs, glee clubs, and sacred and secular groups up to 1,500 singers. This work has been in education and recreation, the latter including choral programs in state hospitals, homes for the aged, and houses of correction for juveniles. She has worked with speech therapists, as consultant and in her own programs correcting speech defects through music; and as music therapist, through University of the Pacific, with mentally ill patients in Stockton State Hospital. Her teaching has been in elementary education and college, and, also, teacher-training, including classroom demonstrations in music teaching (for teachers). She has produced, directed and conducted large-scale musical programs in school and college and for spring festivals, in choral forms ranging from madrigal to oratorio. Special teaching includes music workshops for "gifted" students in Music Educators National Conference, and experimental programs for the Oakland, Calif. City Recreation Department. These projects include studies in theory and composition, organized rhythms and conventional instruments, and extend to creative dance, music and choral forms ranging from madrigal to opera. For radio, Mrs. Kreger wrote and taped hour-long scripts of music analysis and appreciation for high school, college and general adult audiences, in a program: "Let's Begin With Music" for SDSC radio station KEBS-FM, San Diego. She now tutors in music theory and her own principles of "Singing for nonsingers." Her principles are teaching *the reading of music* rather than notation by rote methodology; use of the guitar with folk music; close relationship between instrumental and vocal music; and leading students to inquire into and examine the "inner" world of music (form and structure) as part of music appreciation. She describes herself as consciously working to show students how music relates to life, instead of treating music as a separate and unrelated aspect. Her instruments are clarinet, classical guitar, piano and voice.

CONRAD SUSA is a graduate of Carnegie Institute of Technology and the Juilliard School of Music, and studied dance composition with Louis Horst. Recipient of many grants and awards, including two Ford Foundation grants, and two Benjamin Awards for organ and string music, his composition: "David's Kingly City," won the 1965 annual national Anthem Award (and was published by H. W. Gray). Commuting between east and west coasts, he is Festival Composer for the American Shakespeare Festival at Stratford, Connecticut, and The Old Globe Theatre, San Diego, two of the most prestigious Shakespearean theatres on the continent, and is the resident composer and musical adviser for the Association of Producing Artists (APA) in New York and Los Angeles. A prolific and versatile composer, he has written church music and more than 50 original scores for theatre productions, ranging from Elizabethan drama through contemporary plays, and conducts his own work for regional orchestras. In addition, he has composed music for television, and has collaborated with modern dancers. Conrad Susa is at work on an opera and a concerto for organ and percussion, and is writing a book on the enjoyment of chamber music. Some of his theatre compositions are recorded for "Music for the Theatre" (Corrie Music Publishing Co., New York) and he is guest lecturer on music for Performing Arts Guild, Inc., an educational service group of cognitive teachers in Los Angeles.

The Contemporary Music Project for Creativity in Music Education is administered by the Music Educators National Conference, 1201 Sixteenth Street, NW, Washington, D.C. 20036, Norman Dello Joio, Project Chairman, and Grant Beglarian, Project Director. The Project Policy Committee comprises Dello Joio and the following:

Leslie Bassett, University of Michigan
Ingolf Dahl, University of Southern California
Allen Forte, Yale University
Walter Hendl, Eastman School of Music
Wiley Housewright, Florida State University
Beth Landis, Riverside Schools, California
William Mitchell, Columbia University

Vincent Persichetti, Juilliard School of Music
George Rochberg, University of Pennsylvania
Ole Sand, National Education Association
Jack Schaeffer, Seattle Schools, Washington
William Thomson, Indiana University
Robert Trotter, University of Oregon
Louis Wersen, Philadelphia Schools

"Experiments in Musical Creativity," source of some material in this book, is published by the *Contemporary Music Project for Creativity in Music Education* (CMP). The material is from a report on Pilot Projects in Baltimore, Maryland; San Diego, California; and Farmingdale, New York. These projects were supported by the CMP under grants from the Ford Foundation totalling $1,630,000; the Project also supports the "Composers in Public Schools" program, and a nationwide program of innovative musicianship training at all levels, entitled "Institutes for Music in Contemporary Education."

The CMP Pilot Projects described in this book are from the Baltimore Project, which studied *Creative Approaches to Contemporary Music in the Elementary Education*; the San Diego Project, for *Developing Musical Understanding Through Contemporary Music*; the Farmingdale Project, for two approaches to *Creative Experience in Music*: (1) *Creative Experience in Music Using 20th Century Technique*; (2) *Developing Musicianship through Rhythmic Studies and Movements*.

The Pilot Projects were developed under composer-consultants and teachers working together and also with students in elementary grades within pilot programs. This book is therefore indebted to all these, as well as to the *Contemporary Music Project* for valuable source material.

Permission to include the material in *Children and Dance and Music* is by the kind courtesy of Grant Beglarian, and I am especially indebted to Dr. David Ward-Steinman, composer-consultant, Susan Ward-Steinman, 2nd Grade Pilot Class teacher, and Browning Cramer, Administrative Assistant of CMP for their inestimable assistance.

BRUCE KING is a graduate of the University of California at Berkeley, and received his M.A. from New York University, School of Education. He studied contemporary dance at the Hanya Holm and Martha Graham Schools in New York and ballet under Margaret Craske at the Metropolitan Opera Ballet School, New York, directed by Antony Tudor. Although he works extensively in modern dance forms, he is trained also in classical dance technique. In the 1950s he was a member, for three seasons, of the Merce Cunningham Dance Company. He then danced in summer stock, musicals and in concert; toured the United States, France and Germany as a soloist in his own repertoire. More recently, King has devoted himself mostly to teaching, and performing as artist-in-residence for American universities, although he occasionally performs in concert with dancers of ballet and modern genres. He is best known for his work in creative dance forms, and for his original methods of teaching creative dance to children. He has toured the U.S. with his solo concerts *Design in Space* and *Dances for Children*, and serves as guest teacher and artist-in-residence for numerous colleges. His tenures include those of dance instructor at Adelphi College, Panzer College and Columbia University; Artist-in-Residence in the Department of Dance of the University of California at Los Angeles; the annual Festival of Arts, and the Summer Academy of Contemporary Arts of the University of Oregon; and Visiting Artist at Ball State College, Indiana, Bennett College, New York, and Brigham Young University, Utah. He is on the faculty of the Children's Centre for Creative Arts at Adelphi College, and a guest teacher at the School of Performing Arts, N.Y.C. In addition, King does considerable work in lecture-demonstration, on creative dance forms for children, appearing for conventions and conferences of such organizations as the American Educational Theatre Association, National Dance Teachers Guild, National Recreation Association, Dance Masters of America, and National Catholic Theatre Conference. He is well known for his principles for teaching techniques in creative dance for boys, boys' approach to organized dance forms, and dances for children (some of which are described in this book), and is among the first dancer-choreographer-teachers in the United States to institute teaching methods specifically for working with children in "deprived" or "underprivileged" societies. One of these pilot programs was for Urban Gateways in Chicago, Illinois, under a U.S. Government grant to the Board of Education. In 1967 he was the recipient of a Federal Government grant for developing a curriculum in "Creative Dance in Elementary Education," administered through Montana State University.

Children
and Dance
and Music

Dance and Music

"Dancing and building are the two primary and essential arts. The art of dancing stands at the source of all the arts that express themselves first in the human person. The art of building, or architecture, is the beginning of all the arts that lie outside the person; and in the end they unite. Music, acting, poetry proceed in the one mighty stream; sculpture, painting, all the arts of design in the other. There is no primary art outside these two arts, for their origin is far earlier than man himself; and dancing came first."

HAVELOCK ELLIS: *The Dance of Life*

WE ARE a rhythmic race. Our hearts beat, our blood courses, we breathe, and walk and run, in rhythms. We are creatures of a turning planet whose rhythms ensure life, in day and night, dry and wet, heat and cold. We walk and run, the simplest forms of locomotion, from the instinct by which we dance.

We speak; therefore we sing. Above all other forms of life we are able to make articulate and meaningful sounds as self-expression and communication. With speech and song we declare our identity in the Void, and our highest form of utterance is in music.

It is because we are so shaped and motivated as human beings that we dance, sing, make music and poetry. And because of them, are made to feel and to think. Rhythm and rhyme are marvelous human faculties and, contained in the person, they precede all other arts, such as painting and sculpture, which must be physically made and then transported like goods

[3]

and chattels. The singer and the dancer are the instruments of the song and the dance, and these survive when we are bereft of all other property, including artifacts.

Largely among English-speaking peoples and only of comparatively recent date, dance and music have become separate arts. Although we seldom have dance without music, save as a novelty in art, we have a whole body of music which is neither sung nor danced, kept not only independent but segregated from singing and dancing. This is in the Nietzschean concept that there is Music in which the spirit dances, and Music in which the spirit swims; or that music is of two separate natures: one for the street and the theatre; the other, a purely transcendental thing.

Children have to acquire these concepts because it is natural to them to dance and sing, and to make music with conventional and unconventional instruments. There is no good and bad music for a child, who has the purest sense of wonder and joy that music is, and is music. The first public performance of the dancer Martha Graham was when she danced down the aisle of a Presbyterian church; her first concerts were for the patients in her neurologist father's waiting-room.

A love of music and of music making is a primal racial urge. Music as magic is the oldest form, stemming from the prehistoric time when dance was religion, science, art and entertainment for mankind. For the greater part of time, and the greatest number of people, there have been no divisions between music, dance and drama, and between poetry and song. The modern concept of "pure" music separate from other forms is challenged every time we dance ballets, and sing operas, oratorios, and so on. Lyric theatre of the folkloric concept, totally representative of a people's arts and ideologies, as well as representative of their manners, modes and costume, is the source of modern musical arts, and combines the arts of color and design, the techniques of lighting and illusion. Every major nation supports a national ballet but America does not, as yet, and this may be a reason why we have a less serious regard for our musical arts and artists.

Artists and audiences of "serious" music in symphonic form often despise opera and ballet as frivolous, and set drama and literature outside (and sometimes in opposition to) music. Students study dancing separately from music, as though dance patterns were geometric but not lyrical. Only in the United States have I seen ballet taught without any musical accompaniment, solely to mathematical count, like arithmetic. We speak of going to hear an opera and to see a ballet, while other audiences consciously *experi-*

ence the performance. The French speak of the audience as "assisting" at a performance.

The child makes no separation, as the ancient Greeks forbore to do, between parts of the "Rhythmic Movement" defined as instinctive to mankind. Into adolescence, children dance to music that is both sung and played, especially in this era when a characteristic of rock-and-roll music is the singer, not the song. A child cheerfully undertakes a multiple career as singer, instrumentalist, actor and dancer. In what we call "play," he dramatizes poetry and makes it blood-brother to song. His spontaneous approach is to lyric theatre arts. When he performs he does so as a mummer, putting on fancy-dress, painting his face, assuming props, and taking on an identity —in which he stands revealed. As he sings and dances the actual world is less real than the artistic realm he inhabits. If we look and listen to him attentively we discover things about him that we may never know otherwise, because through dancing and singing a child will express and reveal conscious and subconscious secrets of his inner self.

The primary, instinctive approach to the arts is through the senses. This is the first thing to know about children and dance and music. There is no race without a history of dancing and, unless physically restrained, all children dance. When we see little persons turning and swooping in play and we ask what they are doing, the girls reply that they are dancing but the boys that they are flying. Dancing is as close as we come to natural flight. Atavistic urges make children dance and sing and should you wonder if children need dance and music know that more children prefer to make music than make money, and more of them want to learn to dance than to travel to the moon.

To approach children and dance and music one must know at least a little bit about all three, and that (quoting Wilde): "A little insincerity is a dangerous thing, but a great deal of it is absolutely fatal." Children sense, long before they analyze, what adults feel and think, and the initial approach an adult makes may fix forever a child's attitude and life-long commitment to dance and music. Most persons treat these as play; it is necessary to know that for those who practice them, including children, they are work, and work with merit, as well as enjoyment. Only when we treat dancing, music, acting and painting with respect as well as love will artists become as significant in our society as industrialists, financiers, scientists and politicians.

The adult attitude is important for the child as artist but it is equally so for the children who become the artist's audiences. To dance and to sing and to make music, the urge is not only to express but also to communicate, and in the most personal methods—with the instrument of self. Some of the best minds of our time are concerned with human communication, with the identity of the individual and of the group, within the largest mass. A fully automated society, secure from want, spared from pain, blessed with longevity and leisure, will require greater, not less, human communication. The arts are perhaps the last frontier for the individual in a mechanized age, and the truest means of self-expression of the individual. Useless in themselves, they are unique, as the absolute essence of originality in mankind.

Dance and music are social arts. Painting and sculpture are contained in art galleries, as literature is contained in books; we must go out into the world to see public monuments as architecture. Dance and music are intimate and flexible, and, united with drama, they develop cosily in a corner of a room, arts *in camera*, or sumptuously occupy an immense theatre. A teacher may work within dance and music in her classroom, within the smallest group, and with no other "instruments" save dancers and singers— or she may make use of the myriad physical facilities, the great range of audio-visual techniques with which American education is endowed, until she accomplishes a presentation worthy of an audience in the school auditorium.

Children will discover a lot about the world, and about themselves, by singing and dancing. In this context, the arts are palpably educational, while yielding nothing of their character as art.

Pragmatically as well as artistically, the arts have great values in education. Certain children learn in terms of physical images, others through abstract ones. Some children more readily understand the meanings of cryptograms than conventional language skills—a group of infants may find more pleasure *and meaning* in musical notation than in conventional reading and writing. Other children see paintings and sculptures as images of artistic reality, however abstract or unconventional their forms, and these children most often see dance as dynamic images. They can express, and be communicated with, through corporeal images rather than symbols as numbers and letters.

Musicality and muscularity are closely related in nervous impulse, which is why all children should be educated in an artistic life which integrates the gymnastic one. Arts are not exclusively for the artists, but assuredly for scientists, as well, in "liberal" education. The literal meaning of "liberal arts" is an education in the arts and sciences of free men (differing from a society of industrious automatons).

In education today the arts are particularly important because they are incorruptible in themselves, while science by its very nature is disputatious. There is no "right" and "wrong" dance, and no "good" and "bad" music *per se*, since dance and music must be defined as form in composition and as artistry in performance—on these qualifications they may be judged. There are modes in arts but these cannot negate or void each other.

The arts are inviolate because they do not progress and therefore cannot regress. Scientists disprove their own and their fellow scientists' theories but artists cannot. Picasso is powerless to disprove the art of Raphael or Rembrandt, as Schönberg and Stravinsky are powerless to disprove that of Mozart and Beethoven. Painting and sculpture are no more true and meaningful now than they were in pre-history—only their functional and sacred characters have altered to a character defined as "art." Dance was developed by primitive societies in such intricacy of design, such difficulty of execution, that it serenely withstands comparison with our highest aesthetic standards of theatre dance today. We have invented innumerable instruments but no man now sings more sweetly, with truer pitch, and with greater evocative power for audiences than did the first singer.

Yet with this noble nature, with such cogent character, art is also fiercely rebellious and incessantly revolutionary in form, since its origin lies within the individual human imagination. While the arts may never be described as progressing or regressing, they are forever undergoing change and reform, out of which society distinguishes epochs in art—themselves reflections of epochs of human behavior and philosophy. Criticism, perhaps more than any other sort of thought, is the abrasive and stimulating response to art, in part by other artists of the medium and in part by the audience. There is always a fight being waged in the arts and it is fighting like any other, for causes which provoke sympathy and outrage. History is amply illustrated with examples of exciting artistic controversies. Therefore, art is never stale and cannot become static; it is forever a grand adventure.

Art stirs one up, instead of, as popularly supposed to do by the sentimentalists, "relaxing" one. The artist agitates more than he soothes. We have become used to thinking of science as the energizing factor of this century and art as a soporific for the distraught, whereas, to quote the painter Georges Braque: "Art disturbs; Science reassures." We can affect standards in artistic performance, but art cannot be standardized—for this reason, the artist cannot be crushed by any tyranny, least of all those from political or commercial propaganda.

These are some of the values of arts in education but perhaps the most significant value of dance and music for children lies in their being essentially human involvements with creativity. The musical artist is committed to the most intimate undertaking through the instrument of self. To dance and to make music are human and artistic impulses and to perform these well, to evoke response and establish communication through them, is a challenging task.

To create is to make, to bring into life or being; to perform is: to do. Nothing could be more daring.

The sensual response is the human element in art and it is with this human element that we must be concerned in our initial approach.

Since we know that the child makes his own spontaneous approach, and treats dance and music as functional to life, our approach to dance and music *as arts* must combine the intellectual or cultivated response with the fervid, emotional one.

With this knowledge alone you can begin to work with children in dance and music, prepared to learn more than you will ever teach. The saving grace for parents and teachers is that children dance because they walk and run, and sing because they speak. Moreover, in this cacophonous age, they can be taught to distinguish sounds that are "music."

Begin, then, with pleasure to discover dance and music with the child. And begin with confidence because childhood is a musical time and children are a musical sort of people.*

---

* Approaches must be made with keenest awareness of phases of development and areas of interest for the child or groups of children. Many approaches here, too pedestrian for some, may prove too ambitious, at first, for others. Flexibility in approach, patience and resourcefulness, and a sense of humor about your follies and failures, are the guidelines for every pilot program. Be prepared for errors in evaluating responses, and for surprising results. As the teacher, keep a journal; you will need such reference for analysis and evaluation. As a parent, keep a diary; it will amuse and interest, in later years, the very child you approach as the infant today.

The Child at Home

"Aesthetic feeling, in different people, may make up a different fraction of life and vary greatly in volume . . . Taste is formed in those moments when aesthetic emotion is massive and distinct; preferences then grown conscious, judgment then put into words will reverberate through calmer hours; they will constitute prejudices, habits of apperception, secret standards for all other beauties. A period of life in which such intuitions have been frequent may amass tastes and ideals sufficient for the rest of our days. Youth in these matters governs maturity . . . Half our standards come from our first masters, and the other half from our first loves."

GEORGE SANTAYANA: "The Criterion of Taste," from
Reason in Art, Volume Four of *The Life of Reason*.

"WHEN is a child old enough to know something about music?"

The parent who asks this question needs only to know a little about music to discover that the child responds very early in life to at least two elements of music: tone color and rhythm. The response comes as soon as the child can hear—before he can recognize things seen, including the face of his mother or nurse. The child knows something about music before he can walk and talk and almost as soon as he can do these things he tries to dance and sing.

Five basic elements of music are rhythm, melody, tone color, harmony and form. *Rhythm*, in the complete sense, is everything pertinent to the *time* in music; distinct from pitch. The human ear, quite untutored as a musician's ear, is sensitive to rhythm as "beat," the perceptible presence in music of a unit of time. Music for dancing and marching has pronounced rhythms. The most musically uneducated layman grasps the meaning of "the beat" or rhythm in a piece of music. What is more, he spontaneously responds to it, perhaps by tapping his hand or his foot. In this response to rhythm we are, as a race, born to dance.

Melody is the organization of musical sounds with pitch and rhythm and in its oldest form existed without harmony. In its simplest form we may think of melody as the rise and fall of pitch, within the range of the human voice. Any little tune you hum or sing, is melody: successive musical sounds with pitch and rhythm.

Tone color or timbre is the particular quality or tone sounded by an instrument or voice and is a musical term for the difference between two tones of the same pitch, duration and intensity.

Harmony, simultaneous combinations of sounds of different pitch, is a sophistication, a modern element in music (as compared to music that is truly old, into about A.D. 900, when all music was melodic or consisted of only one line of notes). Harmony has been described as the "dress" of unclothed melody and is a European or Western (rather than an Oriental or Eastern) form of music. To generalize, harmony is technically within the science of music, a province of instrumentation. With form, harmony is the least musical element for the child while tone color and rhythm and then melody compose the greatest sum.

Form in music is the establishment of all the other elements and their relationships to each other within a piece of music, so that the piece has musical coherence. We may think of "form" in music as a kind of blue print for the organization of the basic structure of a musical composition.

If this brief and very generalized description of the basic elements of music are the first and only things you know about music let us see how you can put your knowledge to work in an approach to music for the child.

Almost every adult ear perceives the elements of music and the listener responds to all or some elements out of taste. Largely, the music you say you "like" is music that makes you feel emotions or think thoughts you enjoy, even when they are "sad" ones. Rhythm has the most powerful effect on listeners and changes in rhythms will alter a listener's pleasure to distaste —as when an old and familiar waltz is turned into rock-and-roll. Harmonics, the simultaneous sounding of two or more notes, can also alter a familiar melody, especially with the introduction of discordance. But these "likes" and "dislikes" are formed in adult life or in late childhood; the infant and very young child is the most tolerant listener of music, the great avant-gardist.

His earliest response is to tone color, to which animals are also exceedingly susceptible. You can outrageously insult a cat, a dog and a baby but if your manner is not threatening and if your voice is dulcet the spoken insult will elicit a purr, a tail-wag and a coo.

Small children aimlessly shaking rattles and beating their hands, toys or spoons very soon evince a rhythmic sense. They are percussive by inclination, and this is the oldest kind of instrumentalist. The first flautist, on his reed, was a more sophisticated musician than the drummer. The day your child crawls into your kitchen and finds two pot covers you discover that he is a cymbalist of vigor and persistence. When he strikes together objects made of wood, metal, plastic and glass he is cultivating his musical sense, listening with pleasure to the sounds given out by a variety of "instruments."

And even before becoming the instrumentalist, your child has attempted to sing. Every mother knows the characteristic "songs" of her infant, among which are the tired song with which a fatigued or angry baby lulls himself to sleep; the contemplative buzz with which he lies turning the bright new world over in his mind; and the hum which is accompaniment for an engrossing manual task. When an adult imitates such buzz or hum for the growing baby and identifies it as "singing," the child very soon recognizes sound as song. Thereafter, it is only necessary to ask the child to sing a song to get, in response, a sound made, deliberately and as an intellectual acknowledgment, as singing.

Such song is at first devoid of any of the basic elements of music but it is the child's first intelligent awareness of a form of music, just as the understanding of "to dance" is his intelligent awareness of yet another form.

The child will dance even before he can stand and walk, by joggling his torso in response to music (usually, to rhythm) when he can sit upright. Let him learn to stand, before he can actually walk, and the dancing extends into the knees, which he flexes rhythmically, even while his arms and hands are flailing about to preserve his balance. As soon as he can walk and run he will essay a turn.

Inarticulate and still largely immobile, your child will show his response to tone color and rhythm, and, quite soon in life, his understanding of what it is to sing, dance and make music by instrumentation.

How soon a child perceives melody we cannot know—unless we listen to what the child "sings" as he plays or learns, for all play is learning for him. A baby born one July into a family where there were four older children, was exposed to Christmas music when she was five months old. For weeks, the household revelled in carols off the radio, the phonograph and the lips of the family. When the baby was "singing" soon after her mother and father were astonished to hear (or think they heard) a recognizable tune. Disbelieving, they said nothing to each other, for fear of being sentimental doting parents. But the mother resorted to the tape recorder and after splicing numerous "hums" tried out the tape on unsuspecting listeners. All easily identified the hum as a faithful reproduction of the music for the words of the carol: *Away in a manger, no place for His head*. The baby was then seven months old. Possessed, as was to be discovered later, of absolute pitch, this child was very susceptible to melody as well as to tone color and rhythm. She was a child who, quite literally, sang before she talked and walked.

Since the child knows something about music in early infancy the parent who wants his child to love music can sensibly begin an approach to music while the child is in his cradle.

For centuries, people have sung to babies and told them stories or read them books. Simplicity, rather than sophistication, is the preferred approach to music and literature but from the earliest introduction to these the parent can make them romantic—something the child might think of as love. If an aspect of love is incorporated with music—singing a song to amuse a baby, or one as a lullaby to soothe him—music thereafter will have a certain connotation for the child. The sound of a human voice, however unskilled as singer, is the sweetest introduction to music for your baby. If you want your child to love music, sing to him, speak to him with "tone color," awaken his instinctive response to music as an intensely personal and unimaginably dear thing in life.

Past the first, easy, natural association of music and love there comes the stimulus from music, both intellectual and emotional. Children at home can learn a great deal within and through music, while learning some elementary things about music. Vocal singing often remains, for the first five years of his life, the chief pleasure the child realizes in music. He actively performs with as much pleasure as he listens—but he passively hears even when he is actively occupied at something removed from music. And soon he begins to show his individual "approach," as it were, to music. The better you know your child, the better you can plan his musical education.

Easy and pleasant as this is, it seems a formidable undertaking for the parent who is not a trained musician.

And, too, parents feel a decent reticence about studied approaches to the child and music, since so much of parenthood is spent on force and coercion of the child to conform as a civilized member of society, when he is intent on establishing himself as an individual regardless of our manners and mores. To add one more obligation for the parent and the child becomes, sometimes, insupportable for both.

But to assume that the child, entirely of his own accord, will approach music and develop what we think of as a musical culture, is like assuming that if you never allow the child to share a meal at a "set" table he will nevertheless cultivate the necessary skill and aplomb to share a formal dinner party. It is true that talent will seek the art, like a needle the magnet in a bale of hay, but although all children have responsive instincts to rhythm and tone all children do not have an intensity of purpose about the conventional art forms of dance and music. Past the period where the child, in infancy, shows instinctive responses comes the period when the child responds out of environmental factors, not the least of which is convention or example. Many children begin work in certain media because their environment offers them physical stimuli, as when the young daughter of a good cook takes first prize for her pie at a county fair, or a girl becomes a notable dress model because her mother, an expert seamstress, taught her to like clothes and develop a flair for wearing them.

The American composer Conrad Susa, who has made valuable contribution to this book, had little or no encouragement in music and developed and supported his own intense interest until it was recognizable as talent— all as described later in *The Child as Artist*. This is one instance, not rare but uncommon enough to be out of the ordinary, when the child persists in developing his own musical sense.

Such instances seem to occur more among children who are materially deprived than those who are materially enriched, to a point of satiety. An abundance of musical materials, especially of the kind manufactured exclusively to amuse children with music, may fail entirely to stimulate creativity. They are toys and physical appurtenances but they are not, of themselves, essential for developing a musical culture.

Television, radio, the phonograph and the cinema, provide "canned" experiences and of such strong audio-visual techniques that their polished performance may even quell individual talent, rather than stimulate it, in amateurs. Through the abundance of such "canned" experiences in dance and music (and in drama) we have largely lost impulse and need to create *original* experiences. Professionals, hired by the commercial entrepreneurs of the arts, perform with such facility that we in the mass audience hesitate to attempt amateur efforts. *Children who imitate and adapt "canned" experiences are not working creatively.* The vicarious approach to the arts (especially to mechanistic media of the arts) which is the norm of contemporary society is not the best development of individual artistry.

Yet we cannot separate the child from his environment but must know and consider the norm, and grant that parents must make approaches within it. Indeed, any opposite premise is altogether contrary to my purpose in writing about *Children and Dance and Music*.

Most persons like or say they like music, if only a certain kind of music. Very few people admit to detesting music. But, also, comparatively few persons are trained in a knowledge of music, and are musicians and composers. And many confess that they accept their ignorance of what music really is, and what it is about. The child is a person in the home but, in infancy, totally dependent on the environment. For a study of approaches to children and dance and music we should know the kinds of environments that are the norm, two of these being (a) a home in which music is loved as part of life; (b) a home in which music is not only loved but is also *a way of life*, for parents who earn their livings in music.

Approaches and Responses in Home "A"

My experiences, as mother and grandmother as well as teacher, is that there are two approaches general to young persons and music, and these approaches are determined by the nature of the child. Ask yourself about your child: is he a gregarious person, who prefers a congenial "togetherness" with an adult when he plays and in all that he undertakes as learning? Or is he independent and positive in opinion, someone who likes to discover things for himself, by himself?

For the first kind of child all experiences, including musical ones, are enjoyed the more for being shared, and usually this involves a great many questions for the child, with demands made on the adult to answer them with truth and sincerity. When a child of this nature, aged only four years, listens to music and asks you what it is—tell him. This type of interest, when it occurred among my children, led to conversations like this one:

"What are you doing?"

"I am listening to something."

"What is it?"

"It is music that is called a symphony."

"What is a symphony?"

"It is a form of music that is played by several instruments, all together, in an orchestra. It is something like a choir of voices at church, or a chorus of people singing. These are different from one piano, or one person, making music, alone or in solo form. A symphony is a thing in music played by many instruments."

"Oh!" And as this is a most mysterious and adult affair, invariably there followed: "May I listen, too?" To which the reply was: "Yes, but only if you think you want to enough to be quiet, not to chatter to me right now—because I am *listening*. Sit down and listen, if you like, and when you want to go away go very quietly, so as not to disturb my listening, will you, please?"

The fact that an adult was listening—was sitting down near a phonograph to listen to music—conveyed to the child the same importance attached to an adult speaking on a telephone, and not to be disturbed. Children who adopt good manners for the ordinary affairs of existence will cultivate good manners about music, just as readily. Good manners about music entails, first of all, conscious listening to music—once you have learned how to listen you have made the primary and absolute commitment to music: you *hear* music, in the genuinely physical and sensual way you *see* dance, or look at painting and sculpture, or perform all the cognizant acts by which your mind is informed.

The query might be made: what is the use of telling a four-year-old child that a symphony is a symphony? My children could not understand the *form* of music at that age, but they could dimly perceive that music had forms, one being the symphonic. The description I gave was a very simplified idea of "symphony" but it sufficed, for the child and the moment, as a name to apply to music, a form in which to think of music, itself nebulous and invisible. A child's pleasure in language, from which he invariably finds a name for every person or thing he knows, heightens his pleasure in music. Simply to give him the *names* of some forms and styles of music is to give him an approach to music. Thoughtful teachers, especially the cognitive teachers, make use as much as possible of *conscious vocabulary* about dance and music when working with children. And children surprise inexperienced adults with the facile grasp they make on vocabulary or terminology in the arts.

The premise in this example offered from within my own family is that the truest if the simplest answer should be given to every query the child makes. Never mind if he appears to understand nothing of the musical meaning, and accepts and adopts only the jargon—this is how he learned to talk and learns to read: by recognition of relationship between the thing and its name, and by memory of it, a million times over to cover every thought and idea. A song is a nursery rhyme, a chantey, ballad, love-song, whatever; an idea about the song as form, and the styles of its form, is one which a very young child can seize. He can also be led to understand that while many noises *happen*, music is *made*. The parent who means to have his child trained to play an instrument should make it known, as early as possible in the child's awareness of music, that music in its formal state is organized sound. It is easy to get the child to understand the difference between the natural and the artificial and if the child knows, from early, that music is *created*, on instruments and by fellow creatures, he realizes that music is an art, *man-made*. This realization can have tremendous influence on creativity, leading the child to invent and experiment with the serious intent of making music. Moreover, it inspires him with respect for the craft of composing and producing sounds which are music.

The discoveries that children make, awesome for themselves, are radiant beams of human intelligence. When the child makes a discovery in music he should be praised for it, and the discovery acknowledged as valid in music. A scientifically minded child who rushes to its parent with the news that he has "discovered" what we call magnetic and centrifugal forces, shows his awakening perception of physical laws. And the child who "discovers" that boys sing "the same but different" than girls: that the male voice is usually an octave lower than a female's in a melody, is making a real discovery. This is a primary harmonic discovery, made by the ancient Greeks, and is fundamental to music of the Western nations.

Most children today make their most important discoveries about music through instrumentation. If only through television and movies, almost every five-year-old child knows that instruments, played by people, produce music. In this knowledge, the American child is a sophisticate and sees whole symphony orchestras in full fig, becoming aware of the splendid mass of men and instruments from which the sounds of the symphony emerge as made music. In older times, singing and the piano in the parlor, and the fiddle and the bow, were dear and familiar producers of music, while now we have mechanical means of bringing sight and sound of great orchestras to the child in the home. This allows us to supplement with television the same physical approach the child grasps in theatre and concert hall, and to establish the might and the romance of music making.

The two main approaches that can be made by the parent are through *listening* to music, and by the gradual revelation that music is *physically* made. The listening comprehension is likely to come out of example and habit, and it is safe to assume that your child, in his first response to music, will like what you like—because he will know only what you know and pass on to him. The infant and young child are wholly dependent on environmental taste for their primary approach to formal music. I am convinced that all children, the highly imaginative as well as the pragmatic ones, grasp the sense of music as art when they realize that music is *made*. The sooner the child identifies music within the creation of sound (by players and by instruments) the quicker he perceives the nature of music and its nature as art.

The actual physical substance of music and the miracle of its being made can be approached through simple instruments like "tuned" glasses as well as by a conventional instrument. The best instrument is the piano, large enough to show its detail, as when the opened lid reveals its intricate mechanism; sturdy enough to withstand the child's initial experimentation with sound. Such approaches into music must be undertaken with clarity and conviction—always tell the child that he or the player of the instrument is *making* music. This at once requires an act as *listening*, for by no other means do we know, for sure, that music is made!

We enter here into a secret world, the child's imagination, in which he makes music a thing owned by himself. How much this sense of possession determines a child's approach to music is observed in the frequently noted rapture with which a child finds and makes the musical harmony on the keyboard that musicians speak of as *thirds*, or seeks and finds the same key up and down the major scale. "Come and see this sunset!" I have cried to a young child, when vividly colored patterns appeared in the evening sky. The child has looked, and taken it for granted. "Come and hear me make this noise!" the child has cried to me, excitedly, having "discovered" the magical sounds of the keyboard's *thirds*. When he discovers that he can make music the child feels large, benign, powerful, like God.

A child will often experience a seraphic joy in music. On two occasions I was told by infants that music made them feel like angels, or close to angels—developing, here, the interesting thesis of a famed English clergyman and psychologist who believes that the only approaches that should be made, religiously, to young children, are approaches through music.

My children's celestial joy came not out of a harp but from the lowly recorder. This is a common wooden whistle, a utilitarian instrument in primary schools. It is a relative of the flageolet (which has six holes in front, two behind) and the pipe, a pretty little wind instrument with three holes, in vogue from at least the 12th and well into the 18th century. Musical greats composed for it, sometimes in ensembles, sometimes in solo, but it fell out of fashion during the classical epoch, and is just coming back into serious music again. It will utter sweet sounds and on these children often fall by happy chance, as did one of my sons, aged about five. The resulting thrill lifted his skin in gooseflesh. "Look!" he said to me, "when I play this thing angels walk about in the roots of my hair!" Two other infants, at another time, playing with a pair of recorders owned by their older brothers, miraculously produced several notes in harmony, an experience they described as "feeling like angels inside," where, I assume, the music swelled and trilled too deliciously for human simile.

These were musical voluptuaries, more than aesthetes—but, as has been said and cannot be repeated too often for the adult who makes studied approaches with music, children respond sensually, not intellectually, to artistic experiences.

Nor may we be quite, quite certain what they hear, in their inner, or metaphysical ear. Often, children evince pleasure in discords, some of which afford reasons for gross mirth. But a child, wholly untutored in formal music, will unerringly recognize the quality of harmony, to which he cannot give its formal name, and for which he therefore invents names, or qualitative descriptions—like the heavenly expressions evoked by playing on a recorder.

(This, incidentally, is an instrument every home with a child in it might do well to own!)

The wise parent finds clues to the riddle of when to introduce a certain kind of music, and how, to the child. After the second experience with the "angel music" of the recorder, I was astute enough to go out and find authentic music played by recorders, on a phonograph record. It made an instantaneous hit. This is not at all surprising, since children (although tolerant and avant-garde in tastes) tend to favor baroque music, which is "thin" in texture compared to the thick, rich orchestrations of 19th century classical and romantic music. Perhaps the baroque style seems made for a smaller world, a world closer to the child-sized, than the vast symphonic orations and thundering majestic sounds of the post-Viennese school. But while older children assume prejudices which make music into Mozart sound "tinkly" to their ears, their younger fellows revel in it—as they do in the exceedingly modern styles, which, of course, return to the polyphonic, skipping over the centuries between.

A sense of identity with a true musician is one of the earliest and most lasting pleasures for the amateur, even when he is three or four years old. The discovery that "noodling" (the idiomatic description of playing a recorder) on a foot-long wooden whistle, a thing plainer than some modern toys, is done seriously, by grownups, can amaze and delight a young child. The older child, come to a stage where facts amassed give dignity and importance to an object, is interested to know that there are some 750,000 recorder players in the country, and that an organization called the American Recorder Society has fifty-three chapters and a quarterly magazine: *The American Recorder*. One such child, taking to school the information that Shakespeare, Bacon, Milton and Pepys wrote praising the recorder (and that Henry VIII performed with spirit and grace on his 77) set off such a rash of speculation on recorder music that, in an Eng. Lit. class, high school students were collecting recordings of recorder music by Purcell, Telemann, Vivaldi, Bach and Handel and insisting that the teacher play these for all to hear music made by an instrument whose name means "to sing like a bird." Eventually, a "field trip" was arranged to view, in a music shop, recorders that ranged in size from one to seven foot, and prices from a few dollars to close to a thousand. Moreover, several children bought recorders of their own and played them, since a tyro noodler can produce fair musical sounds in a short time—although it takes study and practice to become a recorder virtuoso.

Parents who wonder what sort of music should be made for children often restrict the initial musical experience. They tend to rely too much on "packaged" music for the young, especially on recordings, and to follow, to the letter, what writers on children, not writers on music, recommend as "children's music." The non-musician must rely on the verbal or written explanation about music and unfortunately the most authoritative statements are made by writers, instead of by musicians. We are too apt to fit a child into a preconceived world of music, as though we were outfitting him at a clothing store for his chronological age's "size" in shoes and coats. Left free in music, the child may show some surprisingly adult tastes, and for many children "children's music" so palls that it becomes distasteful. The child's invariable desire to enter and share the adult's world makes him receptive to "adult" music. But in most instances he must covet it as an adult prize before he enjoys it for itself.

Children of buoyant nature and fine physical coordination are exhilarated by strong rhythms, giving way to impulses to march and gallop, leap and curvet. These are readily seen as children who respond to music. The contemplative nature, and the physically lethargic type, will show less response to singing and dancing, but will listen attentively for music's sake —not for song and dance sake in which music is interpreted in movement or used, boldly, as accompaniment. Very definite emotional and intellectual responses are made by the young child to music and these are more difficult to discern because the child is inarticulate and shy. But many children remember what they first felt and thought because of music, and also what they felt and thought music to be of itself. I have found that the deepest feelings and the most imaginative responses for the child came out of "great" or serious adult music.

The six children in my family were born and approached life and music two by two, with widely spaced intervals of conscious "approach." Although siblings within one family environment they had individual responses and "group" responses, comparable to individual children at home and, to an extent, to groups of children in school. To the parental influence was added a peer influence, by which it is notable that two liked formal music; two were more curious than emotionally responsive; two took music so for granted that they preferred to make music rather than listen to it. None thought (or were ever thought) of themselves as "little" persons relegated to children's music but entered into a knowledge of music *per se*. One of them has described his earliest memory of what he thought and felt about music: "It was a huge mass, like the vastest body of water imaginable, with waves of sounds. Some were tall, thick, dark-green waves, that roared and then crashed and I remember that all of Beethoven's music seemed of this texture to me, as soon as I knew enough to tell Beethoven from other composers. For Mozart, I imagined a multitude of tiny waves, the edges exquisitely crimped, bright, like sunshine, and a rippling, dazzling quality that was in no other music. I suppose one could say that Mozart and Beethoven were my favorite composers, but then that may be because theirs were the kinds of music I first recognized, first analyzed as music and as music like no other kinds."

This child had total recall of incidents and "feelings" from a very early age and this description of his responses (relayed to me in late adolescence) identifies him as one of the beings whose inner eye sees images that are purely aural. If we could discover how every child "sees" as well as hears music psychologists would have an astonishing insight into young minds.

As for "approach" to music, the parent hardly knows when that has been made and in my case the first positive introduction to music as a thing *listened to* (as compared to music taken for granted or used for fun) came out of my attempted rejection of the child as listener.

The two oldest children spent a great deal of time in my company but were barred from disturbing me in my daily phonograph concerts, when I wished a quiet and solitary time for my own listening to music. At first, they accepted this decree amiably enough but soon they become avidly curious and stole in on me, promising to be "good" and meaning to be quiet. On the proviso that as soon as they could not be quiet enough not to disturb they should steal out again, they began to share the phonograph concerts, a little at a time and eventually for the full span. When I turned a record over on the spindle, they asked me questions: what music was this (to which I gave its formal name), who made it, when and where, and, of course, often they asked *why*.

This began at a time when I, for my own interests, was listening intently to changes between 18th and 19th century music. Moving back through Haydn, Bach, Gluck, Handel, Vivaldi, Purcell and Scarlatti I found my children literally entranced by music, by the differences in music, and by the men who had made music. And within this segment of musical history I had ample material for answering their childish questions about music and musicians, even as to *why* the music had been made.

The understanding that music had been composed for persons and purposes was one on which the children laid hold, almost as actually as though I had opened several bolts of satin, velvet and brocade from a store of merchandise and, pointing out color, texture and pattern, told them: "This was manufactured for so-and-so in Italy; this in Germany; that in England." I had no intention of inaugurating a musical education for little boys then aged three and four but they were soon asking me for Handel's *Fireworks Music* by name, for instance, and would have spirited arguments between themselves to decide which composer would hold the floor for the day's concerts.

Their musical perspicacity was soon obvious, and as I read over my journal for the first year I note that one child gaily likened the *Branden-burg No. 3 in G Major* to "a father saying something" (the first allegro, with the main theme); "children all having something to say," (the poly-phonic treatment and the motifs from the main theme, as these are devel-oped); "an argument," (when, towards the end of this piece, the character of the instrumentation is excited) that was resolved "sweetly and calmly" (as Bach's composition does, indeed, end in peaceful unanimity among the instruments).

One day I suggested we might have "a little Beethoven" when they had wearied me with a long diet of Bach. The little boy who looked at me as though I was mad and said: "You can't have a *little* Beethoven," voiced a singular truth in music. I found that my own education in music was being considerably extended through two infants.

The first time these two children attended a theatrical performance it was of a classical ballet, chosen for the combination of music by orchestra and visual image of drama in mime and dance. It was treated as a "treat" in itself, occurring during the Christmas holidays, and incorporated the seasonal theme, this work being a version of *Casse Noisette* (The Nut-cracker) with a score by Tchaikovsky. I discovered that the children so entirely saw this production that they apparently heard nothing of it. They did not recognize the musical score when I played it on the phonograph, although they had certainly heard it before then. What interest they had in the music existed purely in the fact that they had seen it made, by the men and instruments in the orchestra pit. Yet, in the same week, they fully ap-preciated opera as drama in music, when they attended a performance of Humperdinck's *Hansel and Gretel*, whose story they knew well.

After this, I fell into the habit of letting them hear the music of a ballet in advance of taking them to see it, and alternating between these methods of "approach": sometimes, I would tell them the story, and identify, when we listened to music, where the main events occurred in the score; at other times I asked them to listen and then "guess" what the dancing to this music was about. I wrote their "stories" down for them to keep until we had seen the mysterious unknown ballet and then, for fun, compared the children's plots with the libretto—always, I may say, with great disparity between themes and characters, since the children's stories were made up out of their experiences, not the librettists'. I think that they subconsciously perceived then what I later took pains to impress on them in a formal musical appreciation, that music of itself does not "say" something, but is like liquid color which can be poured into a shape or design to transfigure a dramatic form (as in ballet and opera) and illuminate it.

If this seems, on reading above, a simple idea to assimilate by a child, know that it is one which many adult listeners, unaware of the nature of music, cannot tolerate, and resist from their own feelings about music. And it is personal feelings or emotional responses that color music for us, as deliberate use of drama through music, in opera and ballet, colors or imprints mood on music.

The interest my two young sons showed in the orchestra led me to take them to chamber and symphony concerts, always early enough to stroll down to the stage and pit to look at the instruments and whenever possible to exchange a few words with the players of the instruments. "Made music" was a reality to these children.

In the concept of "made music" (which was music in its formal state, as differing from music the children made for fun) a discrimination or development of taste was rapidly manifested. In this "taste" for music I noted the strongest relationship between mood and moment, as when a child, near bedtime, chose the music he wished to hear. Repeatedly, one child (the ardent Mozart fan) requested the *Eine kleine Nachtmusik, K.525,* Mozart's best known serenade, a characteristic of which is the orchestration solely for strings. I obliged, but I should never have offered this music in the conscious choice as a "lullaby"—nor had Mozart offered it as such, it being some of his occasional music. Yet the more I listened, at such times, to *Eine kleine Nachtmusik* the more I grew to agree with my child that it was blissful music to fall asleep by . . .

The little boys, in their most jovial moods, loved Bach—a composer thought of as being as sedate and strict as a schoolmaster. Yet how wrong to think in such terms of Bach, when one listens (if possible, with ears which have never heard Bach classified as a pedagogue) to the *Brandenburg No. 3 in G Major,* the children's prime favorite. They used to dance about the room to the finale, quite carried away with joy, and responded in much the same way to the last movement of the *Brandenburg No. 4 in G major,* and to some (but not the main) movements of the *Brandenburg No. 5 in D major*. Knowing the dramatic theme or anecdote, they would chuckle with mirth at Bach's *Coffee Cantata*, the music of which they liked so much that their enjoyment of it moved me to tell them its basic narrative idea (a father's horror over his daughter's passion for drinking coffee).

I should not have thought to make merry with Bach, as a beguilement for little boys, until then. But Bach has enormous charm for boys, I have since found. For many years, I used to hear my eldest sons whistling, when they were happy and busy, this fragment of melody from Bach's *D major Suite*:

They would not even realize that they were whistling, far less what they were whistling unless asked. They practiced a communication between themselves, into adolescence, with a "signature" whistle drawn from the air.

I next discovered how intensely interested children become in music made by other children. We three found Mozart the main ground on which our tastes most agreeably met and we therefore heard a great deal of his music. Conversationally and in answer to the children's questions about the music and the composer, I told them Mozart's story. This occurred in bits and pieces over a period but Mozart became a very real person to the children, perhaps because when one is five and going on five it is exciting to know that a child of five composed music, as did Mozart. Very soon, the children found empathy between themselves and the composer and attached themselves with love to him and to his music.*

The melodic quality of his name alone pleased them: Wolfgang Amadeus Mozart (as discovering that Gluck meant "happy" delighted them). For a while they revelled in Mozart's gladsome youth and elected to follow his and his sister Nannerl's tours on the atlas, and to find out how people of that time had looked, by gazing into costume books of the period. These were their first conscious lessons in geography and social history. They came, eventually, to the question *and then, what happened?* which led me to tell

* This empathy appears to develop very early in life for the child. American pianist Van Cliburn relates that when he was two and three his mother put him to bed with stories of the great composers. The child had not begun a musical education, had not even yet evinced any talent as a musician, but, as he recalls today: "these stories pleased and excited me very, very much." Van Cliburn's musical talent was revealed when, like Mozart, he climbed on the piano stool and played a tune he had heard his parent teaching a piano student, which the three-year-old Van Cliburn mastered by ear before setting hands on the keyboard.

of Mozart's sad times. The glittering childhood was over and I took, in one quick gallop, Mozart's bad fortune at the hands of his enemies and patrons, and his early death, and told of his funeral on a day when it rained so hard that his few friends found they could not follow the coffin to the cemetery so turned back home; Mozart was buried in an unmarked grave.

The two little boys burst into tears. They could not bear to think that the little boy who had played so many fine airs, with such flourish, traveled about the European continent and been praised, and had as a young man composed delightfully funny operas, had died in pain and poverty, in grief and loneliness. Their rage against Mozart's fate and the pity with which they mourned him, astonished me. They were two very active, good-tempered children, marked by a very strong sense of humor, and all musical experiences until then had seemed to be for fun. More interestingly, they were two well-fed, well-kept, well-loved children whose only tears, until then, had been selfishly spilled, each for his own frustrations, wrongs and woes, never for another soul. Yet, two hundred years later, they wept for Mozart. He had become immeasurably dear and so intimate that they spoke of him with familiar affection, saying that it would be nice if he came and lived with them as another little brother. They knew the characters out of the Bible and European mythology and had delegated Thursday (Thor's day) as the day we heard Wagner, whose majestic uproar they adored for their own gross, hearty roars and rowdy dances, but Mozart was dearer, nearer, for every day.

These children were not only cultivating musical knowledge, they were developing ideas and emotions as sensitive human beings, and they learned selfless grief and compassion, for the first time, through music.

While I was preparing my own ear, through a recording, to attend a performance of *The Magic Flute*, the children became enraptured with Papageno, the bird-catcher, and Tamino—and no wonder, since these are characters as gripping and exciting as those in nursery lore. Mark begged to be taken to the opera and in anticipation of it intently listened to the recorded music, asking me what was going on *here*, what was happening *now*, so that he could follow the drama through the music—in reality, *in the music*.

During the performance (for which he had to stay up far past his bedtime) I whispered to the child: "Are you enjoying it?" He gave me a quick, hard look and muttered through his teeth: "Not now—don't talk to me now!" And at the intervals he preferred to stay in his seat rather than stroll about the foyer, a place where a small child is dwarfed and deafened by giants puffing clouds of tobacco smoke and shouting above their own din. But he showed so little "response" that I might have mistaken his intense appreciation for apathy if he had not eventually revealed the former. On the following day he still had nothing to say about *The Magic Flute* and was so quiet and contained that I thought the night before had exhausted him. But two days later he demanded that I put *The Magic Flute* on the phonograph as he had quite "got the whole thing" in his head and wanted to tell his brother about it. Animatedly, with gestures and some dance steps, he tried to take on himself as many roles as possible out of the opera, to enact it.

I then realized that by concentrating on a photographic memory he "saw" *Flute* after he ceased actually witnessing it in performance. He had retired into silence and as much solitude as a young child can have, to digest *The Magic Flute*. Later, he used to enjoy sitting with his younger brother while the recording was being played, to describe (with less and less correction from me) the events as they unfolded in his head, from the opera, through the music.

As a grown child, going about some task, he would, quite unconsciously, whistle parts of the score, especially the quick, intricate passages. It is true that this child had a nightmare involving the wicked Queen of the Night who struck terror (as Mozart intended she should) as a coloratura, but children need ogres and daemons as much as they require fairies and angels, so I was not alarmed. I preferred to have my child suffer a nightmare about the Queen of the Night than about a green-scaled, goggle-eyed fabrication out of a "comic" book. He had "comic" book experiences, as he grew up, but he knew "classic" experiences in music, myth and poetry before he encountered those.

The next pair of children did not attach themselves emotionally to musical experiences, at first. They would listen, but neither for as long nor as with great concentration as the eldest, and perhaps because he was stern about their behavior when they joined us for listening, with the sharp discipline older siblings show. But these younger children came to their knowledge of music in their own way and time.

They fell into the habit of screaming in unison and also as a sort of "part" singing every evening after being put to bed. It was hard on adult nerves but threat of punishment and coercion had, equally, no effect, while punishment simply turned the screams of mirth to ones of anguish. One evening, Gwenny, the Welsh girl who took care of them, went into the nursery, stood between the beds (over the sides of which lolled the wild-eyed screamers, feverish with excitement at their daring and vocal prowess) and sang the major scale, up and down, in rising volume and tones alternating between high and low. She sang a great deal to my children, but they had never heard her treat wordless music in this way before. Fascinated, they watched and listened as steadily Gwenny put her fine voice to work up and down a musical ladder, eventually lifting it in a ringing sound that shivered the air.

The little boys flung themselves down in bed on their faces, covered their ears and lay still until Gwenny left the room. Then they essayed a few more screams, but half-heartedly, and soon gave up and went to sleep.

The next evening, getting ready for bed, they merrily asked Gwenny to give them a scream. She told them the "scream" had a name: it was a scale, and each note had a name: do, re, mei, et cetera. She sang the notes of the major scale, in the European manner, and the children copied her. They mastered the scale in one lesson, easily—as is readily done through the English tonic sol-fa.

Thereafter, the children and Gwenny used to converse via the 8-tone diatonic scale. Often, arguments were sung, like *We don't want to go to bed now!* by the boys up the scale, and Gwenny in reply: *But to be-ed you must now go!* in descent.

Gwenny had a rich, quaintly flavored vocabulary. A boy would suffer a stubbed toe or a cut finger and bawl, and she would say: "Oh, don't let's make a song and dance about it!"—When the indignant child stopped crying to protest, Gwenny would suggest better subjects and sounder reasons for singing and dancing. These musical turns dried tears magically and returned black moods to sunny ones. They also taught my sons the authentic "jig."

Once, the boys had a bitter quarrel and complained to Gwenny. "Oh," she admonished, impatiently, "it's nothing to harp about!"

Harp! What was *a harp* and *to harp?* With fiendish persistence they fastened on the word and would not rest (nor let the adults in the household rest) until descriptions of harps, pictures of harps, and, eventually, a physical harp and the sounds of a harp were procured for their satisfaction. Gwenny took them to a music store and showed them all the instruments on hand, she plunking and plucking, and blowing into flutes, with a mystified salesman hovering over the trio for fear of injury to the stock. The children were alternately charmed and alarmed by the noises, there and then fixed opinions as to personal taste, and came home from this experience demanding to hear a cello play music out of the phonograph, and a harp "say something."

When these little boys were aged three and four I was seriously going shopping for records they demanded, not by name, but according to instrumentation. The two older had become attached to the symphonic form of music; the two younger leaned to the concerto. Both, by purest accident out of their home environment, found enormous enjoyment in "adult" or "serious" music.

Once attached to a form, the children were adamant in personal preferences—they developed "likes" or tastes with passion. Recently, a mother complained to me that she had heard one record album, by the rock-and-roll group called The Beatles, so many times over that she was going mad. I recall how, about ten years ago, my mind reeled from hearing Beethoven's nine symphonies at full pitch on a hi-fi set for a cacophonous summer during which our children played them without stint all day, every day. I have also been distracted beyond endurance by Beethoven's third piano concerto (*No. 3 in C Minor, Op. 37*) and Debussy's *Arabesques* Nos. 1 and 2—and in between these, heard every word Frank Sinatra ever sung and recorded, and every note the guitarist Django Reinhardt strummed.

Children do not attach themselves to music in sweet reasonableness, but with passion and purpose, and purely for their own ends. Whether emotionally or intellectually motivated, music is functional for children, as is dancing, drawing, painting and the dramatic identification of self in children's storytelling, or lies.

Not easily fatigued, they are not quickly sated and will listen to the same piece of music with conscious and unconscious appreciation for degrees of time that bore, irritate and exasperate the more sophisticated adult ear. It is a sophistication to seek variety; it is passion which permits repetition to stay unalloyed joy, especially for listeners to music. And especially when the child is contemplative.

More active children prefer to create their sounds as music to hearing music, however sumptuous or intricate the sound. Our two youngest children heard music played in the home, and were led into the habit of listening to it (especially at meal times and other congenial social periods) but they from very early showed the disposition to make music for their enjoyment in preference to hearing what our daughter described as "made" music. Nor was the making of music considered play.

I noticed that every weekday morning, in the hours between breakfast and lunch, these two youngest children (a girl and a boy) ran into at least one hour during which they had no interests of their own, as play. Boredom ended in squabbles and I tried to create a diversion (and a studied approach to music) by inaugurating a "music hour" every day, as I had done with my oldest children. These two youngest were unappreciative of the idea of our sitting together and sharing a musical hour but my daughter seized the thought for herself. She pushed the kitchen table against a wall, anchored the table cloth so that it hung down and curtained the side of the table opened to the room, and retired into this underground cave with a set of mixing bowls and some forks and spoons. She fiercely repulsed her brother when he tried to crawl in with her and informed me that she was working and should not be disturbed. To appease him, I made a "music room" for my son, by arranging some chairs to shut off a corner of his room and draping a blanket over the chair backs. He chose his musical instruments from the kitchen and set about making his rival music.

With plastics, metal, wood, china and glass these two children made a brave discordant din, accompanied by their singing and humming, and continued this, voluntarily, day after day, making the pre-luncheon time their "music hour." Charmed, I rushed out and bought two toy pianos. My son thoughtfully took his apart and rapturously plunked the naked keyboard, discarding the lid and legs of his piano. My daughter admired hers so enormously that she decided it was too dainty to be touched by human hand, including her own; she had hers set on a shelf out of reach, for ornament. But both children used the musical glasses I made for them by the simple expedient of filling glasses to varying levels with water, so that a set was "tuned."

Hearing her older brothers talking about music as "blues" my daughter emptied bottles of vegetable coloring into her glasses, apparently to create red, pink, yellow and green music. She was four and it was impossible for me to know what she intended, other than to deduce that color meant something in sound as music. Like idiot savants, who have one forte, this child became adept at playing her water glasses and produced actual form in music. A friend copied down, in a true statement, a thing she played again and again, sometimes incompletely and with improvisations, but with certainty, in it establishing elements of rhythm, tone, melody and a rough harmony.

Taking the child to the piano, he sat her beside him and played her piece. She listened critically, apparently uncharmed, and said: "You're going too fast; it's supposed to go *very* slow."

I kept the musical notation and seven years later, after she had begun to study piano, gave it to her to play for her own ear, with the *Very slowly* injunction she had made. This time, she was charmed, looking back indulgently at the four-year-old composer from a great divide (and choosing to add the bass accompaniment).

"What was it to mean?" she marvelled. "Was it swans?"

But why swans to an eleven-year-old, out of an association at once musical and ornithological? The four-year-old composer had required no meaning; music had been of its sternest function: sounds organized as music within time; and as such it had sense but no sentiment. That a coherent musical phrase could be invented by a very young child was not, in this case, a sign of musical genius but evidence of a musicianly ear—this was the child who at seven months sang *Away In A Manger*. And the changing attitudes towards music is other evidence of children's approaches—the four-year-old was an avant-garde musician, the eleven-year-old was a romanticist, wanting tone color and "meaning" within the musical form.

None of my six children are musicians although all received instruction, during childhood, in playing an instrument. Except for the eldest, who studied violin, all studied piano. While these children were in primary educational grades and their regimes were under parental control they found time for practice and lessons—but when school and social pressures increased and parental control decreased they found insufficient time (a familiar pattern, discussed in *The Child as Artist*). They gave up making music instrumentally but they did not give up music, by any means. And as adults with families of their own, and as adolescents, they have continued to include music in their lives—incapable of conceiving of life without music.

They are representative of the greatest majority of music lovers in contemporary life in the United States, who know at least a little about and have a great deal of love for music despite working in professions we think of as being outside music.

They are typical of children in a large family—the eldest receiving most attention, not out of parental favor, or because the eldest was the most intelligent, but simply because the parent (the mother, particularly) had more time to spend with the first born. By good fortune, the second children came under a benign and stimulating influence as "Gwenny's boys"—incidentally allowing the older children more time to continue the development of the musical tastes they had formed out of a parent's. These four children were from infancy in a somewhat different environment, in a mechanized sense, than the two youngest; for one thing and an important thing, they did not know television entertainment at all, although they knew a great deal and from very early ages of cinema, radio and phonograph drama, dance and music. The two youngest children, post World War II, occupied the contemporary mechanized environment in which all the above were combined with television. They were to one extent more sophisticated about theatre arts than their older brothers, and in another respect more naive. Their initial musical interests were primitive, as described.

Also, there was a geographical shift from an English environment to an American one, and a difference in relationships within a family. The older children lived in a bilingual family and heard nursery rhymes, stories and songs in French and English, and knew a great number of persons from several generations, older and younger. My youngest children lived in an English-speaking family and were totally dependent on influences from their brothers and parents, persons closest their generation.

It was only after all six children had developed in adolescence that their individual tastes emerged one by one out of the three sibling groups or pairs in which they had approached music. In an age range extending from thirty-three to seventeen they have shown the influences of their adolescent eras to varying degrees.

The oldest was the most impervious to such influence, was never attracted to "pop" music, and, from early dedication to Wolfgang Amadeus Mozart, remained true to this first love; he became an opera buff. The second child had intense but passing interest in "pop" music (unerringly picking on the best of the era to appreciate most). He later showed the greatest fondness for the romanticist composers, probably because in his profession as an actor "tone-color" and other characteristics of Romantic music are both appealing and functional for his ear. It is an ear that very early tuned itself to Greek and Shakespearean drama, verse which has distinct meter, rhythm, and other musical forms. The third child, a scientist by profession, is inordinately interested in high-fidelity (hi-fi) and has an enormous tolerance for varieties of music. Such persons have a particular aesthetic of the ear for sounds *per se*, any of which appear to them as "music." The fourth has great musical tolerance but leans in taste towards the classical composers—when he was in early adolescence he described Beethoven as being able to "build a wall" for him, behind which he could retreat to be free and private. The three oldest have exceptionally fine light baritone voices.

None of these four children danced, either in ballrooms or as participants in folk and other dance forms. They were all academicians by taste and seemed to prefer a spectator rather than a participant role in musical arts. They knew theatre very early, and in metropolitan cities where variety and standards were of the best.

The two youngest children, born and reared in the western United States, were altogether different in responses and somewhat different in approach.* For one thing, we were so far separated from metropolitan theatre that their earliest knowledge of this was infrequent—occasional and not regular trips of three hundred miles were undertaken for them to attend performances of ballets, and plays. These experiences were joyous but do not appear to have been so memorable that the impressions made obvious effect. (My daughter has studied ballet as part of her general education, but this is within environmental plan.) True to their eras, these children are dancers

* Musical responses described for these six siblings have close correlation with their behavior patterns as adolescents and adults. The four older, whose first and continuing responses were to conventional musical forms, voluntarily chose to follow familial traditions; the two younger, who rejected standard music and preferred amateur inventions on unconventional instruments, are radicals within the familial norm.

in the ballroom aspect, a form of dancing that was not studied but absorbed, and their own music is now largely within folk song and the guitar (again, true to their times).

But these children also know that music, like other arts, moves through epochs, with certain styles recurrent, sometimes in cycles; and that music is characterized truly by forms and not by phobias or passing fads. With such knowledge, music is not purely an emotional expression (as for adolescent rebellion) but also an intellectual faculty. These young persons have a basic knowledge of music and a better than elementary knowledge of the history of music, through which they understand and appreciate forms and styles in musical arts. They have, we may say, a concept of music as fact as well as aesthetic; as structure in art, and as idea.

Such responses are normal in a non-professional métier, and an environment where the appreciation of music (rather than the personal performance of music) cultivates taste as well as knowledge.

Responses in a musical environment, one in which the musician parent makes a planned, authoritative approach, are similar yet dissimilar, and can best be noted by comparison of the two environments, the former in my home, the second in the home of musician and music teacher Sara Kreger.

These two approaches to the child at home allow insights into what may be described as living with music as a state of mind (within my home) and with music as a way of life (in the Kreger household). Ours is a literary household; we spend most of our time with books. The Kregers' is a musical household, in which most time is spent with music-making.

Approaches and Responses in Home "B"

Sara Kreger writes:

I feel that as parents my husband and I know (as trained teachers) that children do not learn here and there, or now and then, but continuously —and through accumulated experiences. This learning for them has been the same process in music as for all else. Our discipline is 99% verbal and our children have what are considered superior vocabularies for their peers, and in this vocabulary I made music so much a part that it became normal to routine.

We sang to our children and not only lullabies for going to sleep. We have songs for baths, for dressing, for all conceivable occasions of normal life, and our children have accepted them as other children accept ordinary talking.

I want to make it clear that a great deal of this singing, when the children were very young, was "plain," in that it was not concert hall singing. True, it had tone color and elementary melody but it was not formally composed song. It was begun artlessly, out of overflowing love. Music is my language, my trained method of work, and it is natural to me to sing. It seemed, from the first, natural to sing instead of only to *say* words of encouragement, comfort, praise and tenderness to my baby.

I spent a great deal of time rocking and singing to my babies. When I tired of nursery rhymes (although I sang these without stint, as they have sweet melodies and interesting rhythms) I frequently sang what might be called adult songs; for instance, the Schubert arias that I love. This rocking and singing had obvious physical effects on my three babies; as growing children they have shown a fine sense of rhythm, excellent physical coordination, and very early responses to dance and music.

When there were tears over injury, frustration, and so on, I would take the child on my lap and play the piano with one hand, and I found that this instinctive turning to music, on my part, worked like a charm to dry tears and heal small hurts. Long before a child was walking, he would show delight in my playing on an instrument. Each child showed especial pleasure when I played the piano and also when I placed his hands on the keys to prove that he, too, could make sounds. The piano was never a toy but it was positively a tool to divert the children.

The first games we played were games of rhyme or rhythm.

In our family, a universal favorite was the "hand song," which is really not a proper song but a rhythmic recitation, simple ⅔ rhythm. It so fascinated my children and others I have known that it is worth recording here:

Here's a ball for baby, big and soft and round (make a fist)
Here is baby's hammer, see how he can pound (thump the fists)
Here are baby's soldiers, standing in a row (spread fingers stiffly)
And here is baby's music, clapping, clapping so! (clap hands)
Here is how the baby plays at peek-a-boo (peep through interlaced
    fingers)
And here is baby's horn, root-too-too-too-too (curved fingers and hands
    laid one on the other to simulate a horn or cornet)
Here is an umbrella, to keep the baby dry (hands, pagoda-like, over-
    head)
And here is baby's cradle, rock-a-baby-bye. (fingers of two hands linked
    and hands rocked, as for a cradle)

For countless occasions, this pacified and diverted and it did more. Invariably, the children attempted to learn the words of the song and the motions that accompanied it—motions, I may add, that require considerable manual dexterity of a baby.

The setting in which our three children approached music is, I believe, important to note. There is a stable emotional climate in our home; we all work and play together and from very, very early our children have learned that accomplishment is both work and pleasure, as when one performs well. My husband, who is a teacher, continues to live as a teacher when he comes home. He gives good and patient answers to the children's questions and every day of their lives there has been a conscious form of teaching from us. This learning is discovery, as knowledge is experience; it is not dull and fatiguing, but, instead, joyous and exciting.

From birth, the children grew accustomed to hearing me practicing every day, at regular hours. When they were old enough to observe this, they saw me teaching the piano and classical guitar, and as voice coach, work I did in my home after the babies were born. They saw me, also, working with other instrumentalists, flautists, violinists and cellists, and chamber music was the first actual form of orchestration they knew.

Many times, they see and hear their father and me singing together and also to each other, in a sort of recitative, especially when we are joking. The children were included in this kind of singing and soon learned to respond, so that we developed a kind of family opera. I found it easy to sing instructions, like "Have you brushed your teeth this morning?" and "Dinner in five minutes—make sure you wash your hands!"—not as a conscious attempt to be musical or to develop my children's ear for music but because I could not endure asking the same question, or stating the same rule, over and over, in flat speech.

We spent so much time reading, singing, conversing and playing games (in which music was a large part) with Jonathan, our first child, that we determined to arrange our schedule so that with each succeeding child there would be this same person-to-person relationship on which our eldest thrived. Jonathan had no competition for my attention until he was two and a half years old, when David was born. By the time David was one and a half, and demanding a great deal of attention, Jonathan was attending nursery school four afternoons a week, two hours a day. In these absences of Jonathan's, I devoted myself to David, letting him find and then choose his own areas of interest, as Jonathan had done. We read the stories, sang the songs and played the games that were David's, exclusively, and talked about his activities, as though these were the only important ones. When our daughter, Jennifer, was born, I arranged her "own times" with me daily, to coincide with times when her two older brothers were outside, playing together or with friends who were their peers.

In this way, at the earliest development of a child's interest in itself and in the world, I managed (by putting this schedule in priority to all other household ones) to provide "own times" consecutively for Jonathan,

David and Jennifer. During those private times I learned a great deal about each child, and something about his/her natural responses, especially to music.

Beyond these private times, the children's father and I tried always to make time to answer questions *at the time the questions were asked*, to satisfy a child's demand for knowledge when he was most urgent—and most interested in the reply he got. The clamor and intensity of *now, now,* to read a book or sing a song, occurred most frequently when the children were very young, but as they grew older I found them remarkably patient and kind; very soon they could understand if I asked them to wait, they would, indeed, wait.

One of the things that music was helpful for was teaching a *sense* of time. I found, by playing the piano chiefly, that children are very interested in *fast* and *slow*. *Soon* is something like fast—if you make it into *very soon*, and *not so soon*. I should need a whole book in which to describe all the ways in which I used music, quite spontaneously, to teach about all sorts of things outside music!

One of my first tangible approaches to music was through a gift my first baby received, of a nursery rhyme book published in England, with lovely colored plates—rather different from the nursery rhyme books we get in the U.S. which have "cute" pictures and excerpts instead of the old-fashioned paintings and full-length verses. I recall that from the age of sixteen months Jonathan was fascinated by this book, and would sit for long periods of time, half an hour, at his play table, just looking at the book. I knew the tunes to these rhymes and both sang and read the book to him. Some children learn favorite books by repetition—Jonathan made no such effort but applied the book to reality in life. He would step in a puddle and remark that he was like Mr. Foster who went to Gloster in a shower of rain, and stepped in a puddle right up to his middle. By these occurrences we knew that he had actually memorized the verses, and very early after he began to talk. Yet he made no attempt to *sing* them.

Our friends are often musicians and once, when Jonathan was very young, a folk banjo player, who is a virtuoso, visited us for a weekend. Jonathan was enchanted by him, and jigged about dancing for longer periods than I had ever noted—folk tunes have such strong, imperative rhythms that they lure dance. One afternoon, our friend played for hours and during that time Jonathan danced but chiefly stood in front of the player and watched and listened with rapt attention.

He started playing his own "violin," after seeing a violinist friend work with me—just past his second birthday we would see him tuck a sofa pillow under his chin and walk about, "bowing" very seriously. Then, he asked me to lend him my fife, a smooth metal cylinder, and used this for his bow. He made no sounds and was perfectly content to play this soundless violin, for many a month. Although he discarded the sofa pillow it is interesting to know that he did not discard the violin. From about the age of four he talked of playing the violin, and we told him we thought he should wait until he was about six. The day of his sixth birthday, when he received a shiny "two-wheeler" (something he had longed for) he rode it for a while and then came into the house and said, happily: "Now all there's left to do is go and buy my violin!"

[This was in autumn and it was not until the following January that they sallied out in quest of the instrument, an incident properly left for the chapter *The Child as Artist.*]

I remember, quite distinctly, his response to the banjo and to the violin (only one of which he appeared to wish to play, himself, and not even the one which made him the more exuberant!). We did not own a television and he knew nothing of televised music, only of music made in our home on instruments, and through the phonograph and radio. And he was accustomed to long phonograph and radio concerts of classical music; we heard them every day.

The other vivid response was when Jonathan was a baby, just able to say a few words, and we drove by automobile on a lengthy trip, with the child in a car-bed behind our front seats. He would lean over the seat back and once when his father was whistling I whistled in close harmony, in thirds. Jonathan's reaction was unforgettable: he showed not only great pleasure but enormous excitement. Thirds in music are the most pleasing intervals and you may harmonize brilliantly in whistling. The child was enraptured; he shivered with joy and asked us to do it again and again. This event reminded me of Albert Schweitzer's account from his boyhood, when he heard the sounds of French horns playing in harmony. He was in a hall and the musicians were playing behind closed doors in another room. Schweitzer tells how he nearly fainted with the pure pleasure of the sound.

As soon as the children spoke, they learned to ask for their favorite records. Jonathan (as did the others, after him) took records in cycles and asked for the same one day after day—in desperation, from my own boredom, I would suggest a change. If he liked it, he would then make the new record a favorite, the cycle would commence, and he would want it played, over and over. His taste was eclectic. He liked folk songs, not simply children's folk songs but also the adult kind (he was especially fond of Josef Marais' *Songs from South Africa*), and (like Mrs. Maynard's little boys) early formed an attachment for Bach. "Bach," with the correct German *ch* sound, was one of his first words, used to designate an album of this composer's music, which Jonathan identified by its jacket.

He formed the habit of sitting on the floor in front of the record player and holding the jacket of the record being played, regarding it thoughtfully as he listened. I recall his perennial favorites as being, alternately, Pete Seeger (folk songs with banjo) and Bach's orchestral suites; the Limelighters, and Mozart's horn concerti. He would sit and listen, very quietly, for the length of two 33⅓ rpm records, a long span of concentration for a small child. When David was about a year, he joined Jonathan for these concerts—just as now, with Jonathan at school, Jennifer joins David. These concerts began through my putting on records for my pleasure but eventually became concerts in which a child participated, very positively, by asking for music he wanted to hear—and then sitting down, to consciously and seriously listen.

Such concerts were different to times when the children ran about and jigged as dancing, or sang, or seemed to pay no attention at all to the music.

The children were forbidden to touch my guitar unless I could supervise their "playing" of the strings. Once I was practicing Ibert's *Entr'acte*, which obviously fascinated Jonathan, but as I was working for a concert I concentrated on my playing and did not offer to let him "play." He asked for a drink of water and we went together into the kitchen but while I was pouring the water he ran back as fast as he could and strummed the guitar rapidly, as though life depended on getting this music out of his fingers. Such instances showed me that he found some music irresistible.

We live near a college which offers many public Sunday matinee recitals by students and concerts by artists, and the children have attended these from infancy. Often, these are open-air concerts, but we were interested to discover, recently, that the two boys' most vivid recollection of a concert was one outside the familiar college auditorium. They clearly recalled the occasion and all the details that made it "special"—that the performing group was a teen-aged one, the audience "strange" (the concert hall was thronged with Roman Catholic nuns in their habits), the place "beautiful" (this being a richly tapestried hall with more elegant seating than is usual to college auditoriums), and that they (the little boys) wore "concert suits, with bow ties." They recall, too, that the music was by a string trio, violin, viola and cello, from Bach, Beethoven and Mozart.

This is an event not far away in time, in the adult sense, but already "in the past" of their short lives (they are aged four and six at this writing) so that it is noteworthy that they recall all these details, and a happy augury for the future that they speak of it with such pleasure still.

In our conscious approach to music we have never permitted our children to treat instruments as toys but have always insisted that the piano and guitar, and all other instruments in our home, are valuable and precious, *for making music*. We treat instruments with familiarity, but with respect, and with the sort of practical care that only the musician feels for his instrument. I believe that children are drawn to instruments because of the curious sounds, harmonious or discordant, that they make, and also for appreciation of the obviously *precious* nature of an instrument, in adult opinion.

From the beginning, our children have accepted *absolute music* for its own sake, without a literary connotation such as non-musicians often offer children in the belief that it makes a child more interested in music (or makes music "easier"). A Mozart horn concerto, for instance, is sufficient in itself, to be loved for its own sound and organization of sound. *This* is the kind of "musical appreciation" that I cultivate in my children.

While the familial response to music is general, there are differences in individual responses. Jennifer is still too young to express herself articulately but from about the age of thirteen months, when she walked, showed a great response to rhythm, and to changes in rhythm, by dancing. She would unerringly change tempo from adagio to allegro, and, since she was twenty months, has liked to dance, with very fine awareness of changing tempi, through a long playing album of Spanish songs, which range from very fast flamenco through andante, legato with guitars. But she is still among what Mrs. Maynard classes as the great avant-gardists, the most tolerant and uninhibited of audiences for music, who is interested in any sort of sound. She asks for music, when we get into the automobile, and is contented with whatever the car radio offers, regardless of this being static-ridden rock-and-roll, lachrymose Western ballads, or what radio stations dub "light classical music." At home, she will ask for music from a variety of sources, the FM radio stations which offer what I like best to hear, as well as music from my flute, which she enjoys.

Now at age two, this child sings, having begun by singing the last word or words in every verse or line of verse she heard sung, until she gradually built up her own repertory. Alone, she sings nursery songs like *Mary had a little lamb* and *London Bridge is falling down*, but she likes to join in singing with others, tackling even the complicated rhythms of folk songs—and managing to sing a phrase throughout the song, but just a little behind in tempo.

The two boys approached singing as individuals, although both are verbal persons. And from early both these children showed themselves possessed of a musicianly ear. Jonathan saw a performance of Tchaikovsky's ballet, *The Nutcracker*, when he was three, and some time after, hearing the music on the radio, commented: "That music is from the *Nutcracker* ballet we saw." But he was much shyer about singing than David, as I found out by observing David's response to song and comparing it with Jonathan's as Jonathan had shown his own response, initially.

David was a very agile infant and every wriggly task (like clipping

finger-nails and toe-nails, cutting hair, and so on) was soothed and ex-
pedited if I sang to him, whereupon he would sing, too. Before he was
three, he was reciting nursery rhymes in their entirety and singing, in a
delightfully free style. His melodies were musically unstructured but his
simple rhythms were interesting and strong and his lyrics were relevant and
often witty. His idea of music was comparable to the calypso, in its relevance to daily occurrences. Later, as his imagination grew, his songs were
composed with great freedom and commingling of fact and fantasy, as the
song he composed about Mickey Mantle and his cow (Mickey Mantle put
his cow in his piano and the cow was never milked again). "Mickey
Mantle" was a person he knew off the televised sports programs, and perhaps by hearing adults speak of baseball; a cow in juxtaposition with this
personage was something out of David's imagination, but from no correlation that was made for him . . . nor was this a "nonsense" song, but a
seriously composed one, purely for his own entertainment, while he was
supposed to be having a nap. His songs gradually became structured.

Going about his own affairs, David chose to sing, as:

My   shoe,   my shoe,   where is my shoe?

As I have said, I always sang to the children, conversationally, but
whenever Jonathan would smile and reply in speech, David immediately
sang, and when he sang rhythmically marched and pranced to his own
music.

This child always sang or hummed through all his activities and showed marked rhythmic rapport, when swinging a hammer, kicking his heels, et cetera. He loved only certain books and wanted them read repeatedly, with no improvising, and on my asking him why he was so set on just a few books replied that he liked "the sounds of the words." The sense of them, known to him to the point of boredom (one might think) was not so important as the sound or the music of them. One song became his favorite (a thing about Indians smoking a peace pipe) but he never attempted to sing with me when I sang it on his request and seemed to treat it as a listening song. Then I noticed that he would sit quietly with the book open to the colored pictures which illustrate the text. Next, looking at the picture, he took to beating his drum in very measured rhythms, making music that he repeated in exact rhythms. I listened to them and realized that the song he so loved me to sing, about the Indians and their peace pipe, was written in the pentatonic scale with a repeated open fifth in the left hand, resembling the beat of a drum—and the child had found and held this drum beat. It is a difficult melody and, as yet, David has not attempted to sing the song but his pleasure in hearing it sung never wanes.

David had a greater vocal range and sang at an earlier age than did Jonathan. Although Jonathan, our eldest child, joined in singing when we invited him to (and would even sing me a song, when asked) he did so shyly and very rarely of his own accord. When he was four, I was teaching a group of children, of which he was one, to sing *Aunt Rhody*, a song that encompasses a fifth. I discovered that Jonathan had a range of about a fourth (d to g), which is five half-steps in music. This was not a big enough range for *Aunt Rhody*:

Go tell Aunt Rho - dy, go tell Aunt Rho - dy.

Go tell Aunt Rho - dy, the old grey goose is dead.

I did not try to make Jonathan sing; I simply let him sing. I took care to pitch some songs in a comfortable range for him, yet with the upper notes of the song still outside his reach. I listened, and heard that he sang those phrases in his vocal range with correct pitch, so that I knew he could hear and reproduce melody. When the melody went into the upper notes, outside his range, he sang in a lower pitch, but correctly—whereas many children, trying to sing too high or loud go off-key. I think that it has been no more than half a dozen times, in Jonathan's six-going-on-seven years, that I have shown him ways to sing the upper notes of a song, and then only because he obviously wanted help. I knew that to have tried correcting his pitch too often should have spoiled the joy of singing for this child; I knew that time, patience, and lots of clear, light singing would eventually widen his vocal range.

By the time he was five, Jonathan had a vocal range of a sixth (middle c to a) and could sing *Aunt Rhody*, perfectly—and with pleasure! At present, he has vocal range of an octave and a fourth (see above), and his pitch is excellent. Most importantly, when he chooses to sing, he does so with conscious ease of voice and manner.

As a teacher of music I became very aware of the agony some people suffer when they are required to sing, simply because they have never learned to use their voices, and to take joy in singing. Many adults, and children, as well, are humiliated by the sounds of their voices, which they do not really hear until they sing, because they do not listen to themselves speak in ordinary life. I have often had the difficult task of persuading strong young men and women to open their mouths and lift their voices out of their bodies enough to sing a college song or a national anthem, or a hymn, because they were deeply ashamed of their singing. I learned to approach such reluctant singers little by little, first by teaching them to enjoy a song, then by improving elements in singing. And as enjoyment mounted, resistance fell. This was much the same approach I made to my own little boy, when I found he was shy of his immature singing, and sensed that other children had more powerful voices (i.e. higher ranges).

All our children, as a matter of course, will study music and learn to play instruments, as part of "normal" education. I feel the piano to be of itself a sound instrument, worthy of study regardless of the instrumentalist's individual preference for music making. Since our chief pleasure is chamber music, music made in the home, we naturally will try to interest our children in the instruments of the chamber ensemble. Within this ensemble, the child will make his own choice. We have long hoped for a cellist but Jonathan, ignoring our consistent admiration of the cello, elected to become a violinist, from the time he began sawing at the sofa cushion . . . It is sufficient to us that by living with music, and people who make music, influence and direction are there for the child to respond to, as he wishes, and out of his natural bent.

Even if our children were not, from such early ages, responsive to music, we should still have planned on music as part of general education.

We believe the study of music to be a needed discipline, a training for the mind, an insight into abstract thought, and that daily practice on an instrument is a valuable habit for consistency in academics. We feel that such factors as these are important, but that most important in music is making it for its own sake, for the pleasure of creating and performing, and because it is an enrichment in life.

It is normal for our children to study music and to learn to play; it would be abnormal, in our environment, if they did not.

But we do not intend to make our children, one by one, into professional musicians, for our own whim, and to the exclusion of all other pursuits. Far from that, since their father is a teacher of literature, with a great love for science, we hope that the children will develop a whole culture in which all the arts will be appreciated, and the sciences, also. But if the children choose music as a profession then we shall treat their choices as seriously as we should treat them for any other profession, and help them as best we can, to progress in their studies while they are in our care.

The responsibility for us, as parents, is to maintain the balance between approach and response. And the approach is comparatively easy, when we observe each child's tastes and listen to his questions and remarks. Jonathan and David ask a great many questions about music, some quite pertinent: "If the people playing in the orchestra can read music, why do they need a conductor?"—"Ballet is different from other kinds of dancing; does it take a dancer a long time to learn ballet?"—Jonathan has a natural sense of form. He can always tell, when he listens to music that is composed particularly for dancing, whether it is folk dance (with its strong rhythms) or ballet (with greater flourish and subtlety in the variations and coda).

The children can identify a great number of songs, when I play fragmentary excerpts on the piano, and they have learned the names of the instruments in the orchestra. When Jonathan was only two and a half, I hung on the wall of his nursery a set of enlarged drawings of the orchestra instruments and, as a game, we taught him to identify these by name. In turn, David learned these and now both children have distinct knowledge of the shapes of instruments, and are learning to distinguish their sounds, when they hear music on radio and phonograph. When we see an orchestra playing on television, in close-up, they are quick to point out various groups of instruments.

Jonathan already knows the "families" of instruments: strings, brasses, woodwinds and percussion, and can identify them with ease. I often think of the college students I taught, who lacked basic knowledge of musical instruments, even in an age when we hear music at the dentist and in the supermarket. Jonathan has a general understanding, also, of *how* sounds are made or produced. As he was growing up through infancy, and heard sounds such as plucking rubber bands, blowing into bottles and on willow whistles, and striking ordinary objects, he was naturally interested in the noises, and in how or why such noises happened; we took care always to explain, in terms he could understand. And we later helped him compare natural and ordinary sounds with "made" sounds, organized (in sound and silence) as music. He knew all these things before starting to study his violin; he knew a great deal about sound, and something about movement, before he went to kindergarten.

While Jonathan learned from his parents, David is learning from us and Jonathan; Jennifer will learn from these sources, and from David, also. I am continually learning, through my children. I had thought, before I had babies of my own, that there need be no limitation on music for children; now I know there should not be, and a better rule is to allow children preference (or choice). Decided preference occurs very early. Traveling by airplane between New York and California, Jonathan, at five, elected to hear the classical music program on the closed circuit, and said he did not feel like hearing "pop" music on the alternative circuit. Recently, when the radio was playing a series of popular dance tunes, David, now four, asked me if he could have some music "with violins and cellos" instead.

My husband is a good listener, a trained listener, who is really able to hear music—I tend to listen acutely to music when I am working and to enjoy it for relaxation when I am busy with other jobs. My husband has taught the children to actively listen. He was trained in modern dance, and danced as a college student and has a professional familiarity with dance forms that is a good influence on our tastes. We do not have any decided likes or dislikes in music, we are appreciative of the strange and new, and we are also very fond of old friends—familiar, older music. We are not musical snobs, who grade music as to good and bad; we only qualify music in form, style and performance. I work with equal pleasure and academic interest in Bach as I do in American folk songs; and on my piano in the same spirit of music as I play the guitar and flute.

We did not own a television set when David was born but we later acquired one and have made profitable use of it for the children. Through television, they have had some memorable experiences in music. Once (and this they have never forgotten, nor lost pleasure in recalling) we saw a musical documentary with narrator and cartoon drawings—large, animated, speaking drawings—of instruments. The cartoon cello's bridge was his mouth, which opened to tell the history of the cello, what he was made of, and so on, and then the cello sang in its own voice, in compositions for cello. The musically authentic narration was absorbed by my two little boys without effort, while they were entranced looking and listening.

Folk and modern dance programs have frequently appeared on *Cam-*

era Three, and dance of mainly modern style, with religious drama, on such shows as *Look Up And Live*—both, incidentally, Sunday shows on national networks. Jonathan, who from early saw (and enjoyed) live performances of folk dance has been especially interested in television dance of this nature.

I think I may say that in our environment the children are being trained to be musicians, performers of music. They may remain of amateur status or take on professional status, in their adult years, but they will, in childhood, have been trained to *make* music. Jonathan has begun serious instrumental study and we expect David and Jennifer to begin in due course, with teachers specializing in the instruments of the children's choices. But at home I have naturally taught them rudiments of music because music is my language—just as another mother might teach the alphabet and the writing of simple words, or the numbers and simple sums.

Comparisons of Approaches and Responses in Homes "A" and "B"

The chief, and shared, character of the approaches lies in the fact that these nine children had a "person-to-person" relationship with parents in their introduction to musical arts. In the Kreger home, this association was more realistic than in my own home, since Mrs. Kreger's *way of life*, as well as her tastes, were musical. It is obvious that the best encouragement and stimulus for the child lies in the presence of an instrument in the home, and in associations that are close and consistent with musicians. Mrs. Kreger not only amused, soothed and entertained her children with music; she also educated them musically. Hers is the best possible example of parental approach to the child at home.

The Kreger children, two to six, are classical types of children within a musical home environment, and in the extension of the approach and response of the eldest child, Jonathan, for musical training, we gain further insight into this type of child (for which read *The Child as Artist*).

Although Mrs. Kreger insists that, at this phase, the familial response is generally the same, she does admit that responses are individual to her children—chief of these being that Jonathan initially preferred to dance than to sing, that David sang early and with marked talent (but danced only after Jonathan initiated a dance). The personalities of these children must be taken into account, within the sum of their environment. Jonathan, in school, participated in group song and dance, while at home he chose to dance in preference to singing—but it is patent that his genuine participation in song in school comes through his mother's patient, well-informed development of this child as a singer, from which experience he gained confidence, ease and poise to perform.

My less academically informed approach to my children is readily assessed in analysis because my children are a great deal older than the Kreger children, at this stage. The comparisons between homes "A" and "B" are valuable only for illustrating approaches and responses in *kinds of environments*, and as conclusions that regardless of the parental approach to siblings, responses are highly individual, and predicated by the nature or personality of each child.

Cultivating a Musical Environment

For the child as artist, the intimate approach is inestimable. Mrs. Kreger is the rare parent who not only encourages interest in musical arts but is also able to develop potential talents in them. The majority of parents, however, are not, like Mrs. Kreger, *musicians trained as music teachers* (in itself, a particular kind of musician); they are more often people who love music and know enough about it to answer rudimentary queries on the subject.

The child as artist requires expert assistance, as described in the chapter relegated to him. But for the child who is more ordinary than extraordinary in talent, *the child as person*, less expertise, more romance is conducive to developing a love of music—and with that love, a knowledge of music. The heartening thing for parents to know is that, themselves untrained to make music or to teach it, they can develop musical culture and appreciably encourage talent. A great deal of Sara Kreger's approach to her infants is apt for the non-musician parent.

Singing to babies, while rhythmically rocking them, may be the oldest form of musical approach; certainly it is the most natural, the most loving— and the most effortless way to begin a musical culture for your child. But among the young mothers of my acquaintance, the largest majority of them well-educated (college graduates), a great number of professional status (in arts and letters, and in education), it is not by any means the norm for them to sing to their babies, and, later, to make music and play musical games, with their growing children.

Young mothers of this era are the World War II and post-war generations, emergent from an epoch whose culture altered somewhat from an older American norm. In this epoch, the American family, originally contained in grandparents (perhaps, even, great-grandparents) as well as parents, aunts, uncles and cousins to varying degrees, shrank to the nucleus of parents-and-child, and, in many, many instances, to the nucleus of an only child, and a single parent. The mass migration of Americans through and after the war years substantially cut the familial ties which throve in the "small town" atmosphere, regardless of whether families dwelt in cities or villages. Individuals, and splinter family groups, traveled thousands of miles away from their places of birth, became isolated cultural units in the mass American culture. Paradoxically, as the American musical culture is held to have reached its apex in the 20th century renaissance, it is more an adult culture than a child's. We have almost entirely lost our old "nursery culture," as I write in *The Child in School.* The fact is that a great number of mothers of infants do not know nursery rhymes and songs, either because they were not taught them in their infancy or because disuse of these rhymes and songs has caused them to forget those they may have learned.

These young mothers do not sing to their babies, as Sara Kreger tells of herself singing—and not solely because they do not have a nursery song repertoire. A lot of adults are reluctant to sing, even in private (and with as an appreciative an audience as children) because they are embarrassed by their lack of singing talent. As Mrs. Kreger remarks, she found, in teaching, that strong young men and women were frequently ashamed of the sounds of their voices. Unused voices have rusty and faltering tones, because singing is produced by human or physical means. The less you sing, the less abler you are as singer. The way to remedy your faults is to sing as much as possible, with an alert ear (your own) on the elements of tone and pitch or range. Simply by studying Mrs. Kreger's short lesson on how Jonathan learned to sing *Aunt Rhody*, will serve you well in developing your own voice for singing.

Nor is a parent compelled to sing nursery songs; any kind of song you like, and enjoy singing, is good repertorial material for your infant. Our older children, set to care for the youngest siblings, more often sang Gilbert and Sullivan operettas than nursery rhymes, and to the infants' huge delight. The idea is to enjoy singing, to the extent where, in singing to your child, you create music as an enjoyable, loving experience. If you can tell a story or read one with expression enough to please a child's interest, then you positively can learn to sing for him—and to form for him the lifelong association of happiness or solace, *and music.*

Such musical association, a human and sensual one, lays the foundation for an intellectual musical culture. However inept you may be as a singer, you are altogether superior to "canned" music in this earliest, most intimate approach to musical arts for the child.

The best recordings, labelled "children's records," are a poor substitute for music from a warm, human source. The only right way to approach the infant for his true response is through a person-to-person association, a "private time" of love and experience (which is another and perhaps better name for learning). But in our contemporary society such person-to-person association, in private times, is not casually achieved, even between parents and children. Mrs. Kreger, with rare self-discipline and housewifely management, made private times for her children, consecutively. Most mothers find themselves giving more time to the eldest child, when he alone has first demand on them; thereafter, the younger children must share the parental source.

One good way to do this is to take on the group method practiced in nursery school and kindergarten, and, indeed, in almost all schooling. I practiced this method with excellent results among my own six children, who considerably benefited when I extended the group to take in other children, approximately their peers. The necessary "sharing" was put to profitable use, as valuable experience for pre-school children, and as stimulus for individual responses within the group. Any parent, all baby-sitters, and certainly teachers of infant grades may copy this approach, keeping it flexible enough to preserve individual response within the group sharing of a general approach.

All that has been described in the preceding pages, as approaches in my home and in the Kregers' (and much of what I will describe for *The Child in School*) may be used in the "play-school" sharing approach for children at home. It most often is inaugurated as a game, but can turn into a serious undertaking, for parent and child—serious as being a knowledgeable approach to musical arts.

I fell on the method when on rainy days I found myself with several restless children who quickly ran out of entertainment and resorted to rows to offset boredom. My "music classes" (into which I incorporated "storytelling") were so instantaneously successful that they quickly became actual lesson groups, held two or three times a week, and happily, even avidly, attended by the children in our family and outside it.

First of all, the children had a sense of importance—they spoke of going to "music school" and upon my canvassing opinions as to what this meant they gave me replies such as these:

"Music school is where you go to learn music with clean hands."
"Music school is a place to be happy and good."

"Music school is where you are quiet outside, sitting down and listening, and all bubbly inside from hearing music."

"Music school is where I go to sing and play water-music."

"Music school is where I am going to begin to know all about everything." (*We ranged widely if wildly through several subjects in this course.*)

"Music school is where I am finding out all about music so I can dance."

"Music school is for me to know about music so I won't ever be lonesome."

"Music school is to let me find out how to make music so I can make myself glad or sad in music."

"Music school is a thing for people because dogs and cats cannot make music."

"Music school is my best place because I can dance and sing and play water-music and when I do these things I am bigger than being four."

"Music school is to help me hear music so when I am drawing and painting I can listen *to things* [sounds?] *inside my pictures."*

Essentially, the plan for such an approach is simple, and requires enthusiasm and inventiveness more than a plethora of physical facilities. For dancing, of course, we always require a level space, and if possible a round one (which frees the child to turn around instead of dancing backwards and forwards and sideways). For music, a place in which to sit or stand (or loll) is sufficient to sing in and even to make music, instrumentally. Children today are sophisticates at an early age and a too lax and primitive idea of music often bores or embarrasses them. I chose always to go briskly into the adventure as a "discovery about music," and never referred to what we did as "play." This, I found, invariably gave the occasion dignity, of which infants are more than tolerably well aware. But within this serious (as being opposite to frivolous) approach I took pains to see that the responses remained true and voluntary, however wild in nature and wide of the mark as music, and eventually led the group to a form of analysis of *what music is* . . . and what, as an art, music is about. With rudimentary knowledge, you can initiate such play.

To start with, this idea of music lies in knowing that it is *sound and silence*, and that in its organized state (or form) it contains elements which we call rhythm, tone color and melody (investigate harmony when that, by chance, comes into the infantile music-making). Do not set up an academic study but *let the children find out, by their personal involvements as music-makers*, that "beats" measure out rhythms, that tone affects the sounds of music just as color affects drawing and painting, and that melody comes from the rise and fall of pitch, successions of musical sounds. Sometimes a long time elapses, with the children working in these musical elements, before they are sufficiently interested to want to know the elements of rhythm, tone color and melody—but often a *why* and *how*, and *what is this* query inspires an answer, *because*; thereby bringing a marvelous order to music and a remarkable perception, in infants, about music.

I divide musical experiences for children into "made music," a listening experience, and "making music," a creative experience, frankly utilizing the lessons my own six children, as infants, taught me about these. While the listening experience is within music of the widest variety of form and style, some early training in listening should be to pure sound, for the cultivation of an acute ear (it is also a good way to keep consistent check on your child's sense of hearing, and develop his concentration). Guessing games, played with closed eyes, so that the children cannot see what and how you create sounds, test aural recognition and develop powers of oral description. Years after I had initiated this game for my own children and was playing it with children in group work, I found an excellent record: *The Lonesome House*, by Douglas Moore and Henry Brant. This imitates the sounds of an empty house: dripping faucet, banging shutters, and such, and is deliciously eerie for children.*

What succeeds with one group of children fails with another. A kindergarten teacher told me that her first attempt to play the blindman's guessing game to identify noises resulted in distress—too many children in her class were afraid of shutting their eyes and hearing strange noises in the dark. Then *she* found a record: *But Muffin Can Hear*,† about a little dog with a bandage over his eyes who had to learn to trust to his ears to get around until he could see again.‡

After learning to love Muffin, the kindergarten class enjoyed blindfold guessing games, and developed them until they became adept at identifying the characteristic sounds of instruments in an orchestra. This teacher had the good luck to work with the school teacher of band music, who let her bring the children to practice several times, and allowed the students in the band to talk to the littler ones, and to show them their instruments. This kinder-

---

* *The Lonesome House* by Children's Record Guild, New York.
† *But Muffin Can Hear* by Young People's Records, New York, is from Margaret Wise Brown's stories about environmental sounds: *The Noisy Book Series*.
‡ As a rule I refrain from recommending books and records, since it is impossible to keep abreast of these in a book, but the rare ones of everlasting worth like *The Lonesome House* and *But Muffin Can Hear* are exceptions to my rule.

garten class was eventually the pride of the school, happily showing off (blindfolded in assembly) a prodigious knowledge about "the voices of the band," through fragments played, one by one, by the band students on their instruments.

Learning to listen is the primary approach to music and once this is achieved it appears to stimulate the inner ear, the creative source. I disagree with authorities who maintain that a child should exclusively work "creatively" in music, and have no listening experience to formal music, until he has developed his potential. Such a method seems to me a senseless deprivation of an enormous and intensely inspirational source: the music by the masters of music, in mankind's history. I cannot believe that listening to music is stultifying to a child's potential, for then how do we accept that Mozart, an incredibly fecund musical genius from infancy, was born into a musical environment, was reared in it, and knew none other than this environment?

It is my rule to play as much music as possible by the great masters, for the most frequent concerts, when I am working with groups of the smallest children, and to give them the simplest but also essentially correct statements about music, according to their queries, or by observing their responses. In this way, infants quickly learn to distinguish chamber music from symphony orchestration, and, almost as rapidly, the families (or groups) of instruments in the conventional orchestra. Followed up by actual experience of these instruments (through trips to music stores and also to concerts), such preliminary musical knowledge is absorbed long before the child is in school, or begins study of an instrument.

These experiences in no way preclude the child's invention of music, or spoil his appetite for making music by his own methods and through less than conventional instruments. I have described my children's preoccupation with water-glasses, and Sara Kreger mentions her children's interest in very simple, ordinary sounds like plucked rubber bands,—these are part of preliminary "musical" knowledge for the child, on which a parent can build according to the child's curiosity and pleasure. I have found that children are far less interested in musical toys, like miniature drums and pianos, than in make-shift instruments, and in simple types of instruments like the recorder. The child is usually first a percussionist—but there are many things he can play besides a conventional drum: rhythm sticks, the triangle and cymbal, the xylophone, all available in small, low-priced versions suitable for the child or home. The auto-harp is an especial favorite.

In kindergarten, general use is made of these instruments and also of the tambourine, tone blocks, tom-toms and bells. "Finger cymbals" are especially good, since they are small enough to be manually used by an awkward young player.

In all the deliberate uses made of instruments, regardless of their being unconventional or conventional, the child must learn to distinguish musical values. In this knowledge, he separates sounds as noise from sound and silence that is music, a tremendous intellectual feat for an infant mind. "Making a noise," for exuberance, is *not* making music. The indulgent parent who allows the child to think that any sound is music deludes the child, as does the parent who fondly accepts a strut or jump of themselves as "dancing." The initial approach, cultivated in the child, that dance and music have particular sense and being, eventually awakens understanding in the child of dance and music as having art form.

It is my method to sparingly offer the child instruments for music-making, and to alternate periods of music-making with periods of conscious experience of music, by listening to made music, talking about music and how it is made, and inspecting through pictures or in fact the instruments that make music. These infant music-classes therefore include an appreciative listening, during which it is best to leave the child to the privacy of his own thoughts; and active participation in music as singer, dancer and/or instrumentalist.

I cannot overemphasize the need to let the child enjoy music, in privacy. Note the way in which the Kreger children liked to sit and listen while looking at the jacket off the record and at the pictures in a book, and how ruthless my older boys were about not permitting younger siblings to interrupt their daily concerts. Listening to music is in itself a fine piece of work and should be respected as such—and children as infants still have the faculty to listen and hear what we, as adults, assume to be background sound. Try playing, with your child, a game called *Silence*, in which we sit still and listen hard, and then take turns naming the sounds we have heard. You will find that the child hears far more than you do—the watch on your wrist, the electricity in the refrigerator, his heart beat, and the "tick" his eyelashes make as he blinks his eyes. Since musical elements are composed on fast and slow, and soft and loud, raucous sound is not the only one to learn to listen to; we must also learn to distinguish soft sounds, and distinguishing the nature of these and identifying them correctly are far greater tests of the ear than hearing crashing noises.

A good introduction to instrumentation is to tell the child that every instrument has a voice of its own, with which it sings—as various persons have voices with which they sing. Encouraging a child to find his range, in a scale of music, can be an exciting experience, especially when it is correlated with investigation into the pitch or range of conventional instruments (for which see *The Child in School*).

While I set no limits on the music we listen to, I try to keep within bounds of the music the child can make, with enjoyment, in a current phase of musical development. He will hear and understand far more music than he can physically make, as singer, dancer and instrumentalist—make allowances for the physical development being slower than the mental one, most often, as the child responds to your approaches.

The child as singer should be treated as the child as reader, in that he must not be chided and ridiculed when he does not sing faultlessly (even when he sings the most elementary song form) any more than he should be chided and ridiculed when he stumbles in learning to read a new book. A rare few are born with true and powerful voices but in the main, voices have to grow, just as other physical aspects grow. A child's vocal cords are appreciably shorter than an adult man's, and a woman's—which are shorter than a man's even when they are full grown and well trained. Never speak of a child as having a "bad" voice, and as being unable to sing; instead, assure him that his voice grows as he exercises it and trains it, just as his body and mind grow. *Kinds of voices*, as tenor, baritone and bass, soprano, mezzo-soprano and contralto, may be identified for a child (for instance, through recordings of opera arias), to demonstrate the *differences* in human voices. Music's infinite grace and charm lies in its variance, in subtle differences in the musical range. Many a child is fascinated by coloratura singing, and charmed by the brilliant clarity of the counter-tenor voice.

The wise parent does not rely solely on a known approach, even one that has elicited consistently successful responses. One book, and all the books on the subject of children and music are insufficient to guide a parent in individual approach to a child, since each child is worthy of a library to himself. Make yourself aware of *your* child's areas of interests and strive to develop his taste within his choice, refraining from forcing yours, however good, on the child.

Try to save the child from utter discontent and disappointment. When little boys' voices "break," and they have trouble singing on key, suggest that they try to whistle—singing is not the only form of music; if one learns to whistle well it can be beautiful to hear. There are recordings by excellent whistlers; seek these out for a child who wants to whistle or already whistles in tune. If an infant covets an older child's guitar, now by all statistics the American child's favorite instrument, and longs to play it, he (and you) will find that this is not easy for a small, awkward hand. But a ukelele is, and if you make a good approach through this, as an instrument of the stringed family (as is the guitar) your younger child may soon find pride and pleasure in playing this simple, pleasant-toned instrument. If he chooses to call it *his* guitar, don't quibble; let it be a *kind of guitar* for the present— there is time enough, in the future, for the child to learn the difference between ukelele and guitar and a great many other differences in music. Suffice that he wants to make music enough to try to play!

What if, despite your best informed and most thoughtful approaches, your children insist on choosing music that you consider of the most execrable taste, as their favorites? Before you rantingly condemn it, *listen* to this music—not to the musical notes alone but also to the lyrics of the verses. Perhaps the "pop" songs tell your child what he longs to hear, and allow him a species of empathy not only with music but with life. We cannot make preconceived evaluations of what children seek and find in music; the child has a secret world of retreat into which no adult should pry.

And should your child, as the artist, turn to the execrable for his own expression as composer and performer, do not despair— know that Balzac, in his youth, wrote nothing but trash and in his maturity produced nothing but masterpieces. The child has time to learn form in music, and to perceive style; allow him time, too, to learn to love music, and to use it for his own ends.

When the parent has led a child into knowledge of formal music, through experiences as described, the child should be set free to exercise his musical imagination. Some elementary *do's* and *don'ts* include these:

Do encourage him to be selective and also to learn to respect musical tastes. Do this by "sharing" the records you want to hear with those he chooses to listen to. Talk to him about your music and his music with the same enthusiasm and respect; if you are a musical snob, prevent your snobbery from showing to your child. If he chooses, as his favorites, types of music you do not like it may be because you do not know them for themselves; investigate the musical history of these (he will enjoy hearing about the personalities who created or inspired the music, incidentally) and then find *the best music of this kind*, to play on records for the child, and to buy for his record collection. Do plan this record collection with the same discrimination you plan his library, or choose his pictures and books.

The reverse of musical snobbery is musical curiosity, a most rewarding trait to cultivate. Every musical form has a distinctive aspect, *and is from an original source*. As such this is good music because it is truly music, a creative art form. Within every musical form there exists good and bad examples, and *bad* music is music of banality of theme, mediocrity of composition (poor form), and vulgarity of style. *Bad* music is music ineptly performed, a thing in itself execrable for the ear, and *bad* music is shoddy work—the reverse of masterworks. Bad music is usually contrived by hucksters who tastelessly imitate music of true form, and make spurious adaptations of styles. An example might be a sentimentalized arrangement of Saint-Saens' wickedly witty *Carnival of the Animals*, "brought up to date" in a fawning attempt to provide "music for learning about zoos," or a *bête noir* in dance such as "The Little Flower Waltz," concocted out of Tchaikovsky's *Waltz of the Flowers* in the ballet of *The Nutcracker*.

If you fear to accept the criteria of your own taste, out of a feeling of inferiority as a knowledgeable music lover, learn by reading—not by reading the trade "blurbs" on the record jackets or promotional brochures compiled by press agents, but the opinions of informed writers on music. Discover, from reputable sources, who are considered the finest composers and performers of a musical genre, and choose from their works when you satisfy your child's demands for this kind of music.

Almost every child enjoys "Western" music, the ballads of singers who specialize in songs about cowboys, cattle round-ups, lonesome dogies (orphaned children of cows), and such; know that music of the American West is an authentic genre, and a very exciting one for an American musician and his audience. *Don't accept claptrap in the genre; there is an abundance of true Western musical art from which to select your favorites, and for your child to select his.* I consider American Western folkloric material to be the greatest inducement to developing national art appreciation in children. It is heartier in fare than the lyrical but more melancholy repertoire of Appalachia, our "hill-billy" musical genre; and more universally enjoyed than the Southern musical genre, of which the Negro spiritual is one type. I, an American born and reared abroad, was fascinated by the drama as well as the rhythm of Western music as a child, and have remained so as an adult. I recall hearing *Cool Water* sung in England, by a professional troupe at a concert, and finding that my eyes were stung by tears. It does not surprise me to find, frequently, this same response in children born into the atomic age.

Try to hear *Cool Water* from the child's perspective. Its simple melody is haunting, the theme poignant, but neither are soppily sentimental. The essential drama is universally understood and grippingly realistic: thirst. The verse is poetic in expression, while staying true to time and place.

Two men, "old Dan and I," are lost in the desert, dying for want of water. But they do not lie supine—they travel in search of water, doggedly.

The song thus becomes a courageous saga, as moving as anything glorified by troubadours of the European *moyen age. These are knights of the purple sagebrush, fighting a valiant battle for survival.*

From *any* perspective, this is a vividly characterized and plotted drama —and as a song of its genre it is lovely. Easy to analyse and understand why it is so well loved. There are many such, and in other genres. Mountain folk, plains people, the hunters and the seafarers of our country, all compiled large and distinctively styled repertories of songs as did various working classes, for instance river-boatmen and the railroaders. These songs, loosely catalogued as "American folk" arts, are indigenous national music—and should be the best known, at the earliest ages, to American children. Many of them are comical, with intricate rhythms and superb tongue-twister verses. They are among the most laconically witty songs I have ever heard, in any language. Their merits are so great that they should form the first sum of the infant-and-child musical culture in the United States. To this sum should gradually be added all our ethnic and folkloric music.

I advise parents to provide this folk art repertory at home for their children, before they go to school. There are songs that attract the youngest persons, of the least sophisticated tastes—then, paradoxically, next attract collegiates when taken up as folkloric art, but are apt to be entirely neglected by children in between infancy and late adolescence, the phase of faddist or "pop" music.

And in schools today there are so many taboo subjects that even the musically informed teacher is at wit's end to compile a repertory that engages the children, without offending the supervisors and laymen school boards.

Realize that religion is taboo, which rules out all songs of worshipful praise. Children are allowed to chant *Twinkle, twinkle, little star,* (probably a song that could be put under *Astronomy*) but are forbidden to sing *O, little star of Bethlehem* because it commemorates the birth of the Christian Savior. From a *musical* perspective, this is a ridiculous taboo.

Children in America are allowed (in fact, compelled) to share adult entertainment in cinema and television programming, but are prevented from sharing adult art. Many sea chanteys, with their wonderful, poetic verse (some of a decidedly Elizabethan and Biblical character) and irresistible, lilting rhythms, are *verboten* in school, like the magnificently rollicking:

O, what shall we do with the drunken sailor?

Children should not be exposed to such an indelicate character as a drunken sailor, primly decides a school rule—but the same children are exposed to the perils of drink in serious drama and oftener even in comedy. The "falling down drunk" routine is a cliché for clowns, antic personalities universally recommended for juvenile entertainment. By some mores, the child is supposed to be in danger of moral corruption if he sings certain songs and dances in certain ways, although he is "entertained" by crime and violence, and the crassest, most tasteless pornography in cinema and television. I doubt that children singing the lusty song of the drunken sailor take cognizance of the jolly tar's condition; *they* are generally drunk with the rowdy joy of singing the song!

Equally prim is the ban against mentioning "minority" peoples in songs, although America's folkloric arts all come from "minorities"—the immigrants who brought their songs, dances and characteristic instruments to these shores. A pedagogical prudery bans *The Merchant of Venice* as anti-Semitic and an old song about a Negro girl, as "racially derogatory."

In the song, a sailor bewails his bad luck in love, relating that he first had a Spanish girl, who almost drove him crazy; next had a Negro girl—but she was fat and lazy. It is a rhyme-and-rhythm work song, probably for the hauling of sail and such jobs, and every verse ends with *Way-O, away, away-ay-O*. The air is lovely!

One of my sons, at tender age, took this song to school to "share" and was banished in disgrace. He arrived home, bowed in woe, summoning me to a school conference, where I was told that reference to the Negro was highly unsuitable "for schools." Most interesting for me, soon after this experience with the noxious ditty, was to find, while working with a group of "deprived" children in community recreation, this song a prime favorite in repertoire. The children learned the words quickly (they were not all proficient in English, incidentally) and swayed exuberantly to the melody as they "rowed" with their arms and pranced with their feet in our "rounds" or circles. But I discovered that the song was a special "in" joke for them, as well, and made their spirits rocket with laughter; the best "ice breaker" for the shy and aloof ones.

It is a very good song for a group, since (like most chanteys) it can be sung with a lead voice and chorus, and also can be sung in rounds, and developed fugally into most interesting musical experiments. I noticed that the children loved it, always asked for it, awaited it with eager anticipation—then broke up laughing while singing it. I begged to be let in on this joke and found that it lay in the group having a Puerto Rican child who was very sweet and shy, the least likely person in our group to irritate or annoy, —and, also, a little girl with a complexion of blue-black silk, who was very wiry and spry. The children had immediately sensed the incongruity of their prototypes in the song to the girls in real life, and found this excruciatingly funny.

"You see," said the spokesman, "Maria too nice to send you crazy and Ceecee not fat and lazy—her mama call her 'skinny as a rail and brisk as a bee!' "

Even more interesting to note was the clamor from children in other "minority" groups to "get into the song," which made us invent, as a group undertaking, additional lines like "Came a Polynesian girl who hula-ed all the time-y" and so on, all ending with the mesmeric *Way-O, away, away-ay-O*.

For reasons such as those described here, the child's song repertoire depends mostly on his home environment, and, later, on the communal musical arts of supervised recreation in community projects and the church, of which I shall write further in *The Child as a Social Person*. The religious school and the social and recreational groups of a church should concentrate on exploring as much as possible of worshipful music, as dances, songs and instrumental compositions for divine praise. The community recreational program usually has more spontaneity and freedom than the school's, and it is here that "the music of mankind," *the peoples' music* as folkloric and ethnic arts, should be discovered by the child. But in the end (as in the beginning) the child's culture depends most on that of his home environment.

Do value the phonograph, far superior to radio and television for an approach to music for the child, because it allows him to hear what he wants to hear, when he wants to hear it—and as often as he pleases. He learns by repetition, by experiences repeated again and again. If possible, buy your child his own phonograph and records and instruct him in their use and care; treat them as seriously as you would a violin and a bow, so he knows they are not playthings. Allow him peace and privacy with music, and when he sings and dances don't show him off to visitors, like a trained seal. Some children prefer seclusion; if your child is of this kind, respect his nature. Should he incline to making music more than hearing it made, provide him with a corner, as "music room," and make available (but do not dictate) the instruments he should play. Don't gush over a "little musician," even if the child, veritably, is one. Children and artists are not sentimental; instead, they are practical and tough. Give your child music and musical instruments in the same way you set a place for him at your table—in the latter you provide food for the body and brain, in the former, nourishment for mind and heart.

In your attempts to interest him in your music, exercise care in playing records. Don't heap the spindle with albums, let them play through, and flip them backside to play anew. Many an adult, whose parents inveterately "put on some Beethoven" in this manner, thinks the two first parts of the "Kreutzer" and "Spring" belong together, as one composition. Musical schizophrenia, and a pot-pourri record repertoire of "excerpts of great works," confuse many adolescents, whose childhoods were spent in a "classical" musical miasma. The child has an amiable and eclectic taste, ineffable patience, and he is willing to listen, if you will only allow him to hear. Quality, not quantity, should dictate your tastes in the records you buy for him, as well as the books, pictures, and games.

If you make use of televised programs, seek only the best—good material is rare but it can be found, seasonally. Take Leonard Bernstein's children's concerts for a criteria. In that genre, they are the epitome—informed and exciting, the classroom soundly established and brilliantly manoeuvred into theatre. Distrust all artists who condescend to juvenile audiences; better yet: despise them, on principle.

An Approach for the Absent Parent

The approaches and responses described so far have been those growing out of intimate associations between parents and children. In the environments described, the mother worked at home and the children were wholly in her care until they went to school. The musical culture, in its inception, was from such close, consistent and pleasurable associations.

For the absent parent (the mother who works away from home, leaving her child with a sitter for most of the day) it is not so simple to integrate music into the normal routine. Such a child often lives in a single-parent environment; he may be an only child—he is most likely to go very early to school, even if this is of the nursery or play-school category. The approach to music can still be made by the single parent but must be planned to coincide with the child's most congenial times—and his loneliest.

Here I recommend the tape recorder as a machine even more useful than the phonograph, boon that it is for musical approaches. With a tape recorder, supplemented by as much person-to-person association as is possible, the absent parent can bridge the gap left for the child through this absence. When a child associates music with love and comfort, as well as with pleasure, he turns to it for solace as well as for entertainment. Not the least important of music's many-faceted nature is its psychological influence.

For example: a friend named Isobel, divorced when Tim, her only child, was aged three, was compelled to work full time. She found an efficient baby sitter and arranged that Tim's new routine, in their new residence, should follow, as closely as possible, the one he had known in their old home, when the family had been both parents and Tim. The child seemed to accept the new routine equably enough—except every day at his lunch and nap time, when he became cross and then panicky, refusing to eat and crying until exhausted, demanding the presence of his mother. Isobel had been in the habit of reading him stories before he fell asleep, and he had been used to looking at a television program while he lunched, but the sitter as substitute reader and even the television program were not compensation for Tim's loss of Isobel's attention and presence. Isobel tried having regular telephone conversations with the child, just before he ate his meal, but they worsened rather than helped, since Tim was inconsolable after the conversation ended. Also, Isobel, a buyer for a large department store, often needed to go out of town on short trips, had to keep business appointments, and found it impracticable (often, impossible) to make these calls home.

I suggested that Isobel try to create a musical relationship with Tim, which would last through her absences in the periods when he appeared to miss her most. She usually played records in the evening when they were together, and they would listen and talk about music while Tim ate his supper and got ready for bed. Isobel made lists of his favorite records and his favorite television programs, and left these with the sitter, in the hopes that Tim would be diverted by these familiar, well-loved experiences. But she found that the records that Tim liked when they were together were the ones he most detested his sitter to play, to the extent where in rage he broke several of them.

I now suggested that Isobel use a tape-recorder, an ordinary office machine she used at home for dictating business memoranda and letters; she turned on the tape, unnoticed by Tim, during their cosy evening hours and let it record her and Tim chatting together, and the music of the records they listened to in this period. The day after she first did this, she called Tim at lunch-time, talked to him for a while, and then said that although she had to get to work she had left him a "private time" which his sitter would now give him. Dubious as to enjoying this surprise, Tim nevertheless let the telephone conversation end without demur. The sitter then started the machine, out of which emerged Isobel's voice and Tim's, and what Tim called "my own, own music."

As he listened, the child began to cry, but without the vast rages which had shaken him before on such occasions. Soon, he stopped crying to listen and at the end of the tape requested that it begin again. It was played over and over, while he ate his meal and prepared for his nap, these without weeping and wailing. That evening, when he and Isobel talked, he grinned and said he had liked his "private time" and hoped he could have it again the next day. Thereafter, Isobel frequently made tapes of their conversations and the music she played for Tim, until she amassed a store of such tapes. Finding that Tim was happy hearing them over and over (the taped "private time" was repeated by the sitter every day, during the child's lunchtime) and recalled tapes *according to the music they contained*, she labelled tapes by musical contents so that the sitter could easily find and play a particular one that Tim asked for.

Isobel's and Tim's taped "private times" continued for several months, until Tim weaned himself of his grief—which he did completely when he started to nursery school at age four. He was fortunate in attending an excellent school of this sort, where "sharing" is a great preoccupation, and soon asked for some tapes of music to be made, for sharing in his group. This began a musical association for him between home and school, in which Isobel's part was appreciably assisted by the nursery school teacher, a woman with the skill and wit to integrate music into every facet of the children's lives.

Not long ago, I received an urgent telephone call from Tim, asking for a suggestion in music. He informed me that his class was collecting materials to share in a discussion of space, outer space, and space-travel (a subject set off by a news report) and that he had been elected to contribute "a musical idea." I offered him, instanter, Holst's *The Planets*, which he and Isobel put on tape for school sharing.

When the class had thoroughly shared their project, the teacher extended invitations to parents and friends to visit and observe the results. We found that no single shared idea had spurred more enthusiasm than Holst's in music—the class, divided into "committees," had taken it as the source of (1) a little ballet-play with narration; (2) a remarkable fantasy as chart, drawn and colored with paints, of "outer space" and its starry traffic; and (3) the imaginary inhabitation of the planets. Tim, working in the third committee, had chosen *Jupiter* as his theme, from which to create plasticine hordes of male and female and kinder Jovians. It is indicative of his state of mind these days; Holst designated his music for *Jupiter* in *The Planets* as jollity, and Tim's little creatures were indeed a jovial lot.

Tim is what is called a "gifted" child, and attends a school for the mentally superior child, where his teacher works with him (and with Isobel) in an effort to bring him to fullest maturity—not only mentally but also physically and emotionally. Such children, keenly intelligent, are as sensitive or perhaps more sensitive than other children of their age. Intellect of itself does not supercede the emotional and physical needs of the person, and Tim's grief in losing his mother's companionship was in no way assuaged by his superior abilities of reasoning and abstract thought. He remained as vulnerable as any other three-year-old—possibly, his richer imagination, his more than average power of thought, caused him to suffer more than another child of lower intelligence and more phlegmatic temperament might have suffered. Obviously, music was an influence on the change he underwent with his relationship to Isobel and to his sitter. It appeared to make endurable an unendurable condition of life for the child.

Whither does this initial approach lead Tim? He cannot be said to show evidence of musical talent as singer and dancer, and there is considerable evidence that he has the kind of mind called "scientific." He says that he intends to become an astronomer and the confidence with which he discusses this intent (and the manner in which he uses some of the tools of the astronomer's trade) are indicative of purpose and talent. It is sufficient for the moment that in a time of need Tim found succor in music, and that later he turned to music for a bold, functional use *in his line of work*, as he describes astronomy. I believe that in future Tim will turn to music as he chooses, having made it a prized, familiar possession. Music may mean something different to Tim than it means to the Kreger children—but who is to say which meaning has more validity, which of these influences more power?

Tim's example of a very small child finding solace in music is one to prove the worth of musical experiences for infants and children. Isobel was able to make the association between music and love, for Tim—and she was able to do it as the absent parent through the use of the tape-recorder, faithful replica of voice and melody. The same music that Tim violently rejected from the sitter, in his mother's absence (because the music, which he enjoyed with his mother, underscored his loss) was acceptable and enjoyable when it became part of a "private time" between mother and son. Tim refused to be consoled by her voice on the telephone, or by his music, independent of Isobel's attention—communication by machinery was repellent. But he accepted the music in conjunction with his mother's voice on the tape, when the sounds of music and human voice recreated a *real* private time of intimacy between him and his mother. He could then ignore the sitter, or suffer her without anger; he was safe within his "private time."

A child's mind, even when it is *mentally* superior to an adult's, is emotionally immature. Experiences of grief and loss, even brought to a safe and happy conclusion, cause ineffable anguish for the child, until he learns to accept the experience. When a baby cries piteously as its mother leaves, it is not that he wants to accompany his mother on a jaunt, but that he fears he will never be reunited with her again if he lets her go. Such grief can be intense and unassuageable, unless a compensation is found for the child.

My suggestion to Isobel was prompted by my memories of the war, of victims of the blitz, buried out of sight and in the dark, who after being saved declared that their spirits had been kept up through human voices calling down to them, and singing songs to cheer them up until they were exhumed. Children often show response to music as to love, and find a lost intimacy by way of a familiar melody.

Sara Kreger relates having to go to hospital, for a back injury, when David was a baby, and returning home to sit, in which position she could hold the child, although she could not pick him up. He refused to go to her but clung to his father; he seemed to have forgotten his mother, even her voice when she spoke to him. One day she was playing her flute, and her husband came into the room carrying David—who at once smiled and held out his arms to her, recognizing her by the familiar air played on the flute. He sat contentedly in her lap, listening, and thereafter accepted her back from whatever mysterious place she may have gone—to return not in her physical self, or even in her speaking voice, but as that sound (the sound of the flute) with which this baby most closely identified his mother.

Another small child, devoted to her father, consoled herself in his absence on military service by listening daily to tapes he had left for this purpose, on which he talked, played his guitar, and sang for the child—as he had continuously done in person. When the father returned home, the child shrank from him, finding him altogether strange. One day, she came on her father playing his guitar and singing, and threw her arms around him, crying: "Why, here you are inside your new self!"—as though his only *true* self was the self that made music.

Some aspects of the musical responses described in this book may seem closer to areas of psychology than to art . . . but as they are all truly described we must consider them part of the children's musical experiences, and within the character of music, as its influence.

The Child as Artist

"There are two ways of disliking art . . . One is to dislike it. The other, to like it rationally. For Art, as Plato saw, and not without regret, creates in listener and spectator a form of divine madness. It does not spring from inspiration, but it makes others inspired. Reason is not the faculty to which it appeals. If one loves Art at all, one must love it beyond all other things in the world, and against such love, the reason, if one listened to it, would cry out. There is nothing sane about the worship of beauty. It is too splendid to be sane. Those of whose lives it forms the dominant note will always seem to the world to be pure visionaries."

OSCAR WILDE: *The Critic as Artist*

A "musical" person is one who knows music, and, as we say, loves or appreciates the quality and character of music. It is, primarily, a person who *works in music*. The child has musical instincts from birth but the "musical" child, the potential artist, is different from his fellows. The artist is not ordinary; he is *extra*-ordinary, different in certain ways from other persons, including the persons to whom he is most closely related, biologically.

When we recognize the artist in our society, we go against the national grain: we admit that some few are different than, and in certain ways superior to, the many; that in our midst, sharing our place and time, there are one or two so singular in themselves that they are like no others we know. For the parent to realize this, and accept it, especially when it must be accepted as being true of only one child in a family, is not quite as easy and happy as it might seem. It is tenable only in a truly artistic family, where understanding of his kind of mind breeds empathy for this kind of child.

In this chapter I write of the *extraordinary child*, the potential artist, in a different perspective to that in which I write of the child who is average in instinctual musical talents, "normal" because he shares universal response but does not have a particular *artistic* approach to, and concept of, the musical arts. The average child, in what I consider to be his normal musical education (his artistic life which integrates his gymnastic life) is studied further in *The Child in School* and *As A Social Person*. Here, in *The Child as Artist*, let us inquire into the *extra*-ordinary child.

There are two types of artists: creative and performing, and in American musical arts the types commingle to great extent. How such artists develop and manifest their gifts depends partly on environmental influences but more explicitly on the personal will, as well as the personal talent, of the artists. When we study case histories of musical genius we discover that while environment stimulates innate talent, environment does not breed it.

Indeed, there are examples galore proving that genius is wholly independent of environment and continuously emerges from environments that discourage it!

The two most famed women dancers of the first part of the 20th century were the Russian ballerina Anna Pavlova and the American "interpretive" dancer Isadora Duncan.

Pavlova, born of peasant parents, was reared in extreme poverty. Fatherless from childhood, supported by a mother who was a laundress, she was near death at least twice from scarlet fever and diphtheria. At the age of eight, she saw a performance of *The Sleeping Beauty* and was seized with the passion to dance (perhaps to *be*) Aurora. The weak and sickly little girl was refused admission to the Imperial Ballet School at St. Petersburg; she was judged as having no aptitude or potentiality. Persisting in her desire, but with no means of learning dance, Pavlova persuaded the Imperial Ballet examiners to accept her when she was ten. Eight years later, she danced at the Maryinsky Theatre as a ballerina, in the role of Aurora in *The Sleeping Beauty*. Thereafter, she was to make ballet as artistically acceptable as symphony and to inspire untold numbers of little girls to dance.

Duncan's father deserted his wife and older children before Isadora was born, in San Francisco in 1878, to a poor Irish-American family. Nothing distinguished her in childhood except a divine madness: she believed that she was a child of the Greek gods, who ruled her life by signs and portents. She solemnly dedicated herself to Dionysus and to dance, which she propounded as a spiritual and intellectual cult as well as an art—so successfully that serious and prestigious men and women of arts and letters in England and the Continent hailed her as a genius and adopted her precepts in the arts and society. Isadora Duncan is the wellspring of all "modern" dance.

It is inconceivable, today, to think of ballet and modern dance without Pavlova and Duncan.

English and American dance is notably emergent from individual genius rather than environmental stimuli, of the kind which distinguishes major dance dynasties in France, Denmark, Italy and Russia.

The English *primas ballerinas* Alicia Markova (born Marks) and Margot Fonteyn (born Hookham) were children of middle-class British families. The genius of modern ballet, Antony Tudor, was born and reared in Clerkenwell, a lower class London district, and worked in the Smithfield Meat Market until, by chance, he saw a ballet performance and became mesmerized by dance.

The American dance pioneers, Ruth St. Denis and Ted Shawn, and the dancer-choreographer Agnes de Mille (who has based her original con-

cepts for ballet and modern dance movement on folk dance and psychological research) had no guidance and, in the case of de Mille, had to
surmount strong parental disapproval in order to dance. Eugene Loring,
creator of the first American ballet classic *Billy the Kid*, was the son of a
German-American saloon-keeper and amateur boxer, and was trained as a
gymnast as well as a pianist. After high school graduation Loring worked
in a Milwaukee hardware store until he saved enough money to go to New
York and study ballet. Jerome Robbins, perhaps the single most influential
figure in American dance today, cleaned Venetian blinds in a dance studio
in return for lessons, as an adolescent. William Dollar, the first native
premier danseur, worked in his father's modest store in St. Louis, Missouri,
and taught himself to dance out of books—well enough to win a scholarship
to Balanchine's School of American Ballet, then as now the most prestigious
ballet training-ground in the United States.

America's three great *primas ballerinas* of the century, the dramatic
ballerina Nora Kaye, the romantic ballerina Alicia Alonso, and the classicist
Maria Tallchief, are phenomenal individual developments—and Alonso and
Tallchief had to defy familial mores to become professional dancers. Kaye
(born Koreff to a Russian-American family) was a child super at the
Metropolitan Opera, hauled about in a sack as the murdered Gilda in
Verdi's *Rigoletto* and pinched to shriek convincingly as a gnome in Respighi's
The Sunken Bell; from this she turned to dance.

In music, geniuses are developed from environmental influences that
marked those of Purcell, Rameau, Bach, Gluck and Weber, who in childhood
were trained to music as a way of life. In such influences emerged Mozart,
a prodigy who was composing at five and from six astonished mature
instrumentalists with his gifts.

But the musical genius also emerges from wholly contrary environments,
as those of Haydn and Verdi, whose lives are eloquent testimony of the
creative impulse aroused without encouragement and pursued despite discouragement.

Haydn was fired from his job as choirboy (at St. Stephen's Cathedral
in Vienna) when his voice broke in adolescence. Instead of retreating to
his home village of Rohrau, he stayed in the city, living in an attic and
eking out a subsistence as a harpsichord teacher—while he patiently taught
himself harmony and counterpoint. He could not afford to study under a
teacher, so learned from the writings of other musicians—but Haydn became
master of the symphony and one of the most revered musicians of a rich
musical age.

Verdi's father was a poor peasant who, to satisfy the child's inordinate craving for music, bought a spinet and paid for music lessons for his son. But at nineteen, when Verdi applied for admission to the Milan musical academy, he was refused because he had been badly taught and was judged too old to learn anew. Returning home (after a short term of study under a good teacher in Milan) Verdi continued to work at music. He was famous at the age of twenty-nine and by his death (in 1901) had become immortalized as the best loved of all opera composers.*

From the scientific studies that have been made to determine musical aptitude in children (according to age and gender, racial antecedents or nationality, and intellect), I consider the two most interesting generalizations to be these:

1. While the children of musically talented parents are often themselves musically talented they are not always so, and within a musical family (where one or both parents practice music as a profession) there may occur marked differences between siblings as to musical ability. Inherited musical talent is to be observed in the lives of composers, conductors, instrumentalists, singers and dancers—but some of the famed of these categories emerged from non-musical backgrounds. The greatest conductor of the century, Arturo Toscanini, and the most celebrated living pianist, Artur Rubinstein, are two such musical mavericks in their families.† Contrarily, the composer Igor Stravinsky came from a musical background, his father being a basso of the St. Petersburg Imperial Opera. (And Stravinsky's son, Soulima, became a concert pianist.) The Wagnerian diva Kirsten Flagstad's father was an operatic coach and a pianist; the piano virtuoso Vladimir Horowitz's mother was a talented musician.

Notably, there are many famed sibling musicians: José Iturbi and his sister Amparo as pianists; Yehudi Menuhin, a child prodigy and violin virtuoso, and his pianist sister Hepzibah; the great cellist Pablo Casals and his violinist brother Enrique. Inherent musical talent, a matter of genes, may be partly responsible for such sibling musicality but there is also the factor of influence, the older child providing stimuli and creating an environment in music for a younger child.

All the studies undertaken subscribe to the generalization that one is, or is not born with an extraordinary gift for dance and music. We may

---

* For further insight into the careers of these musical artists see Maynard's *Enjoying Opera*, *The Ballet Companion* and *The American Ballet*, *Bird of Fire*, and *American Modern Dancers: The Pioneers*.

† Toscanini was the son of a poor Italian tailor; Rubinstein, of a Polish factory owner—who thought so little of the infant prodigy that he refused to pay for his music lessons.

thus speak of the "born" dancer and musician. But there is, as yet, no positively proved method of creating a dancer and musician, either through heredity or environment. *Genius cannot be contrived, and the creative impulse may and often does impel the individual regardless of uniform environmental or hereditary "norms." Talent is not a product of or the result of education, or training.*

2. Intelligence and musicality are unrelated. In tests to determine normal, supernormal and lower than normal degrees of intelligence it has been found that the superior intellect is by no means the most talented musician's mind. On the contrary, some persons of very high intelligence quotient (I.Q.) and persons considered "educated" as having graduated from university curricula, are musical ignoramuses and are proven to have less talent than persons of considerably lower I.Q. and inferior education. A great musician can also be illiterate, as were many gipsy violinists; an intelligent, well-educated person may be wholly without musical knowledge and have less than average musical aptitude.

Academic proficiency is not an indispensable attribute of the talented dancer and musician, who by necessity devotes himself (his time, energy and faculties) to his art form and not to academic subjects which qualify the student for careers in professions like law and medicine, the ministry and the military. There appear to be physical as well as psychical "types" that are musically gifted, and "born" dancers and musicians may have utterly no aptitudes in other arts—although my personal and quite modest studies lead me to state that many choreographers have the acute sensibilities of the painter, as to spatial relationships for detail and mass, light and perspective.

I.Q. is based on the assumption of ratio between mental and chronological ages, in values of 1-100, and when the mental age is greater than the chronological age the I.Q. is considered to be proportionately higher. In the United States' educational system the premise is that children work and study according to chronological age; only now and then and here and there do American educational administrators qualify the system by mental age instead of chronological, establishing mentally superior children within a chronological age as being "superior" to the norm. And it is too generally propounded that when a child rates as inferior or superior in I.Q. testing his intelligence measurement remains fixed or thereafter alters but little from the established figure.

The arts frequently exert obvious influences for good, in raising the I.Q. percentages of children, because such children respond to artistic approaches—their minds are types of minds which comprehend better through artistic media than along conventional academic lines, or lines which are adopted for general testing of comprehension. My work with children who are aurally deaf, and emotionally disturbed, convinces me that there are such types of minds as perceive through art media what they cannot or will not through other means.

The *musical mind* is a complex, subtle one, impossible to measure by academic standards, and by the rules for testing the machine-oriented or scientific mind. Musicality has to do with physical and psychical factors (among the first being "handedness" and aural sensitivity) in which emotional concepts, *perceptions of music*, allow the musical mind to understand discriminations in rhythm, pitch, tempo, tonality (and dancers: space and levels), too finite and minute for the non-musical mind. The musical artist is specially endowed, much of his endowment is utterly incomprehensible to the layman, but some of his attributes can be ascertained in the *untrained* child, of both genders.

In America we tend to think that more girls are artistically gifted than boys, and I.Q. tests establish girls as being generally cleverer than boys of chronological ages, within like environments, *but only up to a certain age and phase of development.* The apparent artistic superiority of American girls over boys is from the erroneous assumption that the artistic male in our society is inferior to the males who are academic, mechanical, gymnastic and military. Moderately talented girls are encouraged to develop their potential, and receive expert training in dance and music, from early ages, while truly gifted boys realize their potential, generally, by their own efforts, and later than girls—usually, after they have completed elementary and secondary education. This is especially true in musical arts—but all the major composers of the baroque, classical, romantic and contemporary music are male, there is not a single great female opera composer, and no woman has yet exerted a musical influence comparable to any man's!

The majority of parents who discuss children and the arts with me admit a rooted distrust for the influence of the arts on male children, especially the influences on boys who sing in tenor and countertenor tones, play the oboe and violin, and study classical ballet. They express morbid fear that these musical pursuits tend to make a male child effeminate instead of masculine. This fear, which must not be censured or derided since it comes from parental love and concern, stems from the superstition that a boy who is drawn to the artistic life is likely to develop homosexual appetites in love. This genuine horror in parents, especially in fathers, makes several forms of the artistic education *verboten* for young boys, even in pre-school and first elementary school grades. It is an idea that plagues parents of artistic children even more than the worrisome thought of how an artistic child will earn a materially rich living, in a society which does not pay highest wages to the creative and performing artist working in genres that are not popular entertainment but are called "cultural."

The question earnestly asked is: does a boy who is drawn to, and allowed to study and work in music and dance more readily develop homosexual relationships in physical love than his brother who studies to become a scientist, and develops as an athlete? Is the artistic life a sensually "perverted" one, according to social mores, and are not musical artists most often homosexuals?

The factual answer is that homosexuality is not a functional artistic trait, but that large numbers of creative and performing artists, in all media, freely admit to being homosexual. Scientists and athletes do not as freely admit to being homosexual when they are, because social mores impose a rigid virility on science and physical culture but are more tolerant in attitude towards the arts. Yet we know for certain that some famed scientists and famed athletes have admitted, or been proven, despite their denials, to be homosexual. To conclude: some males pursuing the artistic life are homosexual, as are some males in other professions that are not artistic. We cannot assume that the artistic life is a homosexual one, any more than we may authoritatively declare that the scientific, academic, gymnastic life is a nonhomosexual one.

The American distrust of "perverted" sexual appetites is a social morality which is not to be discussed here. But the illogical bias of American audiences to only some (not all) creative and performing artists must be touched on, in this chapter concerning the child as artist. Homosexual relations in physical love (called Lesbianism among females) do exist in contemporary arts and letters (though not exclusively in these); so much is factual. However, a particular art form, its pursuit by the artist, the gear he uses in his techniques and his training, do not cause some artists to become homosexual, above all other artists in other métiers.

For instance, there are no known statistics to prove that a flautist and a violinist are among the highest homosexual quotients—and that all pianists are virile in the accepted norm of masculinity. Sculptors, working in stone, clay and other materials, are not more ruggedly (and morally) "male" as we think of maleness, than the artist of "abstract" genre, even when he employs water-colors. Dancers in ethnic and folk forms, in "modern" dance, and in acrobatic, eccentric and comic dance forms are not established, *by the natures of their genres,* as masculine, while ballet *danseurs,* of the classical *danse noble* type, are to be known, inveterately, as homosexual.

And yet, to take the last example, it is the classical ballet *danseur* who is generally taken to be effeminate and to practice sexual perversion *as part of his nature as the artist.* I do not hear of the "ethnic" American dancer, the tribal Indian or Negro jazz dancer, classified as homosexual, but I am continually informed, by members of the general audience whose knowledge of dance arts is superficial, that all *danseurs* are homosexual, or prone to homosexuality. As far as I have been able to judge, the belief rises out of the costume worn by the *danseur,* which is considered to be revealing to the point of perverted male excitation—but which, in absolute fact, is the same *maillot* (French for "tights" or bathing suit) worn by the acrobatic gymnast, from whom ballet borrowed this particular garment. Male figure skaters may be overtly homosexual in private life but in performance they are invariably accepted as "masculine" by the American audience.

In *The American Ballet,* chapter *Looking At American Ballet,* I have written of the attitudes in American classical dance, as compared to those in other national theatres; the reader is referred there for further statement on this topic, and to the note that in the Kinsey report of a study of the male in contemporary society the greatest percentage of homosexuality was found to exist not among artists but among two strata of the most romantically "masculine" concepts held today: cowboys and bullfighters.

Parents must not stifle musical talent in male children in the belief that encouragement of it morally endangers the child and makes him a social outcast. They should not assume that sensitivity is a feminine proclivity and insensitivity the hallmark of maleness. While it is true that fewer men and more women achieve professional careers in dance and music this is the end product of the system which provides more educational advantages and overt encouragement and approval for women artists than for men artists. In spite of the unequal opportunity, there is conclusive proof that in music the composer, and in dance the choreographer—the *creative* artists in these métiers—are predominantly male, and that more men have musical genius than women, in our recorded musical history. Male genius is predominant over female genius in all creative forms of theatre and fine arts.

In this necessarily brief discussion I hope to clarify the truths about the artistic life and the ethics of genius in art, so that parents will realize that a life in music is as fitting a pursuit for men as it is for women; that the musical education provided at home, in school, and within the community should be equally for the boy and the girl; and that, above all, when the child shows evidence of becoming the artist he must be unequivocally recognized as this person. Teachers and parents alike must accept the *being* of the artist, and the artistic potential of a child, without regard for the sort of child, male or female in sex. Thereafter, the concern is for the *type* of artist, his pronounced area of riches, and the most fruitful means of developing the mature artist out of the immature but potential artist in his childhood.

The first step is logically the parents', who should from early in the child's life become aware of its potential as a whole, including the artistic potential.

Parents ambitious for their children's material gains, for development of their greatest native talent and aptitude, should not only rely on intelligence quotient tests for academic skills, and on biological tests for physical well-being, but should also make studied assessments of children's musical talents. It may be that a child who is inept at gymnastics and sports (perhaps through an abnormal shrinking from gross motor activity and group play) is talented as a musician. And that a child who makes a poor showing in tests for academic courses is a "born" dancer. *This child may be within a wholly non-musical family.*

The area of music (especially when that stretches to encompass dance) is so large and richly varied that it offers unstinted choice and possibilities for development. When a child is less than a creative genius and more the type which establishes the performing artist or the technician in the arts, then music and dance open up for him theatre professions which extend far beyond the stage and auditorium.

The American educational system has not thoroughly instigated music in the normal curricula because the arts are still suspect as being "frills" on the so-called "basic" or utilitarian educational ideal, and as a result musical arts are not fully explored in our schools and colleges. But we generally instigate health and "physical education" within the curricula—and it is through P.E. that dance *per se* has made its greatest gains.

Music should also make its positive and lucid gains through P.E., because of the proven relationship between muscular and musical development. Manipulative and equilibrium testing statistics indicate that the highest musical and muscular scores are counted in the same students. In the newly emphasized national ideal of physical fitness this factor seems, so far, to be largely unexplored.

The child who seems mentally dull and physically torpid; who is considered shy and timid, and "withdrawn," may be a child waiting to be discovered through music because his true nature is a musical one.

Children begin life in a state of innocent savagery and discover crime and punishment, failure and shame. Quite suddenly, usually at about seven into nine, they find that, as they say, they are continually "in trouble" at home and in school. They are either being urged to grow up faster and within a mold different from their natural one, or being retarded by negligence or ignorance about their potential. This "potential" in itself is seen as "resources" that are useful or convenient to the child's society, rather than productive of the best qualities of the child as the individual. Seldom is the child allowed to realize his potential, in an artistic life. More usually, he is obliged to affirm potential, as "performance values," in stereotypes of academic and vocational métiers. His artistic development is incidental and by chance, at home and in school. When artistry develops in the recreational program, it is treated as fun-and-games, as a superfluous frill and not an important element in growth.

Realistically, inquiry into a child's musical mind, his sense about the substances of dance and music, will reveal a great deal about the child and about his potentialities. Nor is this potential only an artistic one. Tests of abstract nature relate to music and dance as well as to arithmetic and physics, *except that the "musical" child responds more accurately and articulately through music than through mathematics.*

In the same week as I write this page I have assisted in tests of "stupid" children in elementary school grades who are failing to maintain "average" development in mathematics because of a mental block or obtuseness in the mathematical jargon. Yet these children have passed, 100%, tests put to them in abstract discussions of dance, as in the queries: *does a straight line have a middle?* and *is half a circle the same size as the other half?* (These questions were chosen from an annual test for *a mathematics contest for high school students,* but put *in terms of movements in group dance to 6th and 7th grade students.*)

There is evidence that paralysis of ordinary thought, especially concerning abstract ideas, can be remedied by applications of dance and musical ideas, when the right approach is made to the child. School psychologists and counselors need to know all such approaches, the better to help teachers and students achieve their best.

Discovering Musical Talent

Marvelling at Bach, scholars have pored over his history, tracing it backwards into his antecedents, and from him, into the famous sons of Bach. But is it not an even greater marvel that another Thuringian family, the Lortzings, were hereditary hangmen for two hundred years and abruptly, on October 23, 1801, produced Albert Lortzing, the actor, singer, librettist and opera composer?

In electrifying ways, the musical genius makes itself known, sometimes as though to assure us that a Mozart will emerge from a household like Leopold Mozart's but, too, that in a family of executioners there may suddenly appear a maker of music (and Lortzing was a composer of *romantic comic* opera, at that).

The true gift takes no thought of place or person but when it is evoked it must be recognized and cherished, or it may wither from neglect, dying before it ever comes to maturity. A gift for composing may be conserved and sustained until a child grows up and becomes independent of his parental environment, free to develop as a choreographer or composer. But for the professions of singing, dancing and instrumental music the child needs parental support and favor, enough to procure him the sound rudiments of a good musical education. A responsible parent, therefore, will treat the musical gifts of the child with the same seriousness that he treats academic or gymnastic promise, in making the child an artist, a scholar or an athlete. Unfortunately, the recognition of a musical or other purely artistic talent is sometimes omitted from parental insight. When the talent is overt, one or both the parents may hesitate to develop it, from sexual phobias discussed here and the belief that (a) the child is better off, as an adult, earning a livelihood at a "non-arty" profession; (b) a naive spontaneity in childhood is a mere frivolity but not a positive indication of real talent, and thus the expenditure of time and money on a musical education is impractical.

Another prevalent parental supposition is that if the child is talented he will develop as a "natural" and be "discovered" by a talent scout, in the myth of the musical and dramatic Cinderellas made famous in fiction. Otherwise, how is the parent to guess, far more to know if the child has potential?

Genius, like lightning, may suddenly illuminate the child's musical career, or it may be a star which has to be sought and identified.

Each person has an individual rhythm and a child's natural rhythm is more easily noted than the adult's, because the child moves with more freedom and less self-consciousness and his clothes do not restrict or alter this natural movement in the ways, for instance, that a woman's natural rhythm is affected by the kind of shoes and corsets she wears. And each musically talented child has an area of richness, in which he will achieve his greatest potentiality. The parent who hopes to develop musical artistry in a child can make some preliminary judgments of the child's gifts and aptitudes— but no parent should attempt to decisively plan a musical career for his child. The most he should do is be alert for evidence of talent and the best he can do, thereafter, is to cherish it, without making the child the slave to parental wish but also without hampering the child's own ambitions. This is a delicate and precarious balance to strike but it can be maintained.

Other than the environmental factors already discussed (in *The Child at Home*) the best passive influence is the presence of a musical instrument in the home, and the most inspiring influence is to bring the child into the presence of the professional dancer and musician, in performance and also through "cognitive" teachers (of which a great deal more will be said in other chapters).

And the parent who knows his children well, in daily existence, will surely be able to distinguish certain characteristics which relate to dancing and music making.

A "natural" dancer has good muscular control, equilibrium and excellent sense of spatial relationships (which dancers think of as locating in space) and better than average kinesthetic reactions.

The body or physical aspect of the "natural" dancer is in reality a particular instrument, notably one of fine proportions and coordination (muscular and nervous), thinner and slighter but *stronger* than the average, organically sound (especially the heart and lungs) and with the quality best described as stamina. Stamina includes energy and resilience and a number of other attributes, and stamina is the fourth ingredient for a dancer—the others being talent, training and the indefinable but infinitely important perception called "soul."

This perception is remarkable in inarticulate or disturbed children, who lack coordination in ordinary tasks but will actually dance with spirit and who find it impossible either to express love or attract affection and admiration, except in dancing. My own observations with children and dance and music lead me to believe that children who will neither act nor sing, and will not or cannot learn instrumentation, will freely express themselves in dance. One type of child who often has a secret aptitude for dance is the physically aggressive child, who obviously enjoys his own body and has at least one but perhaps several notable dance attributes: a natural ability to jump and turn, an acrobatic flair that is not exactly gymnastic but may appear eccentric for being practiced incongruously—sometimes to provoke attention or parental and teacher remonstance; in short: a physical show-off with a touching grace and agility.

Generally, this distinct physical type is also a distinct psychological one, either introvert or extrovert, and most usually the latter. He may be a "loner" or the member of a peer group or "gang" which accepts his eccentricities as frolic and not as dance—but in his heart, if not in his consciousness, this child is desperately *dancing* when he seems to misbehave or to behave in a comical or fantastic manner. If he is a child in a family or school group who does not quite fit into the "nice" norm, and seems to fail or fall short of the median accomplishments set as standards, he may be incapable of achieving his best except through dance.

If all these aspects are combined, in the child, with a bold and original expression in drawing or painting, I would be willing to say that here is a sensitive, searching *dancer* in hiding—waiting to burst out of the active, almost destructive little body, and the moody, provocative, baffled mind. This sort of child is not easily categorized; I find him coming into a group out of a financially and socially "upper class" residential area and, just as often, into a group out of an abysmal slum like one of the black ghettos of today's America. And my conclusions are that perhaps only through learning to dance and working in dance can he be saved from the worst to realize the best in himself.

A "born" dancer has qualities which no teacher can impart: *accent,* the gift of knowing the precise instant at which to emphasize a step to give it maximum effect (this is a rare intuition, but qualifies great dancers who perform always in good taste); *timing* and *projection,* all of which are psychical as well as physical attributes. There are great ballerinas of various styles, and different physiques and temperaments, but all of them bear psychological and pathological resemblances.

A child who has aptitudes for dance will, for instance, be acutely aware of tempo and of rhythm, and will show excellent equilibrium. A very young child (see Mrs. Kreger's description of Jennifer) will show discrimination about speed and intensity of tone, in shifts in dance from allegro to adagio, and from lyrical to brio dancing—these will be shown without prior instruction and as responses native to the child.

Jonathan Kreger (by my own observation) very early showed an almost unerring sense of time duration and tonal fluctuations, by patting or clapping his hands and tapping his feet; had marked aptitude for very quick, very precise changes in movements (skipping, hopping, sliding, gliding, et cetera), and performed all his dances within a musical phrase (not pas by pas, or step by step), ending with a flourish: the arms and hands positioned, the head well set in "line" with the torso and "working" leg, and the feet gracefully and strongly situated. This child showed the strongest awareness of the dynamic image of dance.

Besides, he was physically well formed for dancing, had a strongly developed response to music, and could *move* with remarkable muscular and nervous control, as in turns, fast runs and sudden stops, control of head, arms and torso in opposite placement of hips and legs and feet, partial spirals revolved back within the original turn, and a sense of the *use* of his body, as when he ended a dance phrase on tiptoe, on one knee, or in other well chosen "stops" or reposes. And he performed all his dancing to music and always within the time of the music, completing his dances within a closing phrase.

When Jonathan Kreger was four, after he had been dancing for almost three years in the manner described, he was taken to see an American Indian dance ceremony at Santa Fe, New Mexico, and watched numerous tribal dances within intimate surroundings (a museum courtyard) where the dancers were in informal relationship to the audience, but nevertheless were costumed and in full regalia. After this incident, although no attempt had been made to teach the child, Jonathan included movements from Indian dances in his spontaneous dancing, and adopted some Indian body placements. He perceived the *differences* between his dancing, the Indian dances and, also, folk dance—which he also knew from seeing this form in dance festivals he attended with his parents.

Perception of subtle differences in movement and the ability to quickly learn new movements, are very important attributes for the dancer.

If your child possesses such attributes and innate knowledge about dancing then you can be sure that he is talented as a dancer. You must then find *the best teacher in the dance form best suited for your child to begin studying*, and provide the child with the physical and moral sustenance the dance student requires. Without sufficient training and without opportunity for a professional career the theatre dancer (as opposed to the naive or "expressive" dancer) cannot practice his art.

When a child shows musical aptitude (a love of music and characteristics described in *The Child at Home*) the problem rises as to what instrument is best suited to his study. This, aside from the child's desires, is a matter of what instrument he is suited to, physically and temperamentally. The instrumentalist, like the dancer, must have good equilibrium and muscular control. For the stringed instruments, he requires what musicians call "handedness," good control of strong hands, the right and the left. The singularly strong, adept ambidextrous player is a fortunate person! The organist must develop hands *and* feet. In the main, string players seem to have the most natural sensitivity to music, and percussion players the least. This is a generalization as is the statement that brass instrumentalists have stout and not slight physiques; invariably, they have better than average lung power. All wind instruments require a remarkable tongue agility.

The naturally gifted singer has voice control and a sense of the accuracy of pitch. A child's song sense (and its dance and musical sense) can be tested by noting his responses to ascending and descending notes of the scales, and by his perceptions of diminuendo and crescendo or volume. It is not what he sings but *how* he sings that should be noted, in an attempt to determine the natural singing ability of a young child. *Memory*, the faculty to look and see, to know and to recall instantly when the act is required, is a necessity for dancing and music making. *Motility* and *reaction* play positive parts in dance and music making and can be described by degrees of good, better than average, and superlative, through tests of the child's physical and mental responses—these "tests" giving best results when they are within the child's spontaneous responses to dance and music.

Training the Talented Child

Ideally, every child should come to an awareness of his own musical potentiality, and thereafter develop it, either for his own pleasure as an intelligent and trained amateur, or (when he is truly talented) as a professional musician. If the general educational system included a true musical education the child's potentialities would be discovered and developed when he commenced school. But musical education is generally undertaken by the parent, who must pay tuition fees and buy and maintain instruments, or other gear (as, for dance, specific uniform or practice dress). There is only one kind of teaching: good. Any teaching that is mediocre is, simply, bad. A great teacher will not be able to make a performer of professional standards out of an untalented pupil—but a bad teacher will injure and eventually irreparably ruin a gifted child!

Suppose the parent is assured of the child's natural artistry, and can afford regular tuition and the purchase of an instrument—what then? It is not sufficient to start the child's musical education with a good teacher; this must be the right teacher for the child.

There then arises the problem of time, in real life and not in music. When music is within the general educational curricula then it is a subject like any other and the practice of the instrument becomes like so much homework. This is evident in boarding schools where children study music within the curricula, not as an elective but as a required subject. When the child goes to day-school his day is divided between work and play, although some work is done, as homework, in his "free" period, and within the "school time" he plays, in organized games and sports. It is in his so-called "free" time that he, and his parent, must undertake the musical education. An approach to music must include an approach to undertaking music as work, in theory and practice.

The child may be encouraged by adult influences *but he must be motivated by a personal desire* to study dance and music. This personal desire, in my opinion, should predicate all *formal* musical education for children, regardless of the degree of natural talent. The parent of the talented child must recognize what a musical training entails, for the student and for the family. Immediately a child commences serious musical studies, it necessitates a rearrangement of familial schedules, and, too, a conscious undertaking of a life's plan.

The child who intends to make music a profession must spend two-thirds of his work time on music, but all children should live within the Platonic ideal of an artistic and a gymnastic life. A child who works must also play, and one who studies must also indulge in physical exercise.

Good health, a strong body, are requirements for the musical artist. The romantic superstition that the "poetic" type, frail and anaemic, is the great dancer is void of verity, as in the naive sentimentality that children with long, slender, pretty hands are "born pianists." For a fact, the best pianist hands are shorter than average, with smaller fingers. (Piano aptitudes are distinguished through tests for motility and reaction, not through poetic imagery.) There are characteristic preferences and rejections of instruments by certain types of students. Tuba players, for instance, often have bass voices, some are basso profundo; flautists and violinists have soprano and tenor voices, as a rule; while men who play the clarinet usually sing baritone. (See diagram.) These relationships between instrumental and vocal music are proof of the rapport between the musician and his instrument, but no musician can perform at his best if he is not in good health and with the physical and mental stamina to support an onerous professional career.

When dance and music are taught together, or in correlation, we have

Soprano

Mezzo-Soprano

Alto

Tenor

Baritone

Bass

Violin

Viola

Violoncello

Double Bass

Harp

Piccolo

Flute

Clarinet

Oboe

English Horn

Bass Clarinet

Bassoon

Double Bassoon

Trumpet

French Horn

Trombone

Tuba

Bells

Xylophone

Celesta

Chimes

Timpani

MIDDLE C

RANGE OF VOICES AND INSTRUMENTS COMPARED WITH PIANO KEYBOARD

an easy means of affording a child the prerogatives of the gymnastic life, *within the artistic sphere.* And when the dancer studies music as part of dancing, then he is not simply training as a gymnast but as an artist, combining music and movement as one. These, in dance, are inherent in each other, as great drama has poetry or the poetic concept inherent in it.

The child who means to become a dancer must study the exacting techniques of theatre dance. For ballet, this requires a beginning about the age of eight to ten, and daily lessons for a long period, since development in ballet technique must be perfectly and carefully undertaken both for the dancer's sake and the aesthetic form of the dance. A ballet dancer should plan on completing the general education (through high school gradua-tion, at least) by fourteen or fifteen, to serve an apprenticeship in a com-pany's *corps*, there to develop repertorial styles and company "spirit" or homogeneity within an artistic entity. As a professional, the dancer and the instrumentalist lives a comparatively restricted existence as we think of a worldly or cultured one—yet the great artist in dance or music must retain a place and presence in his era. The artist is *extra*-ordinary compared to his fellows—but he is one of them, a part of society. An artist of genius influ-ences as well as ornaments his place and time.

Ideally, the gymnastic and artistic states should co-exist, for all students, in "normal" education. This co-existence is not yet, in American education, and cannot be wholly developed for the child at home, since the ultimate development is for the child's fullest environmental sphere. The next best thing after general education is community recreation, when it is of a "crea-tive" type. For several decades past, community organizations have fostered childrens' centres for creative arts; therein, many an American artist has discovered his talent, and been discovered and helped to realize his potential. Generally, parents undertake training for the child, as did the Kregers for Jonathan. His mother relates:

> While Jonathan was an infant, in the time that he talked of playing the violin, we took him occasionally to visit a violin maker, where we looked at instruments and talked to the artisan, who became a good friend by the time Jonathan was six, and ready to begin on the violin in earnest. Jonathan knew that the violin was difficult to play, that he needed to be big and strong enough to play even a small-sized one, and that it was a serious matter of practicing and working before playing well. He talked, seriously, to our friends about the violin, including one whose son plays cello with the Chicago Symphony and who was very sympathetic with Jonathan. In this way, the child was helped during his waiting period. He waited well and never deviated from his intent to play the violin—al-though we had piano, guitar and flute at home he was interested only in hearing them played, not in playing them. But he did show interest in piano as reference for musical information. The January after he was six (his birthday anniversary comes in autumn) we set off to buy the violin. The violin maker made a ceremony of the occasion. Before even trying instruments for tone, Jonathan had to be measured for size. He was in-formed that he would need a half-size instrument.
>
> A professor of music was in the store at the time and he told Jonathan that he would grow into a three-quarter size and then into a full-size in-strument. Our new friend tried the half-size instruments with us and we decided on the best one—but then both men, the violin maker and the

professor, advised us to rent the instrument and wait to buy one that we would keep, when Jonathan grew in physical size.

The child showed the greatest alarm. "Rent" is a temporary thing and we could see that the thought of having a violin he did not own was altogether contrary to his long-nourished idea of playing the violin. I know it is sound sense to rent an instrument—but I think it is a bad premise for a child because we infer "we will rent the thing to see if you like learning to play it." Jonathan's own approach had been decisive—he had always stated he would play the violin. Our approach could not be less than decisive; we bought Jonathan his half-size instrument.

He took it with such faith and composure! I wonder how he would have used it if we had shown insufficient trust in him, with a *rented* violin?

Back home, we discovered that he had the mumps, that he must have been running a temperature and feeling ill all day—but had not once betrayed a sign of discomfort, for fear of postponing the violin purchase. We did have to postpone the next step—his first visit to his teacher—but we could not put off letting him *play* the violin although I worried that he might develop bad habits on his own. But on his own, Jonathan decided that he would have to learn how to control strings and bow, and waited patiently for his teacher to begin teaching.

We had carefully chosen this first teacher, and on the recommendation of a woman who has taught college music for twenty years. The teacher was a young man, a high school teacher of music, himself a good violinist.

However, it turned out that this was *not the right teacher for beginners*.

I sat in on the lessons, as was agreed, so that I could correct Jonathan when he practiced at home, and discovered that this teacher used a rote method by which the student does not look at the notes for quite a while after he begins studying. I knew that this would seem odd to a child whose six years of life had been book-oriented and, as I expected, Jonathan was surprised and disappointed that he was being asked to work on the violin without a book. He had already explored rudiments of musical notation at home, simply out of his curiosity, and he wanted something written down to look at, *to read*, in the form of music.

The teacher's assignment the first week included bowing, fingering and other techniques, such as might have been good for an advanced student but that were bad for a beginner, as they were not performed in proper position. This man gave no lesson in holding the instrument and this should have alerted me to the fact that he was a poor teacher for a beginning student. However, since I am not a violinist I forbore to query his techniques, at first.

Jonathan practiced at home for the time alloted for this, did what he was assigned, but it was obvious that it was joyless work. While shopping, at a large music store, I inquired who were recognized as good *beginners'* teachers in the area. The list of names the store supplied me with did not include the teacher I had chosen for Jonathan. I decided to terminate the lessons and we went next to a woman, one of the recommended beginners' teachers. (She was an elementary school music teacher, used to working with young children.)

I saw the difference at once! The first teacher, a tall man, had towered over the child, never stooped down to the little six-year-old boy, and had addressed all his comments over Jonathan's head, most of them to me. The first thing the woman did was to sit down, bring herself to Jonathan's level, and begin talking to him quietly and seriously. I remained strictly in the background, ignored by teacher and pupil. She gave Jonathan a paper with the name of a book he was to buy to study with—we rushed out, thankfully, to get it! Her system was the note and not the rote method and when Jonathan got home he put the book on the violin rack and exclaimed: "Ah! This is better!"

The first assignment with his new teacher was a lesson which paid particular attention to *position*, and only of the violin. The bow was not introduced until the second lesson, as it is quite difficult to manage in itself. As for fingering, (use of left-hand fingers in stopping the open strings) she said that would not be introduced for quite a while. She was warm, friendly but authoritative.

Jonathan responded to her at once because she treated him as a *person* —not as a child, or someone stupidly unaware of the violin, but as a *person learning to play the violin.* It was then that I understood the unsuitability of the first teacher: he was incapable of communicating with a beginner, and with a child, however well he might work with advanced students and adults. There had been, in fact, no rapport between him and Jonathan and this rapport I know to be essential between teacher and student.

Also, the note method was one especially well suited to Jonathan's mentality and his taste as a bookish person, *although this is not always the best method for beginners!*

I was fully aware of the problems of practicing. I have heard innumerable statements of: "I used to take lessons but I gave them up because I had no time to practice." As a music teacher, I hear parents say that they cannot get, or make time for, a student to practice, *regularly*, at home. And as a musician I knew that practice is useless unless it is performed properly, which is the only reason I decided to sit in on the violin lessons and learn from them enough to guide home practice. (This has enabled me to correct Jonathan when he has been wrong and his teacher and I calculate that it has saved the child perhaps 90% of the time that is usually wasted in incorrect practicing.)

Could this be done by a parent who is not a musician? Yes, if the parent and child have a free, loving relationship within music and the child is not placed under a strain in having his parent present while he takes a lesson or practices and performs wrong notes. It is necessary for the parent to be very attentive and very patient—I am especially attentive from being a musician and I am a great deal more patient as a parent than as a teacher!

Two aspects of practicing that I recommend are (1) to refer to the work as "playing at home" (not as practice on the instrument), and (2) always to conclude the practice period after a successful performance—never on the heels of a failure to play well. I arrange a successful climax simply by ensuring that the child tackles the most difficult part of the lesson first, when he is freshest. We save old friends, pieces he knows well, for the latter part of the practice period. This has worked beautifully for Jonathan —he ends his home playing in a glow of pleasure, having experienced success as a musician, and he puts the violin away with reluctance, to take it out of its case, next time, with eagerness.

Before he began studying, we agreed that he would take one practice period in the morning, before going to school, and one in the late evening, and that he would work in his own room. These are times of the day when I can arrange my own schedule to listen. He is still so young that he asks permission: "Mommy, may I go to my room and play now?"— little knowing how relieved and pleased we are that he wants to work. Already, he likes to shut his door and play in privacy, extra to his regular practice periods.

He is very possessive about the violin, refusing to let the other children touch it, or even go near it—he says they are too young to treat it carefully and may damage it. David has been hurt and indignant, since until now the two boys shared toys and had a very close and amiable relationship, with Jonathan assuming a very protective air. But we respect Jonathan's fanatical possessiveness although in secret (when Jonathan was away at school) I have let David gently draw the bow over the strings, just to listen. David now says he wants a violin but we do not take him very seriously as yet—I hope he will play the cello. He has favorite "instruments" of his own, one being an old car radio aerial that slides in and out like a slide-trombone. David has sampled the piano, the flute and the guitar.

Jonathan's artistic life, seriously undertaken at age six, is integrated into his social life. He is a member of our local Little League baseball team, and, I understand, a good player, and he is popular with friends with whom he shares his physical and academic life. He has brought home some of his ruggedly athletic friends, showed them his "real" violin, and on their challenge to "play something," performed a short air with obvious pleasure. Moreover, the friends have shown their pleasure in hearing him play. As he becomes more proficient, we shall encourage him to take the violin to school and play, as "sharing."

My only concern over music in Jonathan's life was what I assumed to be resulting fatigue, especially after his lessons. His teacher gives lessons of an hour, never less; often, more. Once, when she kept him well above the regular lesson period I noted that the child was very silent on the way home, very withdrawn after we arrived home. Detecting this apparent apathy, and taking it for weariness, I became apprehensive that the teacher was making too hard demands on the little boy. Then one day, on the way home, he blurted out: "Oh, I hate having to stop when I am working —I wish we could turn back and I could have another lesson *right now*!" —and then lapsed into his "mood," which I now had the wit to perceive was a purely artistic fever of longing. What I had thought to be exhaustion from overwork was sadness and irritation at not being allowed to work as long as he preferred . . . No words of his could inform us more eloquently than those he spoke; we know that music means something immensely satisfying to him.

I believe it is important to note that private tutoring, from the inception of his studies on the violin, is the right kind for Jonathan, whose state of readiness for serious musical study was completed at home, and extended in nursery school. Other, less musically sophisticated students may require other methods of training, with more emphasis on play than work at the beginning, but for Jonathan the stricter method of formal musical study, and private instruction, appear to be perfect, according to his responses to date. He has begun and will continue to approach music as the *performing* musician, and in his home and training environments we make this precise approach.

This approach to music, ideal for Jonathan Kreger, is not the only one or the one applicable to all children. That it is *an approach predicated on response by the child* makes it a good one; classic of its kind. Such a response comes, usually, from the child who is self-disciplined and chooses to exercise, of his own accord, the stern rules and methods which work well for the artist. It is a response typical of the serious child, the child who is both proud and shy and likes to work steadily and well, and will so work by himself. Some other children are more gregarious and work best within the stimuli of competitive and cooperative forces. They are group workers rather than solitary ones and for them there are other fields of exploring.

In piano training, where revolutionary changes are in effect, many teach-ers advocate group instruction for the youngest students (five and six years old) and most teachers give concurrent private or semi-private tutoring to the advanced students. Other teachers prefer to work with groups for the first two or three years, when the children cannot concentrate hard for long periods, and thereafter to teach the child as an individual in private and semi-private lessons. In the group teaching numbers from four to twenty-four children are the rule but all do not play at once; such classes are usually divided into halves, one half playing pianos while the other half follows along on "dummy" keyboards.

This group method is in effect for piano and organ, and for guitar lessons but, theoretically, could be applied to any form of instrumentation.

If you send your child to a teacher of the group method (either out of his inclination for group work or because you can better afford the lower group-system fees than the higher fees for private tutelage) assure yourself that the teacher teaches good basic finger position, regardless of how limited the technical range taught the beginner. A music teacher should first of all teach the student how to approach the instrument and how to perform on it, manually—as Jonathan was taught to hold and use the violin before beginning to play.

Parents often worry whether the child is progressing surely in his music lessons but when they are totally unmusical they do not know what to observe as progress.

The basic training (say, within a first year course) should make the child a good sight-reader of music in all keys, and the student should know all key signatures, treble and bass clef. He should know or be well along to knowing the tonic, sub-dominant and dominant chords in all major and minor scales. He should have enough musical knowledge to allow him to actually compose, in simple forms. And he should have become proficient in performing a repertory which provides him with music that he plays well—*and that is his favorite music!* Accomplished performers accumulate a repertory of their best pieces, as a matter of course, and good professional (and business) sense, and the student should do so from the inception of his musical education. Playing the music one likes best ensures playing at one's best. Measuring professional accomplishments on instruments it is found that fingering achievement on keyboards and strings is directly related to the instrumentalists' preferences for the music played. What is true for the mature artist is also true for the tyro; in this instance, more so!

Good teachers should be able to teach students to *see* dance and *hear* music, as well as to compose and perform dance and music. A critical perception should be developed for the performer's work and for the performance of music by others—this is the sole practical reason for arranging student recitals, on a regular basis, where children can perform for each other and have their performances discussed and evaluated by their informed peers. Otherwise, I deplore studio recitals because these exert a baneful and hypocritical influence on children who are allowed to preen in a spurious "professional" atmosphere created by doting parents and unscrupulous teachers.

The teacher who, on the sound basis of a "recital" (which is not a theatrical or concert performance) offers students opportunities to perform, for the experience of performing, and also of criticizing performance, is commendable—if she can check parental pride and the witless enthusiasm of local newspapers which describe all females in pointe shoes as "ballerinas" and all pianists and fiddlers as virtuosi comparable to Rubinstein and Heifetz.

Students outgrow teachers and the teacher who is fine for your child to begin with may not be the same one the child should continue with, past the basic training, but this first teacher, and the basic training, may be the most important aspects of life for the child as artist.

When to begin, and at what age to start a child on his education, are debatable and controversial factors. Theorists advise waiting until the child has enough dexterity to physically manage the instrument—but motility varies exceedingly. Children should not begin to study ballet techniques until a certain stage of physical development, because ballet exercises the turn-out, a position in which the hip is rotated in the socket to an angle of 90°; and the upper and lower leg, with the knee and foot, turned out accordingly; the whole body observing aplomb and other characteristics of the classical dance technique. Usually, young children are able to play all the rhythm instruments: drums, shakers or rattles, gongs, et cetera, but may have difficulty striking one key, and not parts of two or three keys, on keyboard instruments. No categorical statement should be made as to age of the student because children have different limitations and capacities at the same age.

I frequently find nursery school, kindergarten and primary grades children confidently (and sweetly) learning to make music not only on percussion instruments but also on the recorder, piano, guitar, ukelele and auto-harp. As a rule, strings, woodwinds and brasses are more readily played by older children; percussion by younger children. It is wise to make the child wait (as the Kregers made Jonathan wait) until physical strength and dexterity manifest themselves enough to assure the child's grasp of the instrument (i.e., the difficult position of violin and bow) and some children elect to wait, in stubborn and sure faith in their artistry. But the child should meanwhile be offered ample opportunity for sustaining his interest in music and the waiting should be an inspiration (something like a squire's portion before attaining knighthood). Mrs. Kreger's treatment of Jonathan's approach to the violin is a sound example.

The reverse of this sane and sensible attitude is the exciting surmise that babies should be taught to make music, not simply left to their devices, as is the contention of the Japanese pedagogue, Shinichi Suzuki, who has taught thousands of infants to play the violin, and whose musical academies in Japan have earned praise from famed musicians, Pablo Casals and David Oistrakh among these.

In the Suzuki method, children are given miniature violins as soon as they can hold them and at age two-and-a-half are taking weekly lessons in schools. Their mothers are given instruction in the fundamentals of holding the violin and bowing and fingering, in order to supervise home practice, and parents agree (sometimes before the children are born) to play recordings of the music of great composers for the child to hear every day. Suzuki's theory is that music inculcated from birth becomes part of the child's mother-tongue and that as soon or soon after the infant can talk, it can perform on the violin.

Suzuki's "Talent Education" methods for string music have been controversial for twenty years with Occidental teachers of conventional systems but meanwhile have produced thousands of Japanese graduates. There are fifty locales and 120 Suzuki teachers currently in Japan, with a student enrollment of 6,000, and American teachers are now adopting many principles of "Talent Education." One project is at San Diego State College, under instructor Theodore Brunson, an assistant professor of music.

Brunson says that the success of the Suzuki method depends on two factors: the parental involvement with the lessons and the child's early introduction to stringed instruments. Infant scholars do not have the inclination, liberty and mobility to pursue distracting forms of entertainment; they are almost wholly dependent on adults for work and play. Despite a short concentration span, the infant can often learn as much about playing music as an older child. And when he forms pleasurable associations with music he feels enjoyment and pride in the ability to create it; far in excess, sometimes, of what his older sibling experiences.

At least one parent of a Suzuki trained child must attend every lesson, actually learning with his child. He must learn to tune the child's instrument, the correct stance and manual procedure, and must carefully observe the teacher's instructions and corrections in order to extend these into home playing of the instrument. Depending on the child's size, physical strength and manual dexterity the Suzuki trained infant commences study on an instrument 1/16 to 1/4 of normal adult size.

Studies begin without printed music or any attempt at teaching rote methods. The parents, through recordings, and the instructor, through recordings and actual playing, familiarize the students with the music they are going to learn. They therefore learn, in this phase, by aural memory or "by ear," and only after they have attained some proficiency on their instruments does Brunson introduce notation, for sight reading. He does so, he says, as naturally as possible, and only after the children have formed pleasurable associations with making music. He avoids all fuss that might alarm the young students about the esoterics of a strange language, and shows them that reading music is following music with the eye, a logical extension of following music by ear.

Brunson favors Vivaldi, Bach and Handel as composers for beginners, and most instructors of Suzuki's "Talent Education" lean on the baroque composers. Suzuki, who regularly visits the U.S. to observe his applied methodology, has composed some music for students.

The growing popularity for teaching by the Suzuki method is being accelerated by the professional demand for string players, of which there is now serious lack by symphony and chamber music orchestras. Always excepting players of popular guitar music, we turn out far less string instrumentalists in proportion to wind players, since American education emphasizes rhythm and marching bands. And yet another reason for the popularity of Suzuki's teaching is the remarkable homogeneity of advanced students who, in mastering a common repertory, are adept at concert performing without a conductor.*

Problems and Perils of the Child as Artist

Whatever the age of the beginner and progress of the early years, the child as artist faces a crucial decision in adolescence, when he must make a choice for or against a musical career. This can be an agonizing period

* In March, 1964, ten Suzuki students, Japanese boys and girls aged from five to twelve years, appeared in a concert at the Dag Hammarskjold Library Auditorium of the United Nations, New York, in a program of works by Vivaldi, Bach and Kreisler.

for a child and his parents, and every such event must be met and dealt with in its own context. Parents who wonder and worry about their child's material welfare realize that very few musical artists become rich and famous and the great majority barely earn a living wage, and are totally unknown outside a very narrow artistic sphere. Against this somber thought must be set the knowledge that for many persons music creates the best and richest life. For such persons, their happiest and worthiest selves are realized only through making music, and no sacrifice, no mortification is too great to endure for it. Mozart was the most miserable of mortals in a worldly estate but the sublimest of immortals in the musical estate.

In *A Majority of One* Sydney J. Harris writes the truest words ever spoken of the musician in America: "A serious musician generally leads a dreadful life in our society. His future is uncertain, his struggles are perpetual, his schedule is either too lax (no engagements) or too intense (six recitals a week). It is a hectic, rootless and abnormal existence in many respects. Yet, with all these drawbacks, serious musicians of talent are the happiest people I have known. . . . It would be an exaggeration to say that I have never known an unhappy musician; but I have never known one whose music did not compensate in full for his personal difficulties. Since none of us, however successful, is exempt from tragedy, how fortunate are those few who find in music a serenity and a sense of achievement surmounting the vexations of the world, the flesh and the devil."

The profession of dancer has an even more precarious economy than that of musician, for there are far more orchestras than dance troupes in the United States. Ballet, more popular than modern dance, is the chief academic training and in America today it is being studied by more pupils than ever before, anywhere in the world. The training is mostly in small, autonomous, commercial ballet schools, all through the country, and they turn out thousands of young dancers, many intent on a professional career. But at this writing there are very, very few professional troupes in the country and only two American ballets that rank in the international hierarchy with big organizations of state-subsidized ballet. These are the American Ballet Theatre, which does not have a resident theatre, and the New York City Ballet, resident at New York State Theatre in Lincoln Center. Boys are at a premium in ballet but girls are a glut on the market.

The greatest majority of young dancers must accept amateur or at most semi-professional careers, dancing with the regional ballet groups that proliferate out of the autonomous commercial ballet schools—but here the dancers seldom work past adolescence, after which they retire into ordinary life. Many potentially great dancers are being lost to the American theatre, for lack of opportunities to mature as professional artists. Yet, those who achieve rank in a professional company must work for love rather than a bare livelihood, and remain, very often, partially or wholly dependent on private means.

In 1967 the minimum wage for a *corps de ballet* dancer, as exacted by AGMA (American Guild of Musical Artists) was $115.00 per week in rehearsal and $132.00 in performance at home (meaning: in the company's residential theatre or metropolitan area), with $174.00 per week minimum for the dancer on tour. If her company has four weeks of rehearsal and six weeks of performance (and some companies have no more than three weeks in a "season" and proportionately less rehearsal time for lack of funds), she earns $1,252.00—and this may well be her annual income in "legitimate" ballet. It is a wry joke among dancers that they are often queried on their annual income tax returns by a government which does not recognize theatre arts as a serious undertaking.

The parent of a child of musical potential needs to know all that I have written here, when he undertakes for the child the beginning of a life in music. But he does not need to divulge these truths to the child, who as artist will discover them, and live with them in music, all in due time. The child prefers to dance and make music on his terms.

In music's loftiest ideal it is sufficient to fill a life but it is better to have a life in music. This means that the musician, especially as a student, should not be concerned with profit and loss but be free to express his greatest potentials in music, while living as a person and as a musician. Almost always, a child of considerable gifts is cherished and encouraged but, finally, expected to earn a livelihood in proof of talent. We read of child prodigies today for whom claims are being made as to rival the legendary genius of Mozart, and we are awed and fascinated but we must wait for time, the acid test, to prove the claims. Even gifted children of dazzling abilities in music are still children—they become musical artists only if and when, in time, they develop all the attributes of the artist. Living and growing, the experiences of the self, are part of the musical experience, and this is something the parent of the potential musical artist must know and remember, for the child to be a whole person as well as a trained musician. The artist as a child is always in peril from adults.

Not only children enjoy seeing and hearing other children perform; adults also enjoy the experience and when an adult has care of a potentially talented child he cannot help but become ambitious. Parental encouragement and management have fostered musical reputations as assiduously as Mozart's father established his son's in childhood. Sometimes parents establish their ambitions before a child is born or begins to be a person.

Frank Alfidi, an Italian-American living in Yonkers, New York, fondly and deliberately named his son Giuseppe (for Verdi) Arturo (for Toscanini) when the boy was born in 1949. At the age of eleven, Giuseppe Arturo Alfidi, called "Joey," was conducting the Antwerp Philharmonic Orchestra in Beethoven's works (at Brussels' Palais des Beaux Arts) and playing his own compositions. The child could then play six instruments and in addition to being a conductor was a composer—of a symphony, a tone poem, rondo and a rhapsody; two overtures, two piano concertos, two sonatas, and eleven sonatinas. His father compared him to a young Mozart while the child admitted to newsmen that his grave problem was the decision as to what he should study to be: a concert pianist, a composer or an orchestra conductor.

Other talented children have a graver problem: how to get training in music while they are young and must depend on parents to pay their tuition fees and provide them with instruments. Every parent cannot afford music lessons and an instrument in the home; indeed, many parents do not acknowledge the necessity for music in the life of the child. From the child's point of view this is cruel and from the musician's point of view, disastrous, but parents contend that they cannot afford and will not be induced, out of a moralistic point, to go into debt for an expensive instrument which the child may never play with genuine proficiency. First, they want proof that the child *is* gifted. They want to know if his gift will earn him a good living.

The social attitude to everything we buy is that it must entertain us, educate us or serve us. Television and high-fidelity phonograph and radio are mechanistic musical means of entertainment, requiring no more manual dexterity than the flip of a switch, and these serve audio-visual interests so well that they almost entirely satiate tastes. These mechanistic means of musical and dramatic entertainment are slickly produced even when of execrable taste, and they make the student and amateur artist pall. Busy and preoccupied parents seldom want to undertake the slow, onerous and tedious task of musical training for the child. They may disguise this feeling from each other as husband and wife but can they successfully disguise it from the child as artist, who is generally more sensitive than the norm?

When the child sings and dances spontaneously, without the excruciating periods of practice, the child is a pleasure and a pride. But children have to work at making music and learning to dance, and they have to be taught by qualified teachers. If a child is a "born" musician, parents say, why need he study, why can he not develop his talent as a free expression of self? If the artist is to work, in professional theatre, he must be schooled and disciplined. Music and dance have techniques and sciences of training, as well as aesthetics. Students of the arts have to *work at learning media,* as compared to infants playing with music and dance for fun.

As soon as the parent concedes music as a study, and begins to pay for the child to study it, he is apt to think of profit and loss within purely monetary terms, and to judge the worth of the musical education by the child's production, as though the child had established himself as a manu-facturer of an artifact. Yet parents accept, unquestioningly, the gymnastic life for children as a part of childhood, without expectation that the child trained to play games and compete in sports will become a professional athlete. Schools provide well-equipped gymnasiums and maintain playing fields, and employ qualified coaches for these activities; all of which are supported by taxes and, in private schools, paid for as tuition fees. Yet many parents cannot treat an artistic education as anything save a profitable accomplish-ment, and they consciously apply the criteria to the child as artist. Few parents take a child's artistic sensibility seriously, or treat the arts with respect. Yet, a musical profession is more taxing, physically and mentally, than a gymnastic one. And for the true artist, the "born" dancer and musician, their professions are in fact vocations, resembling a religious voca-tion in certain ways: dedication, self-discipline, sacrifice, humility, the attri-tion of selfishness in order to contribute to the artistic self. Art, in a word, is a *noble* undertaking. And it ennobles the person.

With such a concept about dance and music, the parent provides the gifted child with ways and means of developing the gift, regardless of the eventual development of the gift. The mortal worth of the training, in its performance value for fame and money, is only one part of the large sum, whose immortal part lies within music, and the child as a person. Never before in our history have Americans so greatly needed the artistic life in its professional and amateur status. Our social goal is a life of ease and leisure and already we face the task of knowing what to do with time and money other than to waste them and ourselves in wasting them. My ideas on this subject are better left to my projected work as *Theatre Arts in Education* but here let us think of a life in music as a purely amateur one.

A ballet teacher of my acquaintance, receiving an industrial foundation grant for teaching beginners, went into the Los Angeles public schools to choose prospective students for classes which they would get free, and within which they would receive allotments for practice clothes and travel expenses. The queries most often made by the children's parents were: what will the child get out of this? how soon will the child earn money dancing? did the training by the teacher include getting the child a job as a dancer, in "legit." ballet, the movies or on TV? All the children were chosen as being potentially or naturally gifted for dancing, so there was no project for obesity, lameness or other physical and mental therapy by dance. But parents thought of dancing and a dance training only as a means of earning fame and fortune and, moreover, required the teacher to undertake achieving this for the children within a set time and with definite goals in sight—before the children had even begun to train in ballet!

This incident and many others, all drearily familiar to teachers of music and dance, are indicative of the pragmatic view our society takes of the arts; the ideal of materialism out of art that parents maintain for the talented child, resulting in brutal pressure being put on the child as artist. I know that the coarsest, rudest demand by the parent is often guided by the most loving anxiety for the child's welfare, but it is a materialistic concept about art which moves such parents to their expectations and demands. Parents, too, are motivated by the predominant standards set in education for the child, by which he is expected to produce by rote, to "pass" on tests of his ability by methods set for the mass and not the individual intelligence, and to avoid, at all costs, failure during any of the set progressions of his life in school. When these principles are set for the child as artist the parent places an onerous burden on both child and teacher; it is the child, most often, who breaks under the pressure and turns away from or yields up his potential estate as a musical person.

The artist makes music for pleasure, not for profit.

Pleasure in music is the first and eventually the fullest worth of music. As a composer, Conrad Susa, describes music ". . . time seems to be stopped or checked. The pitches, rhythms, textures are shaped by the will of the musician through practice. One learns to hear not only what is happening now, but to listen historically (how it must have sounded when it was first composed), and analytically (how music is built and to what purpose). These are the things the musician learns, especially the amateur for whom music is a simple 'pursuit.' *Amateur* is a word that has become debased in our time and language. But *amateur* means: one who engages in a pursuit, study, science or sport as a pastime rather than a profession. It means, too, 'devotee' and 'admirer.' To be an amateur musician is by no means to be an inferior musician and with the passiveness and lack of empathy in our modern communication it is more than ever important to cultivate a love of music without taking thought of pay; to partake of music for its pleasure pure and simple. Much of our 'great' music was written for amateurs—the sonatas of Haydn, Mozart and Beethoven, the hundreds of pieces of chamber music, the hugest repertory of songs. And there is something about *performing* music that a mere listener can never grasp: the tactile pleasure of moving through intricate passages, of being the important note in a chord or polyphonic phrase, of the joy of feeling a composition grow because you are doing your part, of the deep excitement of exploring little known areas of music, both ancient and contemporary, of presenting your achievement to an audience large or small, of sharing your musical experience. Nothing in listening can equal the doing of music!"

This is the statement of a practicing, professional musician who is a composer, and whose work includes composing for young persons as well as for the adult, sophisticated theatre audience. We perceive in this statement that the musical person, professional and amateur, works at making music and in that work gains fulfillment through individual expression and group participation; reflects on time and humanity's concern with art traditions; and finds pleasure or happiness in many ways: by senses tactile and aural, by a sense of adventure within the musical realm, and by a feeling of his own worth as a musician. Who dares say that this is a worthless occupation? Only one who is not a musician and has no sense of music. The child as artist thinks and feels with *a musical soul and mind* and since we are, as parents and teachers, devoted to the principle of making the child good and happy then let the musician's life be a pursuit of pride and pleasure, and not solely of pay.

Conrad Susa is one of the innumerable musical artists who came to fulfillment of his goals through determination as well as talent; his childhood was the opposite of the kind determined for Joey Alfidi and Jonathan Kreger.

The eldest of three children of parents of very modest means, Susa was not given any training other than general education but got this at a Roman Catholic parochial school. He relates:

> As a matter of course, I knew Latin, sang Latin, heard sacred music. I liked all these very much and I remember that while I was still wholly ignorant about music I disliked and disapproved of singing that I later understood was poor or bad. We had a piano at home but no one played it. It fascinated me. I would lift the lid and look at the keys, press one, hear its sound, close the lid and go away. I longed to play the instrument

and I was depressed because I could not. I never strummed it, I did not want to fool about and amuse myself on the piano; I wanted to make music on it.

I would go to my mother, often, and ask if I could have lessons on the piano. She always replied that we could not afford it. I knew we did not have much money and I accepted this without rebellion. But I never gave up thinking of playing the piano. I can remember going into the room where it was, lifting the lid, and looking at the enigmatic black and white keys, which gleamed even in the half-dark, of pressing one and hearing its voice and recognizing that there were different voices inside the piano—separate sounds from certain keys. And of closing the piano and going away. It had secrets that I could never know unless they were taught to me. At school, the nuns gave music lessons but these were "extras" that poorer students could not afford.

Then, I found out that boys could make money selling papers and I got a newspaper route. With the first money I earned I went to a nun who gave music lessons and put the money in her hand and told her I wanted piano lessons, as many as this money would pay for. After that, all the money I earned from selling papers went into the piano lessons. I realize now that the nun who taught me gave me far more lessons than I paid for but then, in my ignorance about money and my greed for music, I did not think about cost and supply. I would practice at home but very badly; I did not know how to work at practicing and no one told me how. This was something I had to learn much later. But I began immediately to "make up" music with utterly no understanding of the composition of music.

I was soon a famous kid in school, composing for groups and arranging musical affairs but still with no concept, musically, of what I was about. The time came for me to take the aptitude tests that students are given, as "Guidance" under educational counseling and supervision. I was in high school and the adults concerned about me (parents, teachers) assumed that I wanted to know how to make money. In truth, I did not give a thought to money, or to making money out of music. Music was most dear to me but the piano and organ (which I was playing) did not affect me as money-making ideas. My mother was concerned about what I would be, how I would earn a "good" living as a man. Music may have seemed a mere frivolity to her; my parents were not musicians though my father played the harmonica. And, of course, they *owned* a piano. Another thing, we spoke Czech at home (my parental antecedents are Czech) and I think the bilingual experience, combined with Latin and church music at school, helped to form my ear. But it was an untutored ear until I began to seriously study music.

I almost never became a musician and almost did become a pharmacist. This is what the test proposed I should be, according to the answers I made to its questions, most of them *yes* and *no*, and all of them offering very narrow margins to think within. The nuns who had been teaching me were astounded to find that I was destined to be a pharmacist. "But you love music, you do well at music, how is it that you have failed to show any talent for music?" they lamented. I did not know how it had come about that I was labelled pharmacist and pegged in the utilitarian board to become this person—but I daresay I might have accepted my fate. Perhaps a pharmacist has all the qualities that a composer should cultivate. . . .

The nuns got hold of my "test" and went over it with me. One question was: *Do you want to work in radio?* I had replied: No. And among the crucial questions for potential musicians was this one: *Would you like to compose a "musical"?* I again had replied: No.

Of course I did not want to work in radio because I wanted to work in theatre; and certainly I did not think of composing a "musical" since I intended to compose an opera. They had asked me their rote test questions and, as the child that I was, I had given them unequivocal answers—but the examiners who were presuming to deal with my future life did not know what to do with the answers to the queries they made.

But for the nuns I might have been pitchforked into a way of life and a kind of work far removed from music; or I might have made my way, tortuously and in an amateur status, into music as a pastime instead of as my profession. Instead, I thereafter worked steadily at music, and I am sure I've never been missed among the pharmacists.

Conrad Susa's childhood experience ended happily: he went to Carnegie Institute of Technology, thence to Juilliard in New York, earned scholarships and fellowships in music, won prizes and awards, was given foundation grants, and in the musical world is counted among the most successful of young American composers. A prolific worker, Susa is known in several genres: theatre and non-theatre music, and music sacred and secular. He is, besides, resident composer and musical director for the Association of Performing Artists (APA), the most celebrated repertory dramatic company in the United States.

This career began when a lonely, thoughtful child, stealing into a room, lifted the lid of an old piano and struck a key, drawing from it not only a sound but a radiance which thereafter illumined his existence, and set a beacon light for his endeavors, from paper-boy to trained musician. . . .

We can never tell when and where it will happen, nor to which child, but the musical gift, like mysterious astral fire, touches and ignites the human soul. When it does, the kindled spark glows more brightly than any other within the person, and to quench it is a form of death. The guardians of such a child must not inquire what material gains will accrue from his gift, nor how shrewdly he will use it, because for such a child making music will be the greatest goodness to know.

Music as National Genius

Some of the world's greatest opera composers are Italian; some of the greatest musicians of German or Austrian heritage; and from Russia come, continuously, some of the greatest dancers we have ever known. But despite tests to identify national genius in art there is not sufficient evidence to allow one nation to claim superiority over all others in an art, because it breeds the artists of that medium. It is, however, clear that certain peoples have a penchant for particular genres and that this penchant is preserved in immigrants, expatriates who assume life in a foreign country, such as the those of our émigré American cultures. Tests, so far, have been with small percentages of peoples, results of which are usually published in medical journals and as academic theses. I have seen some interesting hypotheses but nothing conclusive on the subject, and I have been unable to investigate all the individual environments of the children tested.

One of the pet superstitions about music and race is that the Negro is a "musical" person by nature and that learning music or making music comes easily to the Negro child; *ergo*: he requires no education in music. While the Negro, in general, shows a strong sense of rhythm from an early age, and often "tests out" as rating high in tonal memory, there is no proof that he is superior to Asiatic and Caucasian children of his peer in age, intelligence, or gifts. To the contrary, he usually "tests out" as being inferior to European and Japanese children in the musical arts! Yet his response to music is a most valuable means of integrating him, as the individual, in American society.

I personally eschew "tests" of this nature but I do know, from experience, that children of negroid antecedents, from so-called "underprivileged" social stratas, in the Caribbean islands and Brazil, are more often musicians, and appear to have more natural affinity for music and dance, than negroid children of far more "privileged" social classes in the United States.

Biological scientists tell us that, in general, the Negro child comes to puberty before the white child of the same age and since maturation affects the body and, in it, the organs for the production of song and speech, Negro children's voices usually mature before the voices of their white peers.

The most casual glance at the contemporary musical art world, as "pop" entertainment and within "legit." theatre, shows us that a very large number of Jewish composers and choreographers, singers, dancers and instrumentalists, are ranked among the most famed personalities. A rough estimate is that 50% of string virtuosi in American symphony orchestras and 25% of the "creative" musical artists (composers, choreographers, conductors) in American theatre today are Jewish. The Jewish musician is alleged to excel at the violin because of a biological nervousness which gives innate sensitivity to the delicate, intricate music of this instrument—and this belief appears to be based on more truth than the generalization concerning Negroes and rhythm.

More interesting and illuminating than "tests" are the obvious influences which develop potential, regardless of race or creed, and even of intelligence. I have shown how some counter-irritants, like frustration or total lack of encouragement, develop such potential, while potential is also developed through guidance and encouragement.

The grave concern should be the discovery of potential, in time to allow the child to develop it to his fullest ability and inclination.

If an educated person was always a musical person, then musical arts would be normal or ordinary to the child's environment. In the following chapters I will show means by which they can be made normal to general education, to recreation and to the social climate of religious life. In such précis, not only musical persons would know and enjoy music but persons who were artists in other forms, and craftsmen of all manner of artifacts; engineers, mathematicians, physicists and biologists, too. These persons are immensely important to the artist—they form the audiences for whom he performs or creates his works.

It is the child *per se* as well as the potential artist who should be introduced to the artistic life, so that he may choose and thereafter develop his individual human estate. The human estate is the most important consideration; more so than differences in races and creeds, intelligence quotients, and economic and social castes. *It is a human faculty to create art, not an animal, vegetable or elemental one. It is also a human faculty to appreciate art; the most cunning robots cannot experience this sense of aesthetics.*

The Child in School

"The experience of art, for the child in school and for all of us, is an experience through which we can gain an insight into what it means to be free in emotional response and free in the choice of ideas. The experience of art is a way of enriching the quality of human experience, and of reaching a precision in the choice of values. It is a particular kind of experience which requires for its fulfillment a discipline, freely undertaken, a knowledge firmly grasped, a heightened consciousness, and an intensity of interest in the creative and imaginative aspects of human life. It is not an experience which takes the artist out of the material world or out of the context of his society, but an experience which moves through contemporary reality into newer levels of awareness of what human society is.

"The moral value of art lies in this process of discovery, and in this contribution to the richness of human experience."

HAROLD TAYLOR: "Moral Values"
in *Art and the Intellect.*

$\mathcal{P}$ARENTS think that music is a part of normal school. They say that children "get to know good music" in the primary grades, enough to qualify as a musical culture, and that throughout elementary education children have music enough in which to develop their talents. Such parents assume that every child, as a matter of course, sings in school glees, and sings and dances in school activities of a social and civic nature. Parents also believe that in high school children, if so inclined, can learn to play instruments of their choice, for the school band; and that girls, particularly, study dance forms (modern and folk, as well as ballroom) in P.E.

Music appears in the American school curricula but a musical education is the uncommon, not the common perquisite for the child. The quality of music teaching in American education is widely variant not only state to state, but school district to school district, within counties. Not all school districts employ sufficient music teachers to teach all grades even a basic music course as "arts appreciation."

In high schools and colleges dance and music are elective, not required courses. If the child does not receive a basic musical education in elementary school he is unlikely ever again to have time and opportunity to acquire it. Students today are urged to specialize, to study only such subject matter required for graduating with diploma, and they are counselled by educational administrators to take only the courses easiest for them to pass with highest grades and least amount of study. In this educational system, none but the most self-aware and dedicated music lover elects musical studies in high school and college, except as a means of earning passing grades for total "credits." Parental anxiety to promote students through grades (rather than to *educate* students) now exerts pressure on children from kindergarten, and in the race to graduate in the top percentages students are indoctrinated into stream-lined techniques of assimilating information. In examinations, they are tested to ascertain how much they retain and are able to momentarily recall of this assimilated information.

The norm of American education makes certain subject matter mandatory in elementary school, but in the autonomous United States educational principle there are numerous independent "systems" for teaching, and variant curricula—with widely varying *standards of education*. Within a single county (far less within any one state) some school districts will have better facilities, more experienced teachers, greater ratios of students with potential for higher academics, than those which occupy geographically adjacent districts. Laymen school boards and school supervisors choose and administer curricula so independently of a national "norm" that it is impossible to state categorically what part of the country sets the criterion for American education.

Educators are loathe to initiate new programs, or prone to launch avant-garde ones. These appear as a series of systems, some going back to "the good old days," and others leaping ahead into untested methodologies. Currently, the trend is to develop "national resources" as student material for science and industry, and to disbar the arts as "frills." The pedagogues in favor of an educational system based on "the three Rs" are especially censorious of the creative arts, and the social arts. The "three Rs" is a synonym for Reading, *w*Riting, and *a*Rithmetic; a system lamentably based on illiteracy. The student taught skills in this system is educated to become useful to industry, but is a singularly uncultured person, knowing nothing of art and philosophy, religion and history, and capable of appreciating little social culture outside a laboring or clerkly sphere.

Educational psychology alternates between "permissive" education, with "elective" courses; and "counseling" of students that, in some instances, amounts to brain-washing (*cited*: Conrad Susa's experience with the school counseling program for pegging students in the "aptitude" board).

Education is "programmed" towards promotion and graduation.

Methodologies applied to some forms of teaching in general education are ineffective in an approach to the arts. The practice of art is a humbling, frustrating, arduous and exacting discipline, in which failure is an entity like achievement—but wherein the artist does not have set modes for invariably acquiring success. *Accomplishment*, not success, is the artistic goal. The arts have more abstract than concrete value (their worth as art compared to their estimated worth as art objects). And to undertake to work in an art form is to enter into the pursuit of excellence.

In an educational system which grades, rather than qualifies, teachers and students operate in set patterns of high and low grades, with a median grade on which a student "passes" or succeeds. Moreover, the current trend is to spare the student failure at all costs, to avoid experience of frustration, humiliation and self-doubt. The artist is not spared these sufferings but strives to fulfil an original thought and an individual concept. Observe that I do not say he studies, but that he *strives* . . .

Since the measurement of success in the arts and in education are not by the same yardstick an entirely different approach must be made to art than that which school administrators propound, in current "systems" for education.

The rule for an approach to the arts is basic to ethics of art. These are wholly contained in one cogent law, which is the character of art: *Art cannot be contrived because art is created.*

Philosophers and scientists are eagerly trying to fathom genius, the quality of original thought and individual concept or idea. In education, this is described as "discovering potential." Philosophic and scientific studies are being made on "potential," how to detect it in the young, and, thereafter, how to encourage and stimulate it, usually for projects called "national resources." These are scientific and not artistic, nevertheless it is mainly through the *artistic response* that children show potential for original thought and individual concept or idea.

Experienced teachers, especially of children in primary grades, know this; they know that young students learn most readily through rhythm and rhyme—that, indeed, it is almost impossible to teach kindergarten and first grade students without recourse to *the two true Rs.*

Dance and music, as has been said (in the chapter: *Dance and Music*) are possibly the best means of approaching two main types of intelligence; the aural and the visual. In dance, and in performance of music, a third sense—the tactile one—is added. When children work in dance and music they learn by looking and listening, and by feeling; *they learn by experiencing in the self.*

The younger the child, the lower the grade, the more the teacher must turn to the musical arts.

Principles for a Musical Education

No academic education in the arts should be attempted by the untrained, or by a tyro musician and dancer. Moreover, even an accomplished musician and dancer requires training *for teaching*; assimilation of teaching techniques, chiefly a study of tested approaches and the most universal responses.

Formal study of an instrument, voice training, a dance education, all must be undertaken under trained teachers of the various musical techniques. These techniques have to be learned thoroughly, and they must be scrupulously *and excitingly* taught. The able teacher strictly supervises, patiently tutors . . . and consistently challenges the student. Challenge is progressive in a study of an art form; the challenge for the artist never ceases; it becomes more intense as his standards are raised and his apperception increases.

Such principles of a musical education must initiate the experience as well as sustain it. The student must be properly taught from the beginning.

The accredited music teacher, working in a creditable music program in school, should be able to provide at least a sound elementary education in music, for all children, in all grades. For such a program, a school requires a Music department comparable in size of faculty, and with at least the equal facilities of its P.E. department. In addition, the Music department faculty should be encouraged to promote and produce performances in the musical arts, in the school auditorium for full assembly—plus concert-type entertainments for inter-district schools, and for parents and guests. In fact, the Music department, in the performance and production areas, should have administrative and parental support, and public exposure comparable to that given to sporting events, as baseball, basketball and football games. Musical arts festivals, in school contests, are admirable means of developing challenges for the students—and educating the community audience!

In an accredited music program, under qualified music faculty, every school—and each child in the school—should have opportunities for discovering what music is, and a great deal of what music is about, and dance and drama should be added to establish a lyrical arts program.

The majority of music teachers have no training in dance, while many P.E. teachers of girls' activities do (but this does not always ensure that they have also been trained to *teach* dance). In order to integrate the two art forms the Music and Physical Education departments of all primary and secondary schools should integrate programs, so that the students participate in an artistic and a gymnastic program. Naturally, the musically talented (or those more interested in art than sports) will study more advanced music techniques than those students who are physically and temperamentally better suited to working in gymnastic activities. *But just as all children in school are expected to participate in supervised physical education, unless specifically excused from this by medical certification of handi-*

cap, so should all students be expected to participate in a musical arts curriculum, except those excused for a certified disability.

A "disability" for dance might be through paralysis and lameness, or a spastic and deaf-and-blind condition—but dance as therapy is now in great use with persons so handicapped. A "disability" for participation in the most passive manner (by listening) in a music program might be from deafness—but some deaf persons respond to the frequencies in music (vibrations of air against the human eardrum, and cranial and facial sounding boards).

Indeed, from my own extensive work with the aurally deaf child, and my observation of work being done with spastics and mentally retarded children, I am able to state here that such handicapped students benefit from participation in a conjoined program of dance and music.

On the contrary, and most regrettably, some aspects of the "normal" P.E. program are injurious to children who are coincidentally training for ballet. I know of several instances, especially within recent years (from the newer vogues in P.E., applied as "physical fitness" exercises), of elementary and advanced ballet students suffering ligament and joint strain which adversely affect their dancing. In some instances, a congenital weakness, not apparent enough to appear as disability, has been increased by the alternation between the characteristic ballet training and a too rigorous adoption of certain P.E. exercises, or through participation in certain games which impose stress on the congenitally weakened members. Most frequently affected parts of the body (for the ballet student working over-zealously in P.E.) are the ankle, knee and hip.

If the Music and P.E. faculties of a school would inquire into *approved dance techniques*, enough to recognize, through expert demonstration, those that relate most to (a) the P.E. program of exercises, and (b) *movement in music* (rhythmic exercises, for one), a rudimentary dance program could be put into effect for students, within the integrated Music and P.E. programs, as 'Physical Fitness through Dance.' A program by this name was instituted for the public schools in Atlanta, Ga. by a dance teacher, Dorothy Alexander, and has been practiced for more than 25 years.

Failing this, the Music teacher should work as closely as possible with the P.E. teacher, in attempts to provide a program in *elements of dance movement* within the Music and P.E. courses. Moreover, an entire school faculty (not only two as described) should plan interlocking if not integrated programming in arts and sciences, as described here in *Music in the General Curricula*. And when a school must put such a program into effect without the expertise of a trained Music faculty, then the conventional or classroom (course) teacher must develop her own program, based as much as possible on the approach of the cognitive teacher. Perhaps the best means of the conventional teacher learning how to work with dance and music come from seminars under cognitive teachers. In such seminars, the conventional teacher attends lecture-demonstration programs, is able to participate in question-and-answer sessions (group discussions), and may even be able to do "field work" under supervision.

If, following a seminar course, the conventional teacher inaugurates a pilot program or series of pilot programs (in progressions for the course in the classroom) she should then try to obtain expert assistance in evaluating the classroom work, periodically.

To clarify: the "cognitive" teacher is a term for the genuine creative artist or performing artist; and/or the musicologist and dance authority; experienced in conducting lecture-demonstration, and analysis and evaluation, as well as formulation of pilot programs.

The "conventional" teacher is the regular course teacher—the teacher within the school faculty whose main work is teaching subject matter in the general curricula. She is usually not trained in dance and music, or trained to teach dance and music. In a well-integrated, well effected musical arts program, the conventional teacher, logically, should work within a program established by the school's Music faculty—but in many schools where there is a Music department there is little or no liaison between it and the teachers working in the "basic" curricula. Often, there is not even rapport between teachers from Music and P.E. departments.

In schools without a resident Music faculty (and many schools share one school district faculty for Music, with itinerant music teachers traveling about only enough to look in at the programs under conventional teachers), the conventional teacher works daily throughout a semester; she needs practical guidance for introducing dance and musical arts into ordinary classwork, without adverse interruption of the classwork.

Unquestionably, teachers need help and advice in class work of this kind, and are likely to need these more and more, as the ratio of accredited music teachers decreases in the public school system. It is now comparatively easy to procure funds for large-scale programs in creative art forms for children of "deprived" and "underprivileged" categories, but harder than ever to provide elementary facilities and sufficient teaching in these forms for children from so-called "average" cultures. The physically handicapped are fairly well provided for; the so-called "gifted" are hardly being provided for, commensurate with their particular needs.

Some of the materially richest school districts have decreased instead of increasing musical arts in the curricula. In the 1966 Report to the Governor and Legislature the California Arts Commission noted that, while the arts are flourishing in higher education, and numerous small communities are benefiting from proximity to the college campus, "the rallying place for the arts", opportunities for a musical education in primary and secondary schools are steadily diminishing. According to the California Music Educators Association: *in the last two or three years, many school districts have curtailed music in their schools' offerings by either eliminating teaching positions or not lengthening the school day to provide room for the arts in addition to the subjects mandated by law. As one example of the former, in 1965 the Los Angeles City Board of Education withdrew the special music teacher from 85 elementary schools within its jurisdiction.* During the following year, it withdrew a greater number.

This Board of Education has jurisdiction over the second largest school district in the nation (New York's being the largest), in the state where more students are enrolled in college courses than anywhere else in the U.S., and which has the largest university system in the world.

Through instituting a "basic" principle in elementary education, we have a wholly utilitarian précis, and not a "classical" one. In this premise, it is to the conventional teacher that the child in school must turn, in hope of the artistic life—within the general curricula which has established, through P.E., a gymnastic life as the norm.

When a teacher shuts the door of a classroom she must then choose how to teach—by rote, in strict authority; or "permissively," letting the children, regardless of their past experience, choose what they want to learn. She has a third choice: she can make teaching *discovery*, whereupon the children will *experience*. While I dislike the term "creative teacher" (as much as I deplore the term "gifted child" for the bright child) I favor the term "creative teaching act." It is such an act which transpires when children say they "are getting to know about" something; for example: music, with such intensity that they cannot resist working with it, creatively.

A teacher, however, works within school policies—these over-rule as well as underlie her classroom authority. Autonomous school policy is established in large part by laymen school boards. Education is that type of teaching, by the sort of teachers, a community elects and supports. And a community is made up, in large part, of persons who are parents. The community, like the audience en masse, requires extensive education in

* Stated on p. 28, *The Arts in California*, 1966 Report by the California Arts Commission.

arts appreciation, not only in the aesthetics of the arts but also in their values, in social culture.

Dance and music must not be treated as "activities" in education—even when they are activated within the general curricula. By this I mean: *the approach to dance and music must remain artistic*. Such approach precludes the nauseous habit, shared by condescending writers and teachers, of inanely describing working in dance and music as "having fun and games with dance and music." The "fun" connotation for theatrical arts in America is still within the puritanic colonial distrust of theatre. Many educators overtly treat music as a frivolity ("sweet, seductive sounds") and dance as immoral, because it is over-exhilarating ("abandoned") for the strait-laced bureaucratic mind. And, as some administrators have frankly admitted, in dance and music students do not work "quietly and calmly." Administrators are often alarmed by "the influences of music and dance on animal spirits, with resulting breaches of classroom discipline."

If we are honestly concerned with principles of a musical education, we might reflect on those of John Adams; "I must study politics and war so that my sons may have the liberty to study mathematics, philosophy and commerce so that their children may have the right and privilege to study painting, poetry and music."

More than one hundred and fifty years after, surely our children should have this right. The parent and the teacher, working together, can provide it.

Music in the General Curricula

Administrators with whom I have discussed the principles of a musical education maintain that dance and music intrude on the basic courses, in time, concentration and physical facilities. Invariably, experiments in creativity lead to ambitions for performing and staging works. My premise is that dance, drama and music may be integrated into the general curricula, and to some extent (as in performance) extend to art courses (drawing, painting and sculpture) and the "shop," classrooms for the vocational students, the latter through stage designing. I believe that an elementary course in musical arts should be compulsory throughout primary and secondary education, and an arts appreciation or "philosophy of art" course compulsory (not elective) for all college freshmen.

Every course, in normal school, which touches on the history of civilization, from primitive to contemporary man, involves arts. All civics or social studies should incorporate the arts. The social involvements typical of American education (supervised play) could satisfy ambitions to produce and perform, urges emanating from the desire to communicate, creatively.

Music, more than dance, is easy to integrate in classroom subjects, and can become a brilliant illumination of a subject. The arithmetic teacher and student may discover the system of marking and counting music, the scales in melody, the sum of "building chords," the values of notes and rests, the graduations and skips, as movement, in music. The interval in music has been taken by Leonard Bernstein, a superb elucidator on the theme, to illustrate relationships between atoms and molecules. During the 9th season of his New York Philharmonic Young People's Concerts: *Musical Atoms—a study of intervals*, Bernstein showed that like the atom which requires two particles to create, instrumental music requires two musical notes, a relationship that is called an interval. The layman assumes that arithmetic, the science of real, positive numbers, is a thoroughly logical study, but that music (the art of putting sounds together) is a purely romantic one. In fact, there is an extraordinarily close relationship between arithmetic and music.*

Developing musicianship through rhythmic studies, the Farmingdale Project offered students exercises which incorporated simple and compound subdivisions, and studies of relationships between meters, as described in *Appendix I.*

In science, music might be approached through investigation of pitch

---

* Pythagoras, the Greek mathematician and philosopher, in the 6th century B.C. discovered that the length of a musical string is in exact numerical relationship to the pitch of its tone. From this (he invented philosophy, the study of the principles underlying all knowledge) he developed a theory of harmony. He believed that number was the first principle of the whole universe, propounded a theorem about the solar system that was not too far from the one we have adopted, and about geometry, which remains rudimentary to that science. Existent since the 17th century is the theory that music is an arithmetic process carried to its absolute and logical limit, a theory supported by modern dance and music. Labanotation, the most popular dance notation system, was developed by Rudolf von Laban on principles related to those of the icosahedron, a 20-sided solid figure, and his primary spatial formulae for dance movement are based on the continuous, weaving line of the figure 8. In the 1930's composer Arnold Schönberg's innovation of the unmelodic 12-tone "atonal" system was challenged by Ernest Ansermet, the conductor who began life as a school-master. Drawing on his work as a mathematics teacher Ansermet refuted, by mathematical formulae, the strict 12-tone system as being opposed to the laws of hearing. More recently, the French composers Pierre Barbaud and Roger Blanchard have utilized a mechanical calculator to mathematically compose music as it would compute digital formulae. A good example of music according to mathematical formulae is in the work of Ernst Krenek, as in *Sestina*.

and resonance; the processes as cause and effect of sounds in conventional and unconventional instruments; effects of physical environments (like water, instead of atmosphere) on the sounds of music.

"Art" classes should study relationships between design in painting and sculpture and dance, and examples of such relationships abound in modern ballet and the contemporary (usually called "Modern") dance, from Balanchine's Neoclassical *Agon* in the ballet idiom to the works of modern dancers, for instance: *Cantilever* by Erick Hawkins. Hawkins collaborates with the composer Lucia Dlugoszewski (pronounced *dwou-go-SHEF-Skee*), and sculptor Ralph Dorazio in his repertory for the Erick Hawkins Company, which tours extensively through the American college theatre. Modern dancer Charles Weidman choreographs with "living" sculpture of wire by Mikhail Santaro, in works of dance and sculpture called "Expressions of Two Arts." Many choreographers observe painting and sculptural as well as musical principles and some are artists in other media than dance. Paul Taylor was first a painter and later a dancer-choreographer.

In school "shop" classes students could try making conventional instruments, like guitars, and unconventional ones, including those of original design by the class. Much of the new music of our time is made by new instruments (composer Dlugoszewski designs hers, which are executed as beautiful little pieces of sculpture by Dorazio). Some of this new music is made on "prepared" piano and a variety of unconventional instruments, such as music by John Cage who plays compositions on prepared piano, and Harry Partch, who designs his own instruments.

From the standard "Music" class through classes allegedly unrelated to music, such as science and "shop," studies of the development of sounds as music could become an exciting discovery for students from elementary through college grades. Usually, music is a subject or course unrelated to others in "normal" educational curricula. When it is so taught, under a Music faculty, it is specific to students in the 'music class.' But, often, students outside such a class have little or no introduction to music in school—and may have no creative musical experiences outside school.

The premise that music must be taught as an entirely separate course in curricula ignores realization that a student learns several things simultaneously—and that, very often, one fact absorbed serves to illustrate another. In such premise, music can be integrated into a mandatory or "normal" curricula and an "educated" person might just as readily become a "musically educated" person.

Normally subjects as social history and "civics" require teachers and students to pore over the political governments of world societies, and to investigate regions geographically by naming cities and mountains, and tracing the courses of rivers; and to inquire into the economics of regional or national areas, assaying ore deposits, counting heads of livestock and tons of grain, noting the artifacts . . . and ignoring entirely or barely acknowledging the arts of the people. Contrarily, a "normal" civics class could learn more about foreign peoples by studying their folkways, in which their ideologies are preserved, and getting to know them through their arts, particularly their musical arts.

Educators and politicians are agreed on the urgent and immediate need to establish communication between the peoples of the earth, not solely for the individual material gains of peoples but chiefly so that we may all exist on the same planet without destroying one another. If there is a "modern" and "true" need for education today it is in *communication*, the ability to express one's thoughts, ideas and intents and, also, the ability to listen and hear, and understand, another's. For methods of communication, then, if they are denigrated for being "arts," let educators look to dance and music with more respect than they do as yet in America.

Know that in mankind's history what could not be said, because it was forbidden, was sung—and boldly sung! That which was not sufficiently eloquent and moving when sung alone, was sung and danced. Racial memory and the roots of living cultures are preserved in myth and music, through rhyme and rhythm. And we learn best when we associate ourselves most intimately with the subject under study. These are elementary truths and apply in education as in other aspects of life. And there are certain other elementary truths a teacher must know, in an approach to the child in contemporary society.

What Every Teacher Must Know

"Nursery lore" lies in the musical arts and is a literary culture as well as a musical one. Rhymes are exercises by which memory is developed, and a conscious use of language; they are the beginning of the academic life when they embrace myth and religion, through ballads and hymns. Jokes are the beginning of a civilized wit and humor; riddles the commencement of abstract thought; proverbs and fables the fundament of morality. What children chant, recite and sing as "nonsense" is of unutterable sense later on, and early conscious knowledge of music is the first cultivation of the child as a person.

When a child knows epic character and episode he grows with awareness of the nobility of man, the splendor of courage and self-sacrifice, the sweetness of loyalty and faith. He begins to perceive that racial ideologies, such as are preserved in music, sustain whole peoples through elemental and civil catastrophes, and inspire the themes of the folkloric arts.

A child may be too young to *know* but be sensitive enough to feel, which is why his responses to the arts are spontaneous and exalting.

When a child learns to sing hymns and consciously to know "sacred" music, he begins to understand the meaning of worshipful praise. It is a human need to worship and to express the self, which may be the purpose of the human voice, and we have danced as "the moving creature which hath life" from the fifth day of Creation.

The reasons why children dance are equally profound and when very small children elect to perform "boy's dances" and "girl's dances" they obey an impulse which we recognize in folk-dance where there are dances particular to men, to women and some gregarious dances for partners. We know that our ancestors danced to court a mate and raise a roof-tree, bring game into the forest and grain out of the ground, all for reasons related to survival of the self and, eventually, the society or race. Mankind was here concerned with essential needs like food, clothing and shelter. But man danced for other reasons, some of which have been translated into dancing for entertainment, and chief of these was to importune and placate someone or something which could not be seen or touched or heard but which primitive man perceived to be at one and the same time the author of his being and his end. Children, in an innocent, savage state, dance from native rhythm and from racial memory and the instinct to express and create with the whole self. Since the 1800s, American educators have accepted Friedrich Froebel's principles for rhythmic exercise in 'creative play' for infant education. But we need to know enough about movement in the musical sense, as dance, in order to understand its importance to the infant and child, and to the adolescent.

Formerly, in our society, infants and young children intimately shared an environment with older folk, who were articulate in teaching the children language and music, manners and mores. Recently, from about the Depression, the family norm has altered to parents-and-child; often to a single parent and an only child. Grandparental influences are negative or void in a society that segregates generations, placing persons over the age of fifty in the category of "senior citizens," and establishing them in self-contained, veritable cities of older folk, apart from succeeding generations, especially from the youngest generation: the infant.

Grandparents, the sustainers of a social culture, were traditionally the tellers of tales, singers of songs, teachers of dances. Children sang the same songs, danced the same "rounds" and "squares," and played the same games in a "nursery culture" that lasted for innumerable generations. A rhythm of growth, as surely as a rhythm of time, was established, and even in a modern, urban society we preserved the essential ceremonies of growing from infancy into childhood, childhood into adolescence, in preparation for the adult estate. Proverb and moral, fable and legend were absorbed in rhyme and rhythm, as the child was subtly educated while appearing to be entertained. The identical process continues today and only the approach has been changed, while the responses, *totally human*, remain the same. The approach now is more mechanistic than personal, and in large part by commercial and not cultural media.

Gullible parents and indifferent, indolent sitters delude themselves by saying a child is only entertained by television. In fact, the child is educated and indoctrinated by a medium which, overtly and crudely commercial, uses extraordinary psychology in employing the performing arts as a selling, not an artistic communication. American television is supported by business and industry, concerned with financial and not moral or spiritual gains, and in frantic rivalry for pure profit among competing networks. It is ridiculous and naive for parents and teachers to expect such a commercial medium to provide academic and artistic educations for children, and the recent and sparse attempts at "educational" TV do not yet qualify as "cultural." Television's public services are for topical news events, the time and the weather, (matters more scientific than artistic) and from these children gain valuable data. But the dance on television is not a creative experience for the child and except for the unique contributions of Leonard Bernstein there is no TV music worthy of children.

The child of "privileged" (not "deprived") class has a shallow surface knowledge of the world and little knowledge of himself as a person, and how he relates to others, now giving rise to techniques called "sociometrics," by which he is to be educated in how to live amongst his peers. Through television, a child gains a madly disoriented insight into an "adult" world, where he experiences (participating as spectator) crime and violence (and technical immorality, like the rigged quizzes on television). The child does not so often share the adult art world. Instead, an industry has been developed for "cute" presentations of art for the juvenile.

American children are believed to be bored and without taste, according to the approaches manufacturers and businessmen make to them; more thought and money are expended on the method of approach than on the substance of the "package." Children are subjected to standardized methods of entertainment (much of which, as in the "coke-tail" club, pathetically ape in miniature an adult "cafe society" whirl). Businessmen, not psychologists, have divided the child's world into the pre-school, pre-teen, junior-teen (the "pre-bra" set invented by lingerie manufacturers for sales of apparel that help a child pretend to be an adult), and "teens," this last category an entire world to itself, sharply alienated from the adult world it breaches—and into which the alienated 'teen-ager' is precipitated if he survives his 19th year.

Most of the approaches made to children are audio-visual, cunningly devised to use the child as an advertiser and salesman in its approach to the parent as consumer and purchaser. All "artistic" approaches made within a commercial medium, regardless of the quality of the performance, are salesmanship approaches. The American child's audio-visual education is largely through television, presently the most influential form of communication in the U.S. The older child accepts the cinema, and its "stars," or screen personalities, as arbiter of mores and morals. Now, Education is turning to television and to cinema, and integrating them in the normal curricula.

The child who is left to entertain himself, without supervision, with TV, may see a great deal of dancing and hear a great deal of music, and some of it will be "good" as being of good form in art and good in performance. None of it, however, is within the approach or introduction to creative musical arts, and while they amuse they do not enlighten the child. Worst of all effects are mimicry by the child of adult stereotypes, and the child's acceptance of sales-pitches as songs.

In September, 1965, a kindergarten teacher in an economically rich and socially prestigious school district started the class year with a "song book," to which the children contributed "favorite" songs. Twenty-seven boys and girls of above-average home environments, in a material sense, offered her television themes and "commercials" as songs which they had learned without conscious effort, through repetition of their tiresome phrases but undeniably catchy tunes. If some children in this group knew real songs of the "nursery culture" they forbore to contribute them, since in so doing they should have appeared "different" and therefore alien in the group.

Within the past five years, teachers in schools in the Appalachia area have told me of the gradual loss of traditional songs and dances among their students, who now know only the music they learn from television and, in so learning, forget that which, for generations without number, had been preserved in Appalachia. A teacher writes me: "I go into the homes of these students and see their families living in terrible poverty, but owning a television—often, because a charitable private or government agency has bought the set and installed it as a gift. The houses are hovels, with leaking roofs, split walls and draughty floors, and without any of the common sanitary conveniences. In the same room, where day and night there is no proper light, there is the red glow of an oil stove and the blue glare of the television screen. Between these two household gods the family gathers in stunned torpor, hour after hour, as long as the television produces images and sounds—often, long after the stove has gone out. My children have forgotten to sing, and they do not know how to dance, but commercial folk troupers are making money with bowdlerized versions of the musical culture Appalachia long cherished. The children know nothing that is true and real, *least of all their own music out of Appalachia*! Pop entertainers found this music; has Appalachia lost it for good?"

Children no longer know, as a matter of course, nursery rhymes like *Pat-a-cake, baker's man*; *Little Tommy Tucker*; *Wee Willie Winkie* and *Bobby Shafto*. These songs have been common to English-speaking peoples since 1698, 1765 and 1841, respectively, while *Bobby Shafto* is an old political campaign ditty, dating to 1761, when one Robert Shafto ran for a seat in the English Parliament.

Summer is icumen in, by John of Fornsete, a monk of Reading Abbey, circa 1226, is one of the songs hailing the *cuccu* (cuckoo), an immeasurably ancient rite of spring. Children used to sing it in the nursery; it is preserved by serious adult glees nowadays.

Old songs and stories, like those from the Bible, mythology and folklore, and from 'fairy tales,' have fallen into disfavor with adults in our 'modern' world, which is concerned with the scientific and mechanistic. But older generations relied on them for symbolic values in teaching children human and divine natures, good and evil, and right and wrong. We have found no substitutes so eloquent and persuasive.

The profit of learning nursery songs and stories, and with them a great deal else, accrues after the student has passed through the elementary grades.

Easy reference to "nursery lore" is becoming obsolete for the college student today, and in Spring, 1966, several colleges inaugurated crash courses in mythology and religion, because of professorial complaint that a great mass of literary connotation and allegory is bewildering to students. For about ten years, lecturing on the Romantic era to college students, I have found it useful to relate Perrault's *La Belle au Bois Dormant* as a story, before discussing Tchaikovsky's best ballet score: *The Sleeping Beauty*, since few adolescents know the old, familiar fairy tales, and the Medieval ideas of the Elementals of air, water, earth and fire, who throng literature and theatre and overtly affected individual thought and behavior, art and letters.

During the 1965–66 tour of the Metropolitan Opera National Company, with the opera *Susannah*, by American composer Carlisle Floyd, it was always necessary for me to relate the Old Testament story of Susanna of Babylon, in order to approach Floyd's opera, which is set on Tennessee mountain folk.

Metaphor and simile, like allegorical thought, depend greatly on mythology and religion, and in science as well as art. The furious intent to travel in space has made current the term *Gemini*, the thematic value of which has to be explained to "educated" students; as has the root meaning of chimaera, and reference to a driver like Jehu or an exodus like that of the Gadarene swine. The educational ban on religious teaching in school debars most teachers from referring to the Hebrew or Christian Bibles, and the ruling for a "basic" study "in the three Rs" prohibits all save the most utilitarian courses. For students who lack a "nursery culture" at home there will soon be little opportunity of acquiring it in elementary school—yet children are being sent to school at very early ages, sometimes (to so-called "nursery schools") at two-and-a-half and three. Teachers are now expected to give children the culture that, in an older norm, developed in the home.

If children do not learn to sing and dance as infants they may never do so in later years, or they may accept only faddist styles, generally in adolescent rebellion. School teachers have found that the child who knows no songs also knows no poetry; and that the student totally ignorant of the musical arts is usually without appreciation of painting and sculpture, and, sometimes, of literature and drama. Remedial reading classes are now performing rhythmic exercises, since certain ineptitudes in reading and writing skills appear to stem from insufficient rhythmic development (muscular and sensory) in the infant and young child.

Most importantly, young children who cannot sing and dance withdraw from the group in their first attempts to become social persons. A child who likes to sing will also usually enjoy verbal expression; a child who dances will have confidence to take a place, assume a role, in other forms of work and play.

Then, too, as schools get more crowded and teachers have increasing responsibilities and class chores, active play of itself becomes more difficult to supervise. Song and dance offer pleasant means for children to work and play, together, in large groups—while also providing opportunities for true creativity by the individual child. It is this stimulus to individual creativity which is most sorely missed when a "nursery culture" is destroyed. In the current mode of sending children to school in infancy it falls to the primary grades teachers to sustain an equivalent nursery culture, as foundation for an academic or classical culture for the student in later life. Unfortunately, the majority of conventional teachers rely solely on packaged and "canned" approaches to the musical arts.

"Canned" music and dance are vicarious methods of approach to the arts, which are *living* arts from their essentially human commitment. Music and dance are not only created by the human person; they must also be *interpreted* by the human person. Literature, painting and sculpture, and architecture are solid and static, concrete forms of abstract thought. Music and dance exist only as they are created and continuously recreated in performances by singers and instrumentalists and dancers. Therefore the live approach is the only valid approach. All approaches less than "live," however well achieved in the medium of recordings for music and films for dance, are substitutes, and should so be known by the audience which listens and looks to the canned variety of the living substance.

The teacher often needs to arrange experiences of live music and dance for her students, or suffer them to remain entirely ignorant of these. I believe that from earliest years children should be taken to theatre, there to experience live drama, dance and music. All my "arts appreciation" programs: lectures, lecture-demonstrations of techniques, and lecture-performances of lyric and dramatic arts, are deliberately directed to theatrical experiences of these as conclusive to the program.

For the teacher who must work predominantly with canned dance and music I advise a greater use of cinema film than of television film. Television offers its wares only at certain times, in certain areas, and through certain networks, and many of its best productions are not available to teachers and students within regular school hours, or on a national network. Cinema film, on the other hand, is the servant of the classroom, to be used when the teacher chooses, as repeatedly as she needs to make use of it, and in such an elastic manner that a teacher may halt and hold a picture in a frame, to make a "still" within the film, if she wishes to impress some detail in the whole, such as the bowing technique of a violinist, or the movement of a dancer. She can then run the film straight through, as a performance. Cinema techniques are more flexible than television and far more so than photographs or slides, which are isolated and static.

The phonograph, called the "record player," is an ubiquitous classroom tool and a good one; so is the tape-recorder. But the piano remains indispensable, even for a teacher who is no more than a one-fingered pianist.

In a classroom, a teacher works with raw materials of a group made up on strength and weakness, depending on individual experience and ignorance. The group progresses in ratio to its components. All children do not have the culture of Jonathan Kreger, whose home environment prepared him to look and listen in school. In this child's infancy he learned to hear music, and to perceive dance as dynamic images. He entered kindergarten from a home environment which had prepared him to dance and to enjoy music and although he did not spontaneously sing he sang when required, as part of his group. This child had a nursery culture in literature and already had the rudiments of music—he knew, for instance, that music is written and read, and in a system of notation, as language is contained out of an alphabet. He was, we may say, thoroughly at ease with dance and music.

Few six-year-olds are so well prepared, when they enter 1st grade, and many adolescent children lack the experiences in music which Jonathan Kreger possessed at six, when he began formal study of music, on the violin. More commonly, children begin school without any conscious vocabulary in music, with the most cursory experience in dance, and so ignorant of the human person as he relates to time and space that they are unable to follow simple directions, like telling left from right.

Children of this "space age" accumulate a great deal of scientific information about aeroplanes and rockets, and some fantastic corollaries (flying-saucers), but have small understanding of how *they* relate to space, and how bodies (their own and those of their peers) move and balance by natural, not mechanistic means.

One of the greatest teachers I know, a mature woman whose professional prestige is well known as a teacher of student teachers (in sabbaticals from what she calls her "real work," teaching kindergarten and 1st grade children) has told me that every September she hopes, in vain, to find her new class 100% "teachable." To meet this test, she says, all the children must "know how to go [by themselves, to the bathroom] and when to blow [their over-flowing noses]; and to tell a right hand and a right foot from a left hand and a left foot. This is the preliminary training I beg of parents!"

Children begin first grade in school knowing how to count from one to a hundred, but as yet unconscious of beats in music, so that they cannot follow a tune or a simple pattern in dance. They may be able to babble the alphabet in kindergarten, twenty-six English letters, but are usually ignorant of the seven letters of the common scale. Yet in quite ordinary ways infants will learn a great deal about dance and music, before they are ready to begin learning skills of reading and writing.

Children at home and in the earliest school grades should learn right from left, light from heavy, soft from loud, quick from slow; what it means to be still (but not dead); what is sound and what is silence. They can begin to understand direction, weight, measures of time and speed, degrees of audibility in ways which have been described in *The Child at Home*. They need to know all these things before they can begin to sing and dance and create music.

My principles of an approach to dance and music are based on only two rules: to discover dance and music together and relate one to the other; and to instill in children a critical faculty from the start, so that they may learn to qualify as they create.

Dance and music share a basic vocabulary and may be introduced simultaneously to a group of children if the music (and the conventional) teacher treats dance as *movement qualified by musical elements*.

When the music teacher works in dance, she should know children's anatomical aspects to the same extent as she knows the limitations and abilities of children in median ages when they sing. Muscularity in dance is even more pronounced than in music. I should say that a teacher needs to know about as much of children's anatomical aspects, in a group, for games, as she needs to know for the rudimentary dance-games that are the beginning of creative dance work. The best kind of dance teacher for beginners (young children or adolescents), is one like Bruce King, who works with dance and music. He is musically educated and can play the piano and drum as instruments of reference for dancing. With infants and young children, a teacher must also be prepared to sing!

The teacher should restrict herself only as to quality, as the worth of music, while remaining tolerant of all music that has merit in its genre. When children want to sing songs for me, that sell cigarettes, beer and razor blades, I counter by offering them other selling songs, classics of their kind, like *Simple Simon* (who met a pieman) and *Molly Malone* (who sold cockles and mussels) which have proved their merit by surviving generations of singers.

Children have the breath, energy and inclination to sing and dance, simultaneously, and their song-and-dance repertory should extend to drama and poetry, in a rudimentary form of lyric theatre.

Dancing should be of two kinds: in patterns, as in rounds, squares and other formal designs; and improvisational, or creative. I like to begin with folk dance because many children are often too shy to improvise at first; besides, as Mrs. Kreger has remarked, folk music has strong rhythms and pretty melodies, which are easy to learn, quick to achieve responses. The folk dances are by no means always easy. The *Virginia Reel* is an intricate dance, with a nice ceremonious style which makes it a good choice for coeducational groups, to teach boys and girls to dance as partners. Like almost all such dances it is robust, with enough action to appeal to children, of both genders.

Rely on folk music, whose notable elements are simplicity of form, drama, melody and rhythm, all of which evoke responses in young people. Rely, also, on folk music to be assured of the best music of its kind. The valid and vital dance and music survive; all other kinds perish.*

Nursery culture is by no means static and outworn, since it exists in songs, rhymes, jokes and riddles that children continuously employ in their play. Only some get written down in books and put on recordings; many more exist mysteriously by word of mouth, borne for generations and often from one distant region to another. Perhaps the skipping songs (songs sung by children as they turn and jump rope) have the greatest

---

* For the teacher who knows little about folk music and must rely, to begin with, on recorded material, two recommended recordings are *Music Adventures with 7 League Boots* and *Adventures in Folk Songs*, from a four album series produced by Gloria Chandler Recordings, Inc., New York, N.Y. These, respectively, concern faraway places, to which the listener aurally travels with a 12-year old narrator named Paul, finding out some aspects of peoples' customs and histories with representative music; and a musical American saga covering 300 years of our immigrant, colonizing people. The westward way is particularly good. The other parts of the record series are *Book Adventures*, in which episodes from literature are related with musical accompaniment (not always of the most imaginative choice, but serviceable enough for a rudimentary program) and *Piano Adventures*, originated out of the Toledo Museum by Mary Van Doren with live audiences of children, in discussions about music between the pianist and audience. Folkways Records Ethnic Series is a good source of material. Publications such as the *New York Folklore Quarterly* are informative about folk dance, song and music. Literature about folkways and folk music can become a basic instructional aspect of the classroom, related to musical examples; recommended are *Folk Songs U.S.A.* by John and Alan Lomax, publ. Duell, Sloan and Pearce, New York, and *The American Songbag* by Carl Sandburg, Harcourt, Brace & Co. Inc., New York. There are several others, for which consult library records.

affinity between play and music; almost equal are the songs sung when children play "jacks." Interestingly, these songs are dramatic as retelling of episode and anecdote and they hardly vary in theme (although they vary considerably in accents) in the English-speaking world.

The conventional teacher working with dance and music in the classroom, in an approach to infants and young children, should study these students on the playground, see how they move in their favorite games, hear what they sing as songs without supervision. On such foundation (what they know, what they choose to enjoy as music) she may then develop a musical program which will, from inception, have pleasant associations for the children, chiefly from familiarity with the material.

Clapping and stamping games, marching games, games that form rounds and squares, all may be converted to dances, and when the children relate movement as dance to their games, within music they know and love, they respond almost always as a whole group, giving the teacher more time to develop her theme, allowing her to work with their cooperation.

The conventional teacher, or the teacher who knows more about dance forms, less of song, should be prepared for wide diversity in singing aptitudes, within a group, but must also know that there are generalities about children singing. They have difficulty in reproducing pitch (usually, up to and through second-grade level) and yet they quickly master complicated rhythm, especially when it is syncopated. Children may find it hard to sing *Happy Birthday* and yet be able to sing tongue-twisters, nonsense syllables with complicated musical patterns as melodies. Although there are anatomical rules governing singing, the fact is that a child will sing any song he likes, if he is allowed to sing it the way he can and the way he wants to. And when he wants to learn the song well enough he will even learn to spell the words and write the verse that belong with the music.

Ideally, every classroom in the primary grades should have a piano, and it is fairly usual for kindergarten and first and second grade teachers to have easy access to this instrument. All the schools I know have record players and tape-recorders, which are issued to classrooms on the teachers' requests. If all cannot work freely with dance and music in the classroom, any teacher may help prepare her students to develop a rudimentary knowledge about music. She can begin by helping the children consciously discover what they already know, since a musical culture, like an iceberg, is deeply hidden in every society.

Critical faculties for children are developed by teaching them how to be good audiences as well as how to personally respond to dance and music. The perceptive eye and ear are trained and it is they who inform (or intelligently analyse) the senses that are responsive to dance and music. "Arts appreciation" courses have earned a bad name with musicians and music teachers, from the notion that all "appreciation" is indoctrination; pedantic instruction in what to admire and not to admire in art. On the contrary, true appreciation is a cultivation of natural tastes, governed by discrimination out of knowledge. For the teacher who cannot work physically with dance and music, from being restricted by circumstances that forbid noise and movement, a rudimentary introduction to music as a form, and an "appreciation" through listening to music on records; and looking at dance (on film, and also through a poetic verbal approach by way of a well-informed and eloquent writer), is a good recourse.

All school life should integrate music, since it is in school that the child is integrated within a group and learns to share by expressing himself, and developing the kindness and good sense to let others express themselves. Some administrators have to be approached from the idea of teaching dance and music as lessons in *how to look* and *how to listen*. And they are very worthwhile lessons, too.

Learning to listen, the attribute by which one cultivates a musicianly ear, is a prime educational exercise. Many students, into college, cannot fully comprehend what they hear of oral instruction because they have never been trained to listen and hear. In music, one must do both.

Learning to look, which one must know how to do in order to appreciate dance, is the development of a faculty greater than actual sight, it is visual sense plus the uncanny apperception of the inner eye which analyses, qualifies and evaluates.

Learning to listen and to look are ways by which we develop audience appreciation of art and since only the few are artists, the majority the audience, "appreciation" is by no means a negligible factor in dance and music.

People who play music to shut out other noises do not listen to music; people who hear music are people who listen to it. When a teacher puts a record on the schoolroom phonograph she engages in music production of a sort and with a little planning and effort she can turn this into a musical experience for her students. In the primary grades teachers play music to soothe high spirits (called music to rest by, or to listen to with closed eyes and quiet hands), and also music to color pictures by, scissors-and-paste by, and so on. Usually, teacher tells the students the name of the piece of music;

sometimes, she tells them the name of the composer. She may even letter these on the blackboard, to impress it on the children's minds. Take one or two more simple steps, and teacher makes this into a more extensive discovery, a more intensive experience. She need only formulate a plan out of a program instead of aimless choice of musical material.

The arrival at singing and playing a simple, familiar tune like *Happy Birthday* is the point of departure for a musical adventure out of it. This might be taken via two modern composers who (like many of their peers) have exploited a simple, well-worn tune by exploring it for their individual modes in music. Stravinsky's version of *Happy Birthday* is *Greeting Prelude*; that of the avant-garde composer Harry Partch, an "Afro-Chinese" minuet.

Since young children usually sing in the pentatonic scale, offer them examples of recorded music within that scale, which is 5-toned, thin, delicate and somewhat Oriental in sound to Occidental ears. Children sometimes describe this music as sounding "Chinese" and "Japanese," and the teacher in a standard Music course should, at such times, seize the opportunity of presenting them with true Oriental musical forms to compare with forms of music derived from Oriental modes (examples: Puccini's "Japanese" opera: *Madama Butterfly*; Glière's "Chinese" ballet: *The Red Poppy*). One pentatonic scale can be "found" on the piano's black keys—and greater knowledge of this scale extended into "made" music of composers who have employed it, like Colin McPhee's *Tabuh-Tabuhan* and Bernard Rogers' *Three Japanese Dances*. The more "discoveries" the children make about music, the greater the proportion of their interest and enjoyment.

All forms of music, for young children, should leave room for the improvisational, to develop the creative impulse and also to give the individual child authority within the musical form. As soon as he begins to work with the materials of that form (as singing or dancing, or picking out, as an amateur, musical sounds on instruments), the child becomes involved with the material—thereafter, as he creates or attempts to develop ideas in music, he is committed fully in the doing or making of dance and music. This authority, and the delicious sense of power it diffuses, is the most pleasurable association for the child in an approach to dance and music.

If the teacher has only a rudimentary knowledge of music she can still approach the subject for the child, provided she does so with confidence in her own authority and with pleasure in the task.

The mania to play quiz games is permissible in music as recognition of fragmented melody—such as identifying homespun airs in musical compositions. Examples are the cowboy's lament for his horse, Old Paint, as the romantic motif in Aaron Copland's score for the ballet: *Billy the Kid*; another air in this work is *Old Granddad*, which, with *If He'd Be A Buckaroo By Trade* in Copland's *Rodeo*, derive from music of the American prairie. In *Rodeo* Copland also uses a very old tune: *Boneyparte*. Such examples are legion, and an elementary reading course in music will give a teacher ample material to compile her own program for musical quizzes, through which to trace and link musical modes.

An Approach for the Conventional Teacher

No teacher of infants and young children should be without the *Oxford Nursery Rhyme Book*. Children will dance and act out (improvisations in drama) the nursery rhymes, *while learning to sing them.*

When the rhymes are learned in infancy the plain airs are mastered with the verse, as one—but many young kindergarten teachers nowadays do not know the traditional tunes. Then, learn them by ear off recordings or find them in printed music and pick them out on a keyboard; one-fingered, if necessary. Purely "nonsense" rhymes often have superlative musical elements for your purposes; the majority of the nursery jingles point a moral or make a joke and with these you can inaugurate a modest lyric theatre: singing, dancing and drama, or "action" song-and-dance.

Here, for example, is a universal favorite:

The children draw and identify by name various geometric shapes around a large central circle, to surround this circle or approach it from one, two or all sides. I usually divide groups into two divisions for "performers" and "audience," with alternating characters—one part observing and noting (for eventual criticism) while the other part does or performs, because children readily learn from each other. This allows a nice division, too, between choir and corps of dancers, with the observers cast as singers to accompany the dancers. The movement serves to explore time, speed and direction.

The large circle is called the "well" or "pond" and has to be "reached" by the children who elect to glide, hop, and use various 'danced' movements to *Tommy's fallen in the well* (which is sometimes sung *Tommy's fallen in the pond*):

> Tommy's fallen in the well,
> Do you hear him splashing?
> When at last he gets back home,
> Won't he get a thrashing?
> Ha, ha, serve him right.

The tune of this song uses all five notes of the pentatonic scale and can be subjected to many musical variations. A good idea for the inexperienced teacher is to study its arrangement in *Schulwerk* by Carl Orff and Gunild Keetman, in the English translation *Music for Children*, Angel Records Album 3582 for mono and stereo. This album has a large repertory of songs and spoken rhymes, and is a marvelous song and speech exercise which the inventive teacher can use in several ways—all incorporating movement qualified by elements of music.

The Orff system of cultivating musical interests, and musicianly potential, is one of the best basic approaches to children. If the approach is made without condescension, children far removed from kindergarten and primary grades can enjoy this experience. I particularly like the recording because the voices of the child singers have intonations and accents that are not those usually heard by American children and therefore the very vocal sounds, of themselves, pique interest.*

Whether these records are for home or school use, it is essential that they be used, in the most flexible manner, for the children's pleasure, —not *ad tedium*. Do not put the records on as a group, let each side play consecutively, and then reverse sides and repeat, without intervals for dance movement and class discussion. These are not records primarily for listening, in a passively receptive state—they are records for music and dance, which may be listened to as an entertainment but are the focus of active participation for children.

I find it best to break up the recordings in parts, by taping excerpts, somewhat in the manner of the taped recordings I proposed for Isobel's use with Tim (see page 61; those homemade tapes, incidentally, made a great deal of use of Orff's work), which allows the teacher the most flexible use of the material on the recordings.

With imagination, and with an alert response to the children's approaches, the teacher may capitalize on whatever facet of the music she prefers. In autumn, 1966, the Federal Office of Education (under Title III), distributed funds for a pilot program in the approach of Carl Orff, and teachers who require more advice on using this system should apply for information through these channels. But the elementary uses of the material on "Schulwerk" hardly need more elucidation than the detailed libretto commentary, in printed form, by Walter Jellinek, which comes with the Angel Album 3582.

* Voices are those of the Children's Opera Group, directed by Margaret John; chorus of the Bancroft School for Boys, music master J. G. Wright; and the speech ensemble from the Italia Conti School

Should you adopt Orff's approaches to children and music, you will perhaps wish to develop these approaches on the instruments the composer has designed for these purposes. (Refer, also, to the Introduction by Dr. Sylvesta M. Wassum, Assistant Professor of music at the University of California at Los Angeles, written for the American distribution of the Angel album of Orff's *Music for Children*.)

Singing and Making Music

Young persons do these with gusto—and formerly students "sang" their lessons the better to memorize arithmetic tables (weights and measures, et cetera) and rules of language (from A, B, C, to conjugations). In working with young children the teacher needs to know the limitations of the human voice in range, according to gender and age (for which refer to *The Child at Home*).

You will know that your students are working creatively when they improvise—this also indicates that they are having a high old time with singing, since the more young folk admire a formal art, the more they tend to change it to make it absolutely their own property. Younger children sing in form of chant, a descending minor third:

While there can be no hard-and-fast measurement of progress, it is general to find 1st grade children (median age: six) singing the five notes of the pentatonic scale:

If your students must work within this scale alone, it is still sufficient to teach them rhythmic patterns, the chief interest primary grade students show in music. Moreover, in this scale it is easy to play music on very simple instruments, such as tuned water glasses and the auto-harp.

If you are dextrous and can initiate and carry through a successful workshop in the classroom, your students can make original instruments for their own use as a class "orchestra." This is often the beginning of a very worthwhile program, since it actively (and manually) involves the class, giving the students an acute personal involvement with music and the manufacture of music-producing instruments. (A good book on the subject of home-made instruments is *Creative Music in the Home* by Satis Coleman, publ. John Day Company, Inc., New York. It is chiefly of use for percussive instruments, offering directions for making drums, tone blocks, rattles and tambours. The author, in addition, gives suggestions for the uses of the home-made instruments, in the form of games.)

When a child can sing the fourth note of the scale, he can harmonize in melodies in thirds; when he is able to reach the seventh note of the scale, he is able to sing the full diatonic or major scale (the standard scale against which other scales are valued):

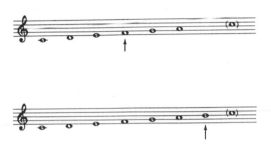

Almost at once, the child can begin to create music, as songs or instrumentally. (Mrs. Coleman's book *Creative Music in the Home*, also includes melodies that should be fairly easy to read, by numbering method instead of regular notation, for the non-musician.) The child will have to learn about pitch but this sense will assuredly improve, quite unselfconsciously for the child, as he works in music, and especially when he works as a singer. Playing by ear to improvise and create, or to attempt to follow a made tune, will give the students elementary techniques in music. As they learn to harmonize, this is usually an excellent time to introduce them to notation. I like to introduce this musical terminology earlier rather than later in a course, so that the children become aware of *reading and writing music*. It is my belief that children are inspired by creative ideas, when they understand that music, a transient aural art, can be recorded, made permanent and kept for future use, *through notation*.

The 3-volume Orff *Songs for Children* can be developed into notation studies under a music teacher, so that students learn to read and write music while they sing. These volumes (in English translation by Doreen Hall and Arnold Walter) are Vol. I—Pentatonic; Vol. II—Major; Vol. III—Minor.

The elementary course (Angel Album 3582) develops chants to triads on the tonic and supertonic, the two chords appearing in harmonization:

Ideally, all approaches to music should be made by a musician but, when qualified teachers are not available, conventional teachers may introduce some elements of music to which young students are generally responsive. Among music instructors there is controversy as to when and how notation is best taught but some remedial reading classes have usefully investigated elementary notation, as a system of "language" by signs that are "drawn" instead of "written." And some pilot programs in music indicate that infants develop skills as sightedness and handedness through experiences with music notation.

With the merest rudiments of music, the conventional teacher can approach notation, the system of recording music. Many children, past 1st grade, are not physically and psychologically ready to acquire reading and writing skills, yet they feel baffled and sometimes guilty when they cannot read, especially when the peers with whom they are in intimate association can read. Such children often enjoy elementary music notation in place of reading and writing, and as even infants draw pictures (long, long before they are capable of writing letters and forming words), they will enthusiastically try to "draw" music. The clumsy results are rewarding of themselves; for one thing, and an important one, children learn to accept musical terminology, recognize it as a "language," and are thereafter prepared to allow music to communicate on its own terms—whereas many adults insist on treating music in a literal sense, as though it can be made to "say" or express in verbal language.

If you are unable to read music as a musician, you can at least train your eye to recognize notes, kinds of notes, and symbols indicating character and uses of note clusters, and others. The instrumentalist reads music in these ways: his eyes see symbols which his ears hear, simultaneously.

The beginning of singing is always without notation, and by ear alone— we hear melody and verse which so affect us that we remember them and thereafter, with truly marvelous aptitude, recreate them as singers. Regardless of the quality of the individual voice, all of us can sing unless we are physically mute—we sing in varying degrees of trueness and power, according to the pitch and volume of our voices. After we experience singing, of ourselves, it is not really difficult to associate music in its recorded form, written and read as notation.

Study a book of songs in which the melody and words are written together and you will find that your eye and ear follow the words in the music, providing you already know the tune. Music "goes" as children say, or moves in directions which an ordinary well-modulated voice follows with fair ease. Common scales have seven different pitches or ranges, from the tonic to its octave duplicate, like C to C. In the major or standard scale patterns of whole and half steps occur, identified by letter or name (the do-re-mi system). Intervals between E-F and B-C are half steps; intervals between other notes are whole steps:

Major scale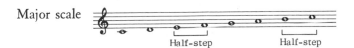

In the minor scale there is a half step between the second and third steps; the interval between the fifth and sixth steps may be a half or a whole step:

Minor scale

Elementary study of music, for listening, should inform sufficiently for sing-ing along with notation, or, even, playing simple airs on musical instruments that are as precise as the piano, or as simple as the auto-harp. Tonal organiza-tion is a good primary lesson to master, and any college preparatory music course or book written as "introduction" to music should give you sufficient material to base your own work on, in approaching elementary notation for the child.

Music is measured or marked out in bars, and a phrase is a unit, generally four measures long, terminated by a musical punctuation called a cadence. Cadence is established by rhythm alone, so rhythm is the chief musical motive in learning to follow along with an air, to sing it or dance it. Instinctively fine dancers and singers follow music by phrases and not note by note, just as good readers scan books by full sentences, not word by word and syllable by syllable.

Cadence is punctuation in music; a half cadence partially punctuates and a full or whole cadence positively concludes a musical thought, in much the way indicated by commas, semi-colons, and full-stops or period symbols in literature.

The unschooled ear easily hears measures in music, and most readily counts these in bars of two, four and eight, the commonest bars in musical phrases. And in Western music, we listen, conventionally, for cadences at regular intervals.

The majority of folk songs, simple rhymes and rhythms, plain hymns and nursery jingles are measured and phrased in these conventions.

The notes in music are qualified by a large variety of symbols, one being the staff on which they are placed. The flat (written with this sign ♭) placed before a note lowers its pitch by a semitone; the sharp (♯), in the same relationship to a note, *raises* its pitch by a semitone. A dot after a note increases its value by half, a piece of musical arithmetic thus: ♩· = ♩♪ and a double dot increases the value of a note by half, plus a quarter, thus:

Bearing these and other elementary rules in mind, you should be able to teach children to follow music of the character of *Old Folks At Home*. Most sheet music or books of collected songs are printed with the words and syllables divided strictly to match the musical notation, thus allowing exact positioning with word and syllable to the corresponding note. In such an early, elementary approach to notation children will sing along by word *and by note* to state the sense of the song in words and music. They "read" off words and music together, or their eyes grow accustomed to this arrangement even though they are illiterate, unable to actually read the printed words; thus, they make a true and good beginning to understanding notation. Moreover, it is an approach they seem to enjoy heartily, many of them describing the system of notes as a secret language, a "code," by which music is stated. I very often discover young children thereafter making up their own music, not for the sake of making music so much as for the fun of making secret statements in music. Supplied with music paper and pencils, they "compose" such codes on the staff and then demand to hear what the music "says" when decoded on the piano keys. Results are more hilarious than musical in the conventional sense, but highly gratifying to the juvenile musicians—and in the vogue of aleatory music these inventions are not altogether spurious.

Reading music through singing music, by following words and music as one off the blackboard, may be extended to reading and dancing music, by moving in the beats of the music sung. Eventually, you will become skilled enough to read music that you do not already know, by ear, by finding the rhythmic pattern of the lyric and following it by singing the words appended, or moving to its pattern by counting beats.

Dancing

The conventional teacher can develop an approach to dance by adapting a familiar song to dance-and-song, *and incorporating locomotor movement in patterns of movement.* Begin with hand-claps and foot-taps, progress to marches, and develop a class repertory of "action" song-and-dance.

Working with children in British schools, one may develop an extraordinarily fine dance-and-song routine out of an old rhyme that dates to Britain's antiquity, and is played (or danced) by dividing groups into two units of lines. One line of children, marching abreast, step in cadence to this:

Have you any bread and wine?—*takes them forward*
We are the Romans!—*takes them backward*
Have you any bread and wine,—*takes them forward*
For we are the Roman soldiers!—*returns them to their "mark" on*

the floor, where they stand, keeping cadence in a straight line by alternating feet in tap-stamps.

The other line advances and retreats, singing:

Yes, we have some bread and wine,—*advance*
For we are the English;—*retreat*
Yes, we have some bread and wine—*advance*
For we are the English soldiers!—*return to their "mark."*

As the verses of the song continue, the plot unfolds for attack and skirmish, which *in dance patterns* wheel the children in half arcs, circles, straight lines, diagonals, all to musical beat and phrasing. This is a dance-game of inexhaustible entertainment for children since its climax is not by rote, and the end or "win" may come about from the dexterity of the Romans breeching the ranks of the English, or vice versa. The point of the game, which lends excitement to the dance, is to move and sing with the music while deploying the two "enemy lines"—the use of music prevents it becoming merely a game, and turning into a rough-and-tumble war. Conscious use of dance is by prearranged choice of steps and directions, and movement in rhythm.

American children are not familiar with this marvelous marching song but a good substitute, and one I find especially so for use with boys and girls in a single class, is the old air:

GIRLS: Soldier, soldier, will you marry me, etc.

BOYS: Oh, how can I marry, etc.

If the teacher has no musical accompaniment, singing, clapping hands and tapping will serve well. Find a steady beat, which may fall on the held note in the bar (meaning, that the beat falls on a *silence*) instead of on the syllable of a word. Above all, choose a song young children enjoy for itself, in air and verse, such as the repetitive *Riddle Song* in 4/4 meter; noting that *cher*-ry, *chick*-en, *ring*, and *ba*-by, are completed *as whole words* before the 4th beat in the bar in which each appears, with no accentuation on the *second* syllable of the words cherry, chicken and baby:

The teacher who knows nothing about dance may still learn enough about locomotion and musical rhythm to teach some rudimentary dance movements and combinations of movements. She should approach the "activity" as dance (not as a game, nor as physical exercise) by qualifying the nature of the locomotor movements she is teaching the children to discover—for example: a *slide*, which generally starts on a downbeat in music, as differing from a *gallop*, which starts on an upbeat.

Taking this primary lesson further into dance, the slide becomes exaggerated into the *glide*, which, performed in 3/4 meter, is the basis of the *waltz*.

Ordinary locomotor patterns that are even in nature may usually be combined with any given meter.

In genuine terms of dance pattern, the *slide* and *glide* are here described, in exactly the same language and notation as used by the High School of Performing Arts in New York, where Dr. Rachael Dunaven Yocum heads the Dance Department:

LOCOMOTOR MOVEMENTS

Rhythmic Pattern in Terms of Long and Short and Music Notation		*Descriptions*	*Meter*	*Speed*
Slide	L.S./L.S./L.S./ etc.	Uneven	Two steps, one foot is brought up to the other foot and weight is transferred to it.	6/8 2/4 3/8	Moderate
	2/4 ♪. ♪♪. ♪|				
	6/8 ♩ ♪♩ ♪|				
Gallop	L.S./L.S./L.S./	Uneven	Resembles slide but differs in execution in that when the transference of weight occurs from rear foot to forward foot, there is a decided knee action (starts up-beat).	6/8 2/4 3/8	Fast
	2/4 ♪| ♪. ♪♪. ♪|				
	6/8 ♪| ♩ ♪♩ ♪|				

Meter or "time-signature" defines the movement pattern of music and dance; it always appears at the start of a piece, as 2/4 or 3/4, which are simple meters called duple and triple. Compound meters are derived from simple meters.

A pattern that falls into a rhythmic *short—short—long* movement is in 2/4, not 3/4 meter, being in uneven, not even beats. A note is not a beat, but the symbol in musical notation which represents one or several beats; i.e. 6/4 equals 6 quarters of

Tempo refers to rate of speed, not to rate of time. If speed accelerates, movements naturally become smaller, in the length of the leap or the height of the jump, altering the pattern of a dance. "Normal" movements (walk, run, hop, jump, leap) are basically even movements, taking one beat to perform. "Complex" movements are based on uneven rhythmic patterns, like skip, slide and gallop—these are *long—short*; or *short—long*, but also take one beat to perform.

We seem to move most easily in 6/8 meter, six beats to a measure in the rhythmic flow of music, and in 3/4 meter, three beats per measure.

Dance movements are *sustained, percussive and swing.* In a *sustained* movement the energy of the dancer moves evenly over an extended length of time and is to be compared to the *legato* quality in music. It is suited to extensions in dance, and to adagio or slow, *sustained* movement. *Percussive* movements are those in which energy is used in sharp and sudden movements, and corresponds to the quality called *staccato* in music. It is useful for sharp movements, and "attack" in dance, also for falls. *Swing* movements are those in which the dancer's energy has a pendulum control, the second impulse or movement beginning before the first movement has died or ended altogether in stillness (or inertia). Swings are excellent exercises for control and studies in movements of varying tempi.

First, young children should spontaneously respond to musical accompaniment, to develop physical awareness of meters, in simple movements like walk, run, hop, jump, leap, (also: brush), skip, slide and gallop. Next, they should be led to a conscious awareness of meters, through dance movement and through music.

In an early approach to music the materials themselves and the manner in which they are used, are important—more than the chronological ages of the students, and their degrees of literacy. Hence, what is described as a primary approach for children in the lower grades may also be applicable to students in higher grades, always depending on their experiences in music and their capacities and limitations for learning about music.

In every instance, the approach to music should be one which interests the particular group and, too, excites it into making discoveries about dance and music. A too pedantic approach, and little or no experimentation by the students, stultifies interest and quells excitement. And it is characteristic of dance and music to exhilarate.

Children, when they sing with gusto, are apt to sing boisterously—they have to be taught to sing softly, as well as loudly, through discoveries of high and low, soft and loud. When they dance in groups they are exuberant, apt to trample and tumble, in gross motor activity—gradually, they learn to distinguish adagio from allegro movement, and to consciously qualify light and heavy movements in dancing; fast and slow movement in music and in dance. But dealing as they are in sound and movement children cannot be expected to sing in silence and to dance without movement!

Many teachers confide in me that they are dissuaded by school administrators from working with dance and music, because of hurly-burly in the classrooms, which distracts the attention of students in adjacent classrooms. A teacher cannot make a good approach or work towards any creative accomplishment if she is restricted to the amount of movements her children make in dancing, and the volume of their voices as they sing. Acoustics for music and space for dancing are major requirements; the large class in the conventional classroom requires a more ideal physical facility for creative work in music and dance. Most schools have auditoriums that are not in use every day, all day; most school cafeterias are occupied only at lunch time and for assembly. The teacher should try to get access to these, or a building removed from classrooms, in order to work freely with students.

New Music

> The history of the Music as of Man
> Will not go cancrizans, and no ear can
> Recall what, when the Archduke Francis reigned,
> Was heard by ears whose treasure-hoard contained
> A Flute already but as yet no Ring:
> Each age has its own mode of listening . . . .
> Nor, while we praise the dead, should we forget
> We have Stravinsky—bless him!—with us yet.
>
> W. H. Auden: Metalogue to The Magic Flute*

From all that has gone before in this book, we understand that in order for the child to become interested in dance and music, to appreciate these arts so that, as we say, he learns to "love" them, he must become committed to them out of responses that form pleasurable associations. The most pleasurable approach, and the most genuine response, come out of crea-

* © Copyright 1955 by W. H. Auden. Reprinted from Homage to Clio, by W. H. Auden, by permission of Random House, Inc.

tivity. The child who composes a song or a musical piece, or choreographs a dance, is closest to knowing and loving the nature of dance and music. *Making music for its sake is in reality making music for one's sake, a profoundly personal joy.*

The personal commitment to music, the personal involvement with music, makes "new" music for the contemporary artist and his audience. When that music is of worth, *in its form as art, or in its emotional associations,* the music is immortalized beyond the contemporary era. It is treasured and it remains alive, through recreation by other musicians for other audiences. In this way, music is preserved as a *living* art. Music recorded and filed away in libraries, never known because it is never played, undergoes a species of life-suspension; it waits, held fast in notes that have been written down, for the touch of the living musician to bring it back to life. When it again lives, it is identified by musicologists as to form and period style, but its verities as music remain tangible for musicians and their audiences as though it had been newly made.

Epochal forms and period styles in music are to be traced in the history of music. This is of itself a romantic story, and when the story is illustrated faithfully with music this history affords a true and lively insight into music through the ages. Pre-historical, baroque, classical and romantic, are the names of some epochal forms, and these, altogether, comprise a "standard" repertoire of what people speak of as "good" music. In twenty-five years observation of music in American education I note a persistent leaning towards traditional or standard music as the almost exclusive approach to the child. Through the consistent ignoring and avoidance of new music, 20th century composers, with very few exceptions, are neglected entirely in the approach to the child in school.

To associate himself with music, a child must know the music of his time.

In order for music to be a valid part of life and education, music must remain viable for the student and teacher. Unless the child understands that music is a *living* art, he will have little regard for it—and perhaps experience little desire to make it, in an original concept as the musician today. However dearly we cherish great music of the past we must also cherish music-making in the present, purely to preserve music *per se.*

Laymen think of "good" music as having been composed in older eras, and when they enjoy such music they tend to value it more than modern works. If they revere such "good" music their respect becomes unctuous and the composers of centuries past become sacred cows, geniuses who existed in a more rarefied atmosphere than ours today. Nothing could be farther from the truth about "old" music and its composers.

The great musicians before our time were frequently required to compose music by a certain date, for certain events, rather like tailors commissioned to make suits of clothes on occasion for their masters. They worked, veritably, for masters as patrons and an enormous amount of the music produced was by command, melody measured by the yard, so to speak, glittering fabric in which to dress state occasions for dukes and princes—and, very often, merchants. Handel worked for the king of England, Bach, Haydn and Mozart for German princes, and numerous composers, through the ages, for masters and mistresses rich enough to afford a resident composer and house an orchestra, whose liveried members were so many factotums in the elegant estate. In that time, *new* music was the absolute craze.

The composer [in the 18th century] . . . had the assurance that when he wrote music it would be performed for an audience . . . And composers were fortunate to be living in an age and in a city where the craze was for new music; there was no hero-worship of dead and gone composers, no desire to treasure their works. Instead, high and low demanded new music in a continuous supply. . . . Not only princes bought or commissioned music (and in batches, so that Haydn would deliver 6 symphonies at once) but tradesmen as well. Haydn would be required to turn out half-a-dozen quartets for a merchant who wanted them performed for the entertainment of his customers.

How ironic to hero-worship Haydn and others of the era today, at the expense of barring living composers and their new music!

Contemporary dance (the dance technique called "Modern") is "educational" dance in high school and college; ballet, the classical dance whose academic form dates from the 1600s, is not so much "educational" as it is theatrical. But while educators have adopted a purely 20th century dance form there seems to be an unspoken rule that the correct approach to the student must be through old music, and that this approach should be historically based, through a survey of composers and their works, in chronological order.

This rule entails beginning in pre-history or at least the baroque era and travelling steadily through the centuries into our own time. Since music is very old, a thorough chronological research, civilization by civilization, to reach good perspective for international musical history today, should consume several years' comprehensive studies for the student, working under teachers who are thoroughly informed in their subject. For this course of study in music to correlate all phases, it should be undertaken as a program wherein consecutive approaches by teachers contribute and eventually build the course to fruition for the student.

In fact, very, very few American students start and complete their elementary education in the same school system; even fewer receive a correlated musical education from kindergarten into the university, and all students working in elementary grades now will not progress to junior and senior high school, and then to college. The insistence on an approach to music by chronological studies of composers is hardly feasible. Surely it would be more logical to combine studies of the standard and contemporary repertories in elementary school and also later, in high school and college, to give all students representative music of all eras.

In such an approach, a student could independently research a composer's works, or a form in music, or a particular style of music, which he encountered and which interested him so greatly that he was attracted to it beyond the cursory approach in school. Or a whole class, indicating such vivid interest, could then be led to explore the particular form or style as an outgrowth of the initial approach. My own work with children convinces me that more response would be initiated and more interest sustained by such methods—less ennui suffered in school by children who already know a normal or general approach to music at home.

A factor hardly recognized in school is that children who make good approaches to music at home generally do so through traditional, not modern music. Parents usually initiate a child's first approaches; as a rule parents today offer their children music of the classical and romantic eras, in the belief that "old" music is superior, as art, to "new" music which is strange and, perhaps, ugly.

Some of the beautiful old music we cherish now was considered reprehensible when *it* was new, and was therefore strange and controversial. To the survivors of the baroque age, the classical and romantic modes were avant-garde. Many a musician sternly upbraided the change from the baroque as did Rossini in a celebrated diatribe in 1817, when the "new" music of the 19th century had become the vogue. Reading Rossini is uncannily like listening to an anti-modern musician railing against the modes that are new in the 1960's, for these, like Rossini, aver that the new modes are wrong, that they pervert the ear and Music itself, and are likely to destroy music. Despite these gloomy forbodings, era after era, music survives with uncommon energy and aplomb.

A good musical education includes, matter of factly, a sampling of representative music through eras of art, and such sampling should be the choicest selection of the most representative composers in order to give the student succinct knowledge of music, and of changes in musical forms and styles. In this sampling of representative music the teacher should include the music of the student's times, rather than approach the student exclusively through music of the past.

The notion that all old music is good and "beautiful" is as erroneous as the idea that all new music, yet unproved as of artistic merit, is bad and ugly. It is truer to say that some unconventional modes as new music are "strange" and therefore entail for the listener a more strenuous approach than music of older eras, which, from being familiar, have become conventional sounds to our ears. Music that is referred to as being "good and beautiful" is *traditional* music, which we enjoy without strenuous listening, since it has been subconsciously appreciated without conscious approach to qualify it as "arts appreciation." Familiarity does not inverately breed contempt; more often, as in music, it breeds habit and contentment.

There is no "bad" dance in a moral sense, although Salome's seven-veiled performance cost John the Baptist his head and served as aphrodisiac to Herod; nor because, in Medieval dance mania, dancing was treated as demonic possession.

There is no "bad" music in a moral sense, although a great deal of music was suspect by the Puritans of Colonial America; or because a Pope, in Medieval times, forbade certain chords in music on pain of excommunication from the Roman Catholic church.

Bad dance and music are choreographic works and compositions without good form, unredeemed by originality (which sometimes lends a mediocre form a distinctly brilliant style). *Banality* is a sin in dance and music; when a choreographer and a composer lack true gifts, or are undisciplined artists, or do not possess sufficient technique, they create poor works rather than works of merit—but such mediocre or bad works sin against *ethics of art*, not against ethics of social morality.

I believe, emphatically, that children should know new music as well as old, and should know the music of their times. Our children live in *their* times, and are accustomed to their "modern" environment to an extent that makes them more the people of this time than any people who came before them. Our children accept, as part of their world, the extraordinary means by which we now travel and distribute news; the explorations of physical space and the human psyche; the experiments in the sciences, particularly in medical science and physics; and innovations in education that are startling to their parents: "new math.," learning by computerized tutoring devices, and learning while sleeping, or under hypnosis. Some of the common affairs of this age that are calmly, indifferently accepted by our children, are not only startling but incomprehensible to us as their parents and educators.

In this strange, new world there is strange, new music—the musical idioms now are "new" but so are idioms in language, mathematics, science, painting; even religion. The child is approached in school by way of many new idioms—*except in music*. If he grows up thinking "good" music is antique, serious music will have little validity and vitality for him.

The San Diego project (*Experiments in Musical Creativity*) was prompted by concern over the limited emphasis given to contemporary music in schools. In an attempt to offer approaches and teaching techniques to teachers in elementary education, the San Diego Project's staff conferred with teachers—many of whom admitted that they believed children should always approach standard works before being introduced to the works of modern composers. Most teachers who accept this principle of approach cannot sensibly qualify it as being the soundest.

Approaches to students in primary grades fail to support the unspoken rule for teaching music chronologically. As has been said, infants and young children are the most tolerant, aesthetically, and have the most eclectic tastes in the arts. Although they show marked affinity with the baroque composers, probably because they respond more to rhythm than harmony, the latter element characteristic of 19th century music (from which we draw most of our "good" and "beautiful" serious musical repertoire), they are equally drawn to some modern composers. In general, their favorites are Bach and Mozart—and Bartok, Stravinsky and Copland. Modern music is more polyrhythmic than harmonic and some of it deliberately returns to 17th and 18th century modes. Young students are agreeable to investigating music of the 1600s or the 1960s, and they show no aversion for atonality: absence of key or tonality in the traditional sense.

Admittedly, adolescents are more loath to accept unaccustomed sounds and unorthodox techniques of composition, generally because they have assumed prejudices and accepted adult "labels" for art modes. But they are intensely interested in their "pop" music, art in the vernacular, and when they discover the "contemporary sound" of serious new music they recognize it as being, too, music of their own times. As soon as they make this identification, their interest is whetted.

20th century music's contemporary sound is strongly influenced by jazz, which should make it of particular interest to American students. It also has mechanistic and electronic elements which, however strange to adults today, make it authentically music of its era. The young person should be as aware of new music as he is of new literature since the musical and verbal means of expression are equally representative of his place and time. Introducing him to music, one can hardly make a better approach than through music with the immediate interest of being identifiable with these.

A good method of combining old and new musical modes is through investigation of themes in music, or through instrumentation. In the latter instance, a teacher making an approach through the clarinet is not compelled to begin in the 17th century, when this instrument came into vogue, and thereafter plod through every clarinet composition, in consecutive order . . . a task that could not easily be contained within the normal school curricula.

But the teacher can, for example, offer sufficient data about the clarinet (and should bring a clarinet into the classroom to aid the discussion) to interest and inform her students—then program clarinet music of as varied and representative modes as possible, *taking care to include music of the 20th century among the examples.*

The clarinet is used here as an example because it is a wind instrument, of the family of instruments most ordinary to American schools and therefore readily available, with a player, for demonstration in the classroom. It is also a very expressive instrument, more mobile than the oboe, with greater nuance of sound than the flute, and it runs the gamut from the sublime to the ridiculous since the bass clarinet has a noble sound and the E-flat clarinet's shrillness lends itself to musical grotesquerie.

As a listening experience, the teacher might begin with playing a recording of Copland's *Concerto for Clarinet and String Orchestra*, composed for famed virtuoso Benny Goodman (and used as the score of a ballet: *The Pied Piper* by Jerome Robbins for the New York City Ballet in 1951). Next, the teacher might program Mozart's *Quintet in A-Major, K. 581,* composed in 1789 when the clarinet was about 100 years old, to be followed by his *Clarinet Concerto, A-Major, K. 622,* composed in 1791.*

When a teacher treats old and new music as being of equal worth and

---

* For briefest note: the clarinet is featured in compositions by Mozart and Weber in the *concerto* form; Mozart, Weber and Brahms in *chamber* ensemble music; clarinet in E flat by Richard Strauss in *Ein Heldenleben* and Ravel in *Daphnis et Chloe*; and bass clarinet in Tchaikovsky's *6th Symphony* and Meyerbeer's opera: *The Huguenots.*

interest she broadens the students' tastes and inspires their individual responses. The conventional teacher, who relies more on the social than aesthetic attributes of the arts, should develop the human aspect of music, leaving the technical instruction to the qualified Music faculty. Composers living and working within the 20th century, like Copland, and artists of the time, like Goodman, are of extraordinary consequence to students; the fact that they share the same time and place especially endears their music to young persons. They are equally touched by human aspects of old music and dead composers, when these are interestingly presented.

Tell them that Mozart's Quintet for clarinet and strings is nick-named "the Stadler," because it was composed for Mozart's friend, the clarinetist Anton Stadler. This piece is said to have made the clarinet musically acceptable whereas before then composers had used it merely as a piercing orchestral sound. Tell them (whose music is subject to intense criticism from some of their elders) that Mozart's music was sometimes so strange and new to his time and place that his clarinet concerto was described as being unfit for ladies' ears . . .

A good discipline for the teacher is to read about contemporary music, the better to arrive at an understanding of *why* it is as well as *what* it is, as music. Wilfred Mellers' *Music in a New Found Land,* publ. Alfred A. Knopf, 1965, is an excellent work for the layman who seeks to comprehend themes and developments in the history of American music—and American music, especially the new music, should be obligatory inclusion in the student's education. By making an appreciative approach to contemporary music the teacher will have prepared herself to make continual discoveries about new music as they are contained as experiences for her students in arts appreciation.

Experiments in Musical Creativity

The Contemporary Music Project's experimental or "pilot" programs in three school districts, in California, Maryland and New York (see *Bibliography* sources and *Appendix I*) are examples for the teacher who initiates similar approaches in the classroom, and particularly for the primary grades.

There is good evidence that younger children, from infancy into median age eight, are most receptive to new and unconventional music—coincidently, research into teaching languages suggests that children most readily assimilate native inflections of tongues during this span, when they are tolerant of strange, new sounds and do not consciously think of speech and music patterns as normal or abnormal. It appears, on the basis of such research findings, that an eclectic approach to music, *and one which includes contemporary music,* should begin in kindergarten, and in the 1st, 2nd and 3rd grades of normal school.

The San Diego Project, under composer-consultant Dr. David Ward-Steinman, was set up for "developing musical understanding through contemporary music."*

Objectives of the project were to provide an opportunity for a selected group of music teachers to broaden their own understanding of contemporary music, under leadership of a specialist in the métier; to investigate aspects of contemporary music that appeared most interesting to children of various ages at various grade levels; to test the materials in selected classroom activities (through pilot programs); and to develop teaching techniques and approaches for presenting these materials within the typical or "normal" school curriculum of music.

Two hour seminars each week were conducted by Dr. Ward-Steinman for teachers enrolled in the course; the course was developed and intensified (for teaching techniques) through classroom implementation of three pilot programs from grades 2nd, 6th and 7th.

Organization was in lecture-demonstration format by Dr. Ward-Steinman as composer-consultant, and the project seminar content focused on the elements of rhythm, melody and harmony, as used by contemporary composers, *with the formal structure of music being considered in relation to the contemporary compositions studied.* Representational music, non-representational music, music form, were chief aspects of the seminar outline. A general survey established these as being pertinent to the development of "new" music (new sources of sound which characterize modern music):

The sound sources of an era influence the musical styles of an era, and vice versa. The history of instrumental development from primitive to 19th century music supports this statement.

Characteristic of "modern" music, contemporary composers sometimes simulate the use of "literal" sounds: Gershwin with taxi horns in *An Ameri-*

---

* The coordinator was Mary Val Marsh, and the Project staff comprised Charlene Archibeque for the 7th grade pilot class; Mary Val Marsh for the 6th grade pilot class; Susan Ward-Steinman for the 2nd grade pilot class; with Joann Ford and Douglas Massey assisting the project. All of the San Diego City and County Schools.

can in Paris, Respighi with the recording of a nightingale singing in *The Pines of Rome,* Rogers with sandpaper on drum (to simulate the serpent's tail) in *Leaves from the Tale of Pinocchio,* and invent entirely new and unconventional sounds, for example:

harmonics	*Mikrokosmos,* Vol. IV, No. 102	Bela Bartok
"prepared" piano and percussion	*Amores*	John Cage
	Dance	
	Toccato for Percussion	Carlos Chavez
harmonics from sympathetic vibration of unstruck keys	*Piano Variations*	Aaron Copland
	The Aeolian Harp	Henry Cowell
plucking & hitting piano strings	*Banshee*	Cowell
voices used instrumentally	*Sirènes*	Claude Debussy
sympathetic vibration of strings fingered only while one player plays	*Time Cycle for Soprano and Orchestra*	Lukas Foss
tack piano, simulated gamelon sounds	*Suite for Violin, Piano and small orchestra*	Lou Harrison
chanting chorus with percussion accompaniment	*Les Choëphores*	Darius Milhaud
	Concerto for Percussion and small orchestra	Milhaud
use of new instruments; 43-tone octave	*Plectra and Percussion Dances*	Harry Partch
	The Wayward (U.S. Highball)	Partch
	Thirty Years of Lyric and Dramatic Music	Partch

2nd Grade Pilot Program

Sound Source discoveries began through asking the 2nd grade children to think of sounds they might hear early in the morning. Here, the children were introduced to "made" music by composers who have employed "literal" sounds, or by inventing new instruments (Gershwin, Respighi, Partch).

The students used conventional and unconventional instruments, all available to the normal classroom, on which to produce their sounds. These sounds were identified, by guessing what they represented, and as part of "early morning" sounds. The theme here derived from the song *I Wake in the Morning Early*, in a 2nd grade music text book. David Ward-Steinman, the composer-consultant, explains that this procedure was largely an "ice-breaker" for the group of students. It also made them aware of the variety in sounds, and the infinite possibilities of putting sound to musical use.

Throughout this pilot program, instruments were emphasized as being "tools" which the composer uses—and which the students used to better understand the music they listened to in the program. Ward-Steinman states that "involvement by the students with sound not only gave them a better grasp of sound sources and of rhythm, harmony and other musical elements, but allowed them a form of elementary expression."

Equally strict was the emphasis for the Music teachers participating in the program as to the precise nature and values of "sound sources" in approaching the students. Apparently, some teachers have mistakenly supposed that anyone may "compose" by beating on pots and pans or turning rows upside down. Students in the San Diego program were never led into this erroneous supposition, yet they worked within a theme (that of "early morning") with appreciable development of "sound source" intelligence.

The children were asked to bring to class, to "share," something from home which might contribute a new sound for their classroom music. Promptly, following this request, the students contributed instruments for their "orchestra" and originated the playing of these, as follows:

INSTRUMENT	HOW PLAYED
baby food jars	filled with water, to make a tuned scale
band-aid can	struck with a metal spoon
bracelet	jangled
clothes hanger	struck with spoon

INSTRUMENT	HOW PLAYED
coffee can containing gravel	struck and shaken
coffee can containing pennies	ditto
circular tin (pie plate)	struck
two of above	used as cymbals
glass bottle with ridges	scraped with spoon
pieces of tin suspended on a bar	struck with a pencil
rubber bands of various sizes stretched over cigar boxes or shoe boxes	plucked
sand in a paper bag	struck with pencil
soft-drink bottle, empty	air blown across mouth of bottle
soft-drink bottles, filled with water to various levels	struck with a large bolt
padded mallet (soft surface)	struck and stroked on piano keys
vegetable grater	scraped with fork
ditto	struck with metal rod

Some of the discoveries about these sound sources led to incidental discoveries: when an instrument is grasped, while being played, its sound is dulled; instruments need resonating chambers; sounds are made by striking, plucking, blowing, shaking and scraping objects in various ways; the larger the instrument, the lower the sound, and vice versa.

In composing music in the classroom (see fig. A and B, and later version) the children were asked to use a meter other than 2, 3 or 4, and chose 5/4 meter for a three part ABA form using can, pan, scraper, shakers, bells, bottles, and piano and cymbals. Their quiz included "new" sounds by composers Cage (his "prepared" piano, which they at first called drums) and Debussy (voices in *Sirènes*).

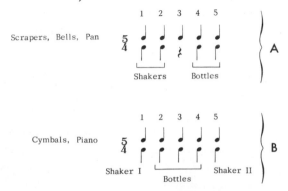

Later version:

	A	B	A	Coda

Can

Bells, Scraper

Pan

Bottles

Piano

Cymbals

Table I-II

Table III

Rhythm and Meter were discussed, the children being asked to think first of meter as regular beats, relating to themselves as heart-beats, breathing, chewing, walking, arm-swinging; and to ordinary life as clocks ticking, water faucets dripping. Favorite songs were sung, to discover their meters, and the class recognized 2, 3 and 4 meter.

The children were next introduced to unconventional meter: 5 in Ravel's *Quartet in F Major* and 7 in Brubeck's *Unsquare Dance,* and tried to count 7 while listening to Brubeck's composition, through physical involvement with the rhythmic patterns, in clapping and stamping.

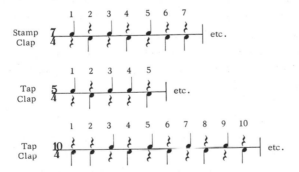

The first important innovation of rhythm as a structural element is in Stravinsky's *The Rite of Spring* (see also the 4th movement of Charles Ives' *First Piano Sonata* for example of an American use). Syncopation, which is achieved through a variety of techniques, was explained to these students as (1) accenting a beat other than the first beat of a measure; (2) rest on a strong beat; (3) accenting a short note or partial beat, and the teacher played a familiar syncopated song *without* syncopation; following this the students listened to *Dance of the Adolescents* from Stravinsky's *Rite*.

To experience *changing meter*, the class composed a song using five selected resonator bells (d,f,g,a,c).

An - i - mals   are   nice;   An - i - mals   are   pret - ty.

These are cows, cats and crows, man-y, man-y more, man-y, man-y more to name.

The students sang *Little Bird, Go through my window*, from *Music Through The Day*, which employs changing (2 and 3) meters, observing the metric pattern written for them on the blackboard, and listened to Brubeck's *Three to Get Ready* as observation of the rhythmic pattern.

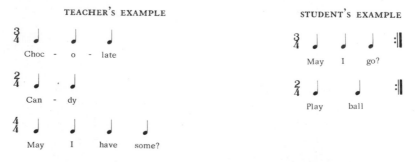

The students investigated *altering familiar meters*, examples being played by the teacher of *Twinkle, Twinkle Little Star* and *Did You Ever See A Lassie* in 3/4, 4/4, 2/4 and 5/4. They listened to the original triple meter of the Jarabe melody which Copland used in *Billy the Kid*, altering it to 5/4 and sometimes 4/4, and to *free meter* (shifting accents, no apparent down beats, syncopation) in Harrison's *Suite for Violin, Piano and Orchestra*. They discovered *polymeter*, for which the teacher offered this example: 'chocolate—candy—may I have some?'—and then made up examples of their own, as 'may I go?—play bill' recited sumultaneously.

Melody through scale sources, gapped scales, harmonic sources, et cetera, was discussed for the class, starting with early church modes (which are not consistently employed by contemporary composers); as examples:

Dorian	*Dance of Puck*	Debussy
Phrygian	*String quartet* (beginning)	Debussy
Mixolydian	*The Sunken Cathedral*	Debussy
Aeolian	*Daphnis and Chloë*: "Daybreak" theme	Ravel

The whole tone scale was frequently used by Debussy, to a lesser extent by Ravel, but is not frequently used by contemporary composers. An early example of use of whole tone scale is in Mozart's *A Musical Joke* (in the violin cadenza) in a scale gone awry. Debussy's most concentrated use of the whole tone scale is in "Voiles," *Preludes*, Book I.

The 2nd grade class heard the melodies of *Yankee Doodle* and *America* with piano accompaniment, and separated the parts (bass, alto, soprano) when identifying the melody. They learned that melody may be placed in the bass, the middle or very high register. Altering melodies, a technique by which contemporary composers displace conventional melody, was at first described (to this 2nd Grade class) as "spreading out notes," and later described by the correct term "octave displacement." As an example, the teacher played *Yankee Doodle* on the piano in its ordinary version, and, immediately following, with "octave displacement," or by "spreading out the notes":

The children listened to the two versions, while looking at the teacher's fingering of the piano keyboard.

Another example of altering conventional melody was Stravinsky's *Greeting Prelude*, altered out of *Happy Birthday*. A portion of a recording of this composer's *Agon* was played to illustrate "music which spreads notes of the melody throughout the orchestra, giving notes to many different instruments." (The first music to be correctly identified by this class was by Stravinsky and Copland.)

After hearing Partch's recorded version of *Happy Birthday* as his Afro-Chinese Minuet, the children fragmented the song with resonator bells playing "Birthday" and a drum playing the two beats for a person's name, while the teacher played the remaining notes on the piano. Each child had a turn at being sung to, in this instrumentation.

(*play* 4 *times*)

Coffee can   Tin can   Hollow bar   Towel bar "chimes"   Water jar   Rocks in milk carton

The children composed other versions of *Happy Birthday* by playing it backwards (retrograde), upside down (inversion), and backwards and upside down (retrograde-inversion). They adopted these techniques for the following songs:

"Little Ducks"   sung as written
next, sung with each child supplying one word fragmentation

"Goodbye, Old Paint"   sung as written
meter determined by class
sung again with whole class conducting

(Children were asked to identify composer and the melody; Copland, *Billy the Kid*.)

"Grasshopper Green"   sung as written
instruments then added as accompaniment

"Sky Bears"   sung as written
melody located in piano part—in left hand, below accompaniment
resonator bells (c & g) added

Creating melody was discovered by selecting five resonator bells (c,d,f,g,a) which five children at a time were selected to play. The five tones were played in a determined sequence (f,g,d,c,s) until a meter was established (3/4); whereupon the teacher wrote the melody on the staff—and the tones of the first phrase backwards to create a second phrase. An

accompaniment by drum and sandblocks, and cymbal with mallet, was added, and the teacher eventually "spread out" the melody on the piano keyboard.

At this stage of the project, the composer entered the classroom, bringing to the children realization of a real, live composer working in music. He composed two pieces for the class, harmonization of the familiar *Twinkle, Twinkle Little Star,* and *Happy Birthday.*

The composer discussed the difference between improvisation and composition. The class chose four pitches in two groups, on which he improvised on the piano. The students were then asked to improvise melodies for the words *now sing and play.* The four pitches were used for melody, organized into a form as rondo (ABACABA), each melodic idea also written retrograde.

The 12-tone row was introduced: the twelve notes counted and the sharp and flat name for each black key on the piano discussed, prior to choosing 12 notes, at random:

but in identifying this as a "tone row" the students also learned that a composer would seek organization, not fall on haphazard sequence. They chose a meter of 7 and counted it, for an example, as the composer played:

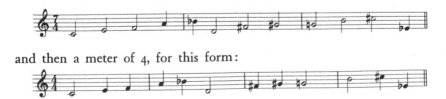

and then a meter of 4, for this form:

The class then listened to a portion of Schönberg's *String Quartet No. 4* (beginning of third movement), to note a composition which uses a 12-tone row.

Harmony was introduced: familiar airs were played with and *without* harmonization, the students identifying which versions had harmony. The class identified traditional harmonization (parallel thirds) and newer harmonic modes (parallel seconds), and discussed the comparison, noting the characteristic "new sounds" of contemporary music. The students heard Haydn's *Symphony No. 67* and Stravinsky's *The Rite of Spring*, for comparisons, and a Bach *Brandenburg Concerto* and Copland's *El Salon Mexico*. Traditional chords and "tone clusters" were also compared with those in *El Salon Mexico*.

Continuing this trend, a teacher could discuss:

Polyharmony: music that combines two or more chords or triads of different roots, sometimes in two or more keys (Honegger's *King David*); *bitonal* or polytonal harmony: simultaneous sounding of two or more keys, or tonalities, that can be separately analyzed (Britten's *A Ceremony of Carols*: "There Is No Rose"); *pandiatonic* harmony: a free chromatic enrichment of an essentially diatonic harmony (tone clusters in Cowell's *Advertisement*).

Eventually, a class would proceed to discovering jazz, "Third Stream" music of the genre advocated by Gunther Schuller, and electronic music, with the French development as *Musique Concrète*.

Typical of the reviewing in this class (reviewing was done at almost every class session) are these queries:

Name a 20th century composer whose music we have heard.

Name one of his compositions.

What is it written for?

What instrument is prominent at the beginning of the composition?

What are some of the things especially notable about this music?

The two closing sessions of the seminar were devoted to reviewing material from previous classes, and on the last one the children produced, voluntarily, a song they had composed as a going-away gift for teacher. It utilized some of the 20th century compositional techniques the students had discovered during the pilot program.

6th and 7th Grade Pilot Programs

The pilot classes for these two grades followed the general sequence and content of the 2nd Grade classwork, extended to suit the older and more sophisticated students at higher grade levels. (For example, technical explanations of modern harmony were not given the 2nd Grade students.) In the main, the same musical examples were basic for all three pilot programs but these were elaborated for the 6th and 7th grade students.

Grade 6th	*Grade 7th*
SOUND SOURCES	**SOUND SOURCES**
Rondino (for percussion), Warren Benson	*Tamboo*, Les Baxter
Variations on a Handmade Theme (for hand-clappers), Benson	*Percussion Sounds* (of) Martin Denny
Dance (for prepared piano), Cage	*Plectra and Percussion Dances*, Partch
The Aeolian Harp (for piano) Cowell	*U.S. Highball*, Partch
The Little Train of the Caipira, Heitor Villa-Lobos	
RHYTHM AND METER	**RHYTHM AND METER**
Billy the Kid: "Street Scene," Copland	*Blue Shadows in the Street*, Brubeck
Golliwog's Cakewalk, Debussy	*Far More Blue*, Brubeck
American Salute, Morton Gould	*Rain in Autumn*, Ernest Gold
Merry Mount Suite: "Children's Dance," Hanson	
Kirgiz Suite, Alan Hovhaness	
Pumpkin Eater's Little Fugue, Robert McBride	
MELODY	**MELODY**
Composition for 4 Instruments, Milton Babbitt	*Concerto for Orchestra*, Bartok
Pagodes, Debussy	*Le Marteau sans Maître*: 1st movement, Pierre Boulez

MELODY

Saudades do Brasil: "Laranjeiras," Milhaud

Music for Children, Carl Orff

The Parting of the Ways: Canon, Arnold Schönberg

MELODY

Pagodes, Debussy

For the First Time: "Mists," Hanson

Tabuh-Tabuhan, Colin McPhee

Symphony No. 4: 1st & 2nd movements, Walter Piston

Four Pieces for Clarinet, Violin, and Piano: 2nd movement, William Smith

HARMONY

The Red Pony: "Circus Music," Copland

For The First Time: "Bells," Hanson

King David: "Fanfare and March," Arthur Honegger

Three Places in New England: "General Putnam's Camp" Charles Ives

HARMONY

A Ceremony of Carols, Benjamin Britten

Advertisement, Cowell

Les Choëphores: excerpts, Milhaud

Saudades do Brasil: "Copacabana," Milhaud

The 7th Grade class was the largest (65 students) and studied for a longer time (four 55-minute periods a week). It was divided into ten groups of six or seven students to a group and the groups worked together throughout the entire semester. This pilot program was the most extensive, and enabled the students to experiment with composition, in addition to the other discoveries made in the program. Volunteers (incidentally, all boys) chose instruments, including resonator bells, bongos, sandpaper blocks, cello, maracas, and strings of the piano for their sound sources. The point of departure was through examples of music by Harry Partch (which were introduced to provoke discussion of sources of sound used by composers). Following a brief review of the four basic elements of music, the class listened to *U.S. Highball* and wrote answers to such questions as:

How would you describe the rhythm of this piece?

Do you hear any order or form in this composition?

Additional listening experiences were for discussions of the music devices employed by the composer, in theme and variation, repetition and contrast, development, rhythm, melodic structure, tonal contrast, and texture. Students were encouraged to contribute musical examples of the techniques discussed.

In the study of rhythm each group created a rhythm score in 4/4 meter, using three percussion instruments; and percussion scores, employing four and more instruments, were written later, in unusual meters like 7/4 and 5/4. A study of syncopation and polyrhythm prepared the class for listening to *The Rite of Spring* as an example of the use of rhythm in contemporary music.

Melodic ideas were explored by playing and listening to pentatonic scales, illustrated by examples from the compositions listed under Melody. (See *Appendix*.) Students were asked to bring instruments to class, to contribute to the class orchestra of black keys on the piano, orchestra bells and tone bells, which provided a background for creating pentatonic compositions incorporating the unconventional (the project referred to them as "original") instruments chosen by the students. Two and three note ostinati and rhythmic patterns were created to accompany melodies written by the groups, culminating in a student composition titled *Japanese Workshop*, which was tape-recorded for listening and evaluation.

The origin of the 12-tone row and serial music was discussed in preparation for creating a row, with variations employing retrograde, octave displacement, changing meter, and rhythm accompaniment developed by the groups. Listening experiences included music by Babbitt, Smith, and Boulez.

The study of harmony was preceded by a review of intervals and triadic harmonic structure. Musical examples illustrating tone clusters, quintal harmony, polytonality, and polyharmony were offered—but no compositional experiments were made with these, for lack of time.

Evaluation of the San Diego Project and that at Farmingdale, New York (which was a summer pilot program for students in 6th, 7th and 8th Grades), indicated that children readily respond to "new" music, and do so with pleasure, especially at youngest age levels. The Farmingdale Project was explicitly directed to exploration of the interrelationship between creative experiences in composition and the development of musical resources through training in rhythmic studies and movement (and is referred to in *The Child as a Social Person*). Conclusions drawn from these projects confirm results evaluated as responses in my own approaches to children—a primary conclusion being that exploratory or "discovery" work is the best means of stimulating original and uninhibited self-expression for the child. The extent of the experience is chiefly through freedom to discover and explore; the earlier the experience, the greater the enthusiasm. The San Diego Project staff is of the opinion that 20th century music should be offered children in primary grades, for them to know it as an enjoyable experience, before they are able (or inclined) to approach it from an intellectual point of view. The use of synthetic scales in modern music appears to incite the young child to creative work, improvisation, and original attitudes towards the arts. And a "background" in traditional music is positively not a necessity for the student, before he makes an approach to contemporary musical forms.

A need is seen for teacher education in contemporary music, and for greater inclusion of 20th century art modes in general education, and studies should be made to determine the modern composers, and compositions, which might be the best representations of the contemporary genre for inclusion in general music courses, for primary, secondary, and college education.

The Baltimore Project, under composer-consultant Emma Lou Diemer, was set up as a teachers' seminar, to develop creative approaches for musical education in elementary schools. Efforts were made to identify contemporary music suitable for classroom use and to formulate approaches that would encourage improvisation by students.*

The pilot classes were far more various than those of the San Diego Project.

Kindergarten and 1st Grade (from a city school in a low socio-economic level neighborhood) children were provided with opportunities to respond to contemporary music through movement. Class projects included:

> composing songs
> experimenting with irregular meters through percussion instruments
> singing and dancing songs in contemporary idioms
> some improvisation

This group's story compositions with sound effects was its most original and distinctive contribution. The children gave convincing performances for observers, and audiences of other children. *Report*: "Not only was development noticed in the creative abilities of the children, but there was evidence

---

* The Project coordinator was Alice Beer, Supervisor, Elementary School Education, Baltimore Public Schools, Maryland, and the 30 elementary school teachers enrolled in the seminar studied examples of contemporary music (which emphasized basic elements of melody, rhythm and harmony); utilized techniques and ideas from contemporary music (at the outset, from material available in the school: *Music for Living Series* and RCA *Adventures in Music Series* recordings) in original compositions, and analysed and evaluated these. Four schools participated in pilot classes.

of growth in oral language skills and reading; improvement in oral expression; extension of speaking vocabulary."

1st and 2nd Grades: students

    sang songs in contemporary styles

    composed song

    experimented with percussion instruments

    experimented with *Musique Concrète*

    explored almost all the ideas discussed in the seminar, for the 30
        teachers enrolled under composer-consultant Mary Lou Diemer.

These children were from a school within an average socio-economic level, located in an old section of the city. Their music teacher made extensive use of drawings and charts illustrating line and color in music, from which the students developed understanding and feeling for contrast in music such as long-short, high-low, smooth-jerky. Free expression was so well cultivated in this program that children who, at the outset, were inhibited and reserved, responded, eventually, with great freedom and expression, to contemporary music.

Their experiences with creative rhythmic movement in music and dances was the most original and distinctive contribution of this program.

3rd Grade and 4th Grade: from a school in an above-average socio-economic residential area; the students' median age was eight. They

    improvised, with singing and percussion composition

    experimented with *Musique Concrète*

    explored several aspects of contemporary music

    composed on unconventional instruments

The exploration of the 12-tone row held greatest interest for this group. They were inordinately proud of their tone-row compositions; when the rhythm of a familiar folk song was played in this row, it became one of their favorite compositions. They made several important discoveries, one being the necessity for resonance in instruments (rattle of crushed cellophane does not have enough sonority to be included in a "composition"). *Report*: "It is difficult to reconcile the extraordinary growth in musical understanding [of this group] with the fact that the majority of the students were only 8 years old."

5th and 6th Grades: students came from a suburban school, in a high socio-economic level. They

    sang, played, and listened to music presented

    developed marked skill in identifying the characteristics of music
        that is contemporary sound

composed melodies using church modes, and learned how these
scales differ from major and minor scales

transposed and adapted folk songs to various modes

improvised

undertook self-evaluation and criticism

Although the class program included experiences with 12-tone compositions it was evident that some of these students felt this style of composition
too restrictive. Their knowledge of music theory and their skill in playing
classroom instruments enabled them to harmonize folk songs bitonally with
considerable ease. *Report*: "There seemed to be no limitation regarding the
amount of information this group could absorb and use."

Three main topics were studied in the Project's seminars: *Sounds
Around Us—Creative Interpretation of Contemporary Music—Improvisation
and Composition.*

The important contribution of the first topic was to open the ears of
teachers and children to contemporary musical sounds and to stimulate the
children's creativity and desire for self-expression through the use of sounds.

The familiar nursery rhyme *Hickory Dickory Dock* (rhythm sticks and
tone blocks for the tick-tock; glissando for the mouse running up and down;
triangle for clock striking) was played, without identification by title, for
teachers to determine the nursery rhyme by the representative accompaniment.

This example was correlated to ways in which composers have used
instruments to represent an object, image, idea, or painted pictures through
sound: Haydn's use of pizzicato for the clock ticking in his *"Clock" Symphony*; Beethoven's use of percussion in his *Sixth Symphony* to represent
a storm. Contemporary examples of music of this type included Schuller's
The Twittering Machine, on themes of Klee, and Cowell's *Conversation
in a Chinese Laundry.*

(Other examples are Respighi's nightingale in *The Pines of Rome*, the
cannon in Tchaikovsky's *Overture 1812*, score calling for the sounds of two
airplane engines in Antheil's *Ballet Mécanique*, the serpent's tail in Rogers'
Pinocchio, and the taxi horns in Gershwin's *An American in Paris*.)

Electronic music was introduced—it also featured in the San Diego
Project, as did *Musique Concrète* and Aleatory or music "by chance."

Teachers discussed the second topic, searching for ways in which children
could express themselves creatively: through oral and written language,
through the use of art media, through bodily movements, including dance
and pantomime, and through singing and playing instruments. Mood, story
and picture music, and structure were discussed.

The third topic—*Improvisation and Composition*—was explored in a variety of ways, one being to study a known element of music and then to make changes and additions in it. *Little Liza Jane* is a simple song in three rhythmic ideas:

These ideas are arranged as follows in the folk song:

(1) (2) (1) (2)

(3) (2) (3) (2)

Teachers rearranged rhythmic patterns in various sequences, orchestrated them with a variety of instruments, sometimes incorporated them in an original tone row. The same idea was applied to instrumental selections, such as Virgil Thomson's *The Alligator and the Coon.*

Some teachers experimented with different ways in which instruments apparently carry on a musical conversation, suggest the names of children or birds, reproduce the rhythms of television commercials familiar to the students. A steady 4/4, 2/4, or 3/4 meter was used as a unifying element for free improvisation. In some instances, irregular and changing meters were introduced through the use of Brubeck's *Three To Get Ready* and *The Unsquare Dance*, rhythmic ideas readily seen and heard when charted:

Three to Get Ready

$$\frac{3}{4} \mid \; \mid \; \mid \; \mid \; \mid \; \mid \quad \frac{4}{4} \mid \; \mid \; \mid \; \mid \; \mid \; \mid \; \mid$$

$$\frac{3}{4} \mid \; \mid \; \mid \; \mid \; \mid \; \mid \quad \frac{4}{4} \mid \; \mid \; \mid \; \mid \; \mid \; \mid \; \mid$$

$$\frac{3}{4} \mid \; \mid \; \mid \; \mid \; \mid \; \mid \quad \frac{4}{4} \mid \; \mid \; \mid \; \mid \; \mid \; \mid \; \mid$$

$$\frac{3}{4} \mid \; \mid \; \mid \; \mid \; \mid \; \mid \quad \frac{4}{4} \mid \; \mid \; \mid \; \mid \; \mid \; \mid \; \mid$$

The Unsquare Dance $\frac{7}{4}$ **L** R **L** R **L** R R | **L** R **L** R **L** R R | etc.

Classes in this Project were encouraged to share their accomplishments as much as possible and the Music staff helped children refine and clarify communication, and tried to stimulate thought and idea. Parents were invited to visit classes; auditorium programs were presented to acquaint the public with the Project in music education; interschool "festivals" were popular; and three televised programs from the project were presented as public service by the local NBC network station (WBAL-TV) in Baltimore.

On numerous occasions, classes spontaneously shared creative work with other classes and individuals. Some classes set poetry to music. One class volunteered to study Japanese music as part of social studies on Japan; and, as a result, composed music in the style of the Japanese. Often, an abstract musical idea was used as a point of departure for original expression as when, following a discussion on some of the means composers use to build a climax in music, a 10-year-old boy composed a piece for percussion, illustrating the way he achieved a climax in his composition.

Children in this program often asked music faculty members for evaluation of their work and requested suggestions for developing their ideas. Sometimes there was no attempt at formal evaluation, and students worked through trial and error, obviously gaining greater satisfaction in their work.

These projects could not have been developed without the supervision and assistance of qualified music teachers, and the aid of the composer-consultants; and their very success underscores the need for Music faculties in schools.

What may parents do to preserve the Music faculties in American public schools, and ensure that general education integrates at least an elementary musical education for children?

Parents can first of all learn more about the arts, and *the values of the arts*, in civilized society. The arts, most often taken for ornament by the layman, are in grave need of an appreciative audience en masse, sufficiently well informed to develop discriminating tastes. From such an audience en masse will naturally come responses that demand excellence, and that encourage the pursuit of excellence. Eventually, we should have, in American society, a culture in which the dancer and musician, the painter and sculptor, the architect and writer, are first-class citizens, like scientists and politicians, financiers and diplomats, men of the ministry, medicine and law, industrialists and military officers.

We shall have come, we may say, to an intellectual response to the arts, as civilized persons, with no less ardency than we responded to the arts in our older, savage human state.

Parents who want to keep Music faculties in public schools, especially for children in elementary education, should support the school boards that appreciate the arts for their intrinsic values, and refrain from electing to the boards such candidates that despise the arts as superfluous frills on life, forbidden to the masses who are to be given only "basic" courses, while the arts, presumably, are to be kept apart for the elite class. Parents should speak as citizens, concerned not only for a single child or the children from a single family but for all children, who are a national trust and a social investment for the future. Parents and other citizens should write their congressmen about their opinions on Music in the general educational curricula, make them known in quarters where opinions of the citizenry affect laws.

And we all can interest ourselves seriously about education, *in its fullest aspect* as the cultivation of the intellect and the development of the human person, as well as in its "basic" skills. Parents can treat the mental and emotional needs of a child with as much seriousness as they treat the "basic" needs of food, shelter and clothing.

Accredited music teachers working in the schools must continue to develop their careers, not simply by teaching by rote in posts which they already hold, but by a consistent and ever-extensive pursuit of those careers. A large number of teachers in today's Music faculties in schools have been teaching for twenty years, and hold Master's degrees or equivalent in credits; many more have been teaching for five to ten years. But the greatest majority of these teach by rote, in systems that have been persistently maintained not for their values as approaches to students, but because they are perfunctorily set by administration.

How may a teacher know if her system of teaching is productive of good results? *By evaluating the responses to her approaches, and by analyzing these approaches for their strongest and weakest methods.*

In working with children in elementary education the approach must be one which encourages the student to respond, not merely by dutifully performing classwork but by self-expression. Students should form definite opinions, even if these need to be enlarged; they should have positive ideas, even if these need to be qualified. *Children working with dance and music respond when they show us that they feel and think.* So doing, they discover and experiment, they improvise and compose; they create experiences in dance and music which fulfill them as persons. The music teacher cannot afford ever to forget that dance and music are social arts, and that they involve the whole person. Respect the arts for their values, and the child as a person, not a statistical little pot waiting to be filled to the brim with only so much, of such-and-such "musical knowledge."

At the commencement of every semester, when the music teacher prepares her materials, let her ask: does this material create interest *at the beginning?*—does its plan or program have a decisive ending?—does it have a recurrent pattern through which we shall experience some basic aspects of music, melodic, rhythmic, harmonic, in the greatest possible range?—does the material have contrast, in that old and new (and all other contrasts) illuminate each other?—will the material, when the children make use of it, have a feeling of tension and relaxation, qualities inherent in dance and music?—is there a climax dramatic enough to give students a sensation of accomplishment at the end of the course?

All through the school year, all through the career of teaching, the music teacher should ask herself questions like these: am I keeping up with the ever-expanding field of teaching techniques and compositional developments in music?—am I being stimulated by new materials and new ideas, while maintaining my initial comprehensive knowledge—and respect—for traditional music?—do I know the steps and devices for creating sound sources in *this* time, my students' own time?—am I maintaining a tolerant but critical acquaintance with new composers and their avant-garde music?—am I consciously inspired by Music *per se*, so that I teach with confidence, out of love of music, and thereby my concrete use of materials in music education is sustained as art?

Conventional teachers in general education must learn more about dance and music, about movement as dance, and the qualification and organization of sound and silence as music. Teachers in the schools should work in closer collaboration with dance and music, simply in order to work in more intimate relationships, and on infinitely more rewarding terms, with the children who are their students.

Parents and teachers alike must recognize that the moral value of the arts lies in the process of discovery not only of the nature of the arts but of the experiences these bring to the human person. For the child, as Harold Taylor tells us in *Art and the Intellect*, a discovery out of art is an insight into what it means to be free in emotional response and free in choice of ideas; it is a way of enriching the quality of human experience, and of reaching a precision in the choice of values; a discipline, freely undertaken; a knowledge, firmly grasped; a heightened consciousness, and an intensity of interest in the creative and imaginative aspects of human life. Finally, and here it affects not solely the rare person who is the artist but all of us, who are society as a whole, the arts are an experience which relate to our material world, which moves through the contemporary reality (here and now) into newer levels of awareness of what human society is.

So qualified, so estimated, judge then, as parents and teachers, what dance and music mean to children.

Dance and Music in Physical Education

In schools where there is no true standard of musical education, the child depends almost entirely on the physical education teacher for music and dance. Since we are predominantly an athletic people, rather than an artistic people, the largest part of American dance education stems from P.E. in elementary schools and colleges. Almost all P.E. teachers today have basic knowledge of dance forms, mostly of folkloric content; many have studied modern dance under pedagogic systems; few, in elementary school teaching, are trained dancers but are nevertheless able to apply some rudimentary dance principles (folk and ballroom, especially) for student activities.

The role of the P.E. teacher in a school system dedicated to a "basic" course of instruction is doubly important to that in a school with a true music curriculum. She may be, at least for girl students, the sole inspirational source in musical arts, and perhaps in dramatic arts. In any school, the P.E. teacher has an advantage over other conventional teachers, in that she commands a greater physical facility as space.

The child in the gymnasium occupies the largest space in school, excepting the cafeteria and the playground. In classrooms, he sits at a desk which is fastened to the floor and addresses himself (and is addressed) in a single dimension: that wall or area which is the teacher's background. In the cafeteria he is marshalled in and out in "lines," either to eat at meals or to attend assemblies; he is required, generally, to be still and quiet. School playgrounds are too diverse in character and physical facilities to be determined, here, and are omitted from a realistic study of musical arts in schools—although infants and young children spontaneously undertake dance-and-song games which have rhythmic structures. Skipping, for instance, is an interesting development of the song-and-dance game, in that rhythm and rhyme are integrals, requiring the children to practice mental concentration and physical coordination. Teachers can utilize elements of this song-and-dance game in the classroom and gymnasium.

In the gymnasium, music accompanies or states movement rhythms, from music for calisthenics to music for true dance forms, like marches. In every instance, the gym or P.E. teacher can enlarge this ordinary musical experience into an extraordinary one. If she works in a school where there is a qualified music teacher, then both music and P.E. teacher might collaborate on semester programs for children.

In preparation for the best achievement, the P.E. teacher must plan to use her attributes of space and motility, normal to the gymnasium, with disciplines for a "creative" approach and response. Children come to the gymnasium in a state of mind (and a sensible mode of dress) conducive to a much freer expression than is considered a norm for the conventional classroom. They become aware of their bodies, and of space, and of the sounds of their voices, magnified in a large, open P.E. facility. When they are led by the teacher into *conscious* knowledge of how their movements relate to music in rhythm and tempo they can approach elementary forms of dance.

The P.E. teacher works with large groups, generally larger than the group in the classroom—far larger than the small groups of children, or single child, that it is general for autonomous dance and music teachers to work with. She must accomplish dual purposes: gymnastic and artistic, for her group. It is usually a group of girls, which limits certain aspects of teaching, but enables the teacher to concentrate her approach within its margins.

Almost invariably, the P.E. teacher's approach to dance gains immediate response, since the children are acclimated to physical activities in the gymnasium. The response to singing and conscious appreciation (knowledge and discrimination of taste) of instrumental music come from a studied approach by the P.E. teacher, and most particularly when this teacher works in collaboration with the music teacher. Marches, for instance, are a good primary approach for strongly rhythmic movements.

I am told that ballroom dancing is often taught in P.E. classes, and when this is done the teacher should make a point to investigate "dances of the past" within the context, for comparison with "dances of yesterday and today." By relating the music as closely as possible *in form* to such dancing, the P.E. teacher will be working in music as well as dance.

As time and ingenuity permit, the P.E. teacher can develop her program into social culture of dance and music, within physical education. One teacher who has done so with great success, and in very large groups (50 to 70) of girls, is Audrey Patterson Tyler. Specifically employed as a P.E. teacher, but finding that her students (the majority of them Negro, from "deprived" socio-economic environments) had little dance and music cultures, Mrs. Tyler developed a program in which musical arts are integrated with physical education. She teaches students in junior high school, children in growth phases that fall into early and mid-adolescence, and makes a flexible approach, according to group experiences and abilities.

Her dance programs are formal (folkloric, modern and jazz) structures, and experimental or "creative" forms, and she undertakes some "scientific" studies, as to the relationships of dance and music (movements, and sound and silence), and studies of human involvement with these. She makes her students write, design and perform music and dance compositions; they also paint and model, and are encouraged to choreograph and select music for dance patterns. These extensions from P.E. classes lead students into the history of dance and music, of drama and theatre history (as social history through epochs of arts), and into painting, sculpture and architecture through studies of costume design and scenery, and theatre architecture through the ages.

Mrs. Tyler stages full-scale student lyric theatre in school assemblies, which combine dance, drama and music, stage design and mechanics. When she encounters a form, or a style, in dance and music with which she is unable to cope (from her own knowledge and available material), she invites a cognitive teacher to join her project, as enrichment resource (for direction of research and also for guidance, analysis and evaluation). She enlists the aid of college student teachers who are dance majors, in her program of integrating dance and music within the gymnastic life, and finds that these teacher's-aids are predominantly modern dancers.

Lecture-demonstrations in music and dance are preliminaries to theatrical experiences of "live" dance and music for Mrs. Tyler's students—but, at this writing, this resourceful teacher has found it easier to call in outside resources, like myself, than to work in an integrated program with school district music faculties, in so far as a program of P.E. music might emerge as an artistic experience within the accredited gymnastic one.

She is wholly without partisanship regarding artistic genres, and plans each of her programs to suit the particular needs of an individual group. Thus, she has no conventions about continuity in music, such as the school music teacher usually advocates—with the result that by the time a music course has consecutively investigated past epochs, the child has graduated out of school, perhaps never having encountered music of his own time (excepting for music of faddist types in the "pop" genres). Mrs. Tyler is apt to use avant-garde, "pop," romantic and pre-classical music, in the same program (sometimes, in one day's lesson) and to teach the *Virginia Reel* to the same group which is also studying (and experimenting creatively with) dance in forms of jazz, or preparing to attend opera or ballet.

Twenty years ago I foolishly believed that all musical arts needed to be introduced by accredited teachers. While I am insistent that all *technical* instruction must be made by them, I have discovered that some conventional teachers are qualified to make initial approaches in dance and music and that a great many P.E. teachers, dance-trained or at least dance-oriented, are making considerable contributions to the American child's musical culture. Audrey Patterson Tyler (whose work I observed in San Diego City Schools) is one such and she extends her work, as do many conventional teachers, into community recreation.

Recreation of the "educational" type (meaning: recreation for young people under supervision by teachers, usually Physical Education, Music and Drama school faculty teachers) normally is within a physical facility comparable to the school gymnasium and auditorium. Space and acoustics are important quotients of such facilities, making them better suited to working in dance and music than the regulation classroom. In *The Child as a Social Person* the conventional and the P.E. teacher will find material readily adaptable to use with *The Child in School*.

The Child as a Social Person

"The value of art lies in making people happy, first in practicing the art and then in possessing the product . . . Happiness is something men ought to pursue . . . If happiness is the ultimate sanction of art, art in turn is the best instrument of happiness."

GEORGE SANTAYANA: "Art and Happiness," from *Reason in Art*, Volume Four of *The Life of Reason*.

*I*F a child lives in a home where there is no musical appreciation, and attends a school which shuns all artistic life as extracurricular to a "basic" education, he must find other resources for dance and music. As a social person, he shares a life among his peers, in school, in the community as he plays and in his church as he worships. The two main recreational-educational resources are in the community and the church.

Church social activities generally include music, unless the church is of a religious denomination which forbids music and dance, even as worshipful praise. Largely, religious denominations in the United States are musical religious denominations and some of these (the Mormon church in particular) may be said to be religions which favor both dance and music. The subject of music and religion (touched on lightly, later in this chapter) requires a study all to itself, especially if one subscribes to the idea of singing and dancing in praise of the Divine Being.

Community activities for children invariably include dance and music, and in particular as "recreation" centers for children of all classes. One type of community recreational source for the arts is the settlement house, usually founded by an individual if later maintained in part or whole by civic authority. Out of the American settlement house artistic life there have already emerged artists of consequence—the best known example is the Henry Street Playhouse in New York City, most noted for its modern dance.* Here there are not only classes for students (in modern dance

---

* The Henry Street Community Settlement House was founded in 1915 by Alice and Irene Lewisohn, the latter of whom was a student of the Delsartian system of dance. She inaugurated dance education derived from the *plastiques* of the Duncan school, Oriental dance, and Delsartian movement. The Henry Street Community Settlement Dance School and the Henry Street Playhouse Dance Company are emergent, the latter currently most noted for the work of avant-gardist Alwin Nikolais. The Henry Street Settlement House is an institution primarily devoted to social work in Manhattan's Lower East Side. Among its most famed alumni is modern dancer-choreographer Helen Tamiris, who died in 1966.

and drama) but also seasonal concert schedules by distinguished artists and tyro choreographers and playwrights, giving students an education *per se* in the arts as well as an early awareness of professional theatre.

Settlement house centers for children working in creative arts are more often set up for children from "deprived" socio-economic societies, meaning that the students are offspring of impoverished parents. The best kind of creative center is open to all children, whether of indigent or prosperous class, and regardless of social caste, and is overtly concerned with the artistic development of the child, rather than with social welfare. The approach I favor is designed to provide opportunities for the child to explore art forms, for purposes of growth of the child *as a person*. In essence, such approach provides a climate in which the child works to discover his artistic powers, and accomplishes or creates through experiences.

In principle, I like to develop this climate through a confluence of graphic and musical arts, within a broad lyric theatre approach. In my opinion, this is the best approach for the child from infancy into adolescence, the last period being the one in which he is compelled by his parents and teachers to specialize, or to prepare to specialize in order to become self-supporting as the adult. Unfortunately, education is more often compartmentalized, so that the student of science is "channelled" away from the arts, which are considered (and which he comes to consider) as being useless and time-wasting and "not for him" as a scientist—or a craftsman in preparation within "vocational" and "shop" courses in high school.

Unless a student graduates into a liberal arts college, he may never approach the artistic life during his educational years. And as many students do not even complete high school grades it is essential that they discover the artistic aspects of life in the elementary (preferably, the primary) grades. The younger the child, the more spontaneous the response; hence, the easier the approach. But many high school students have told me, with obvious grief and regret, that a first approach to the arts in high school is "too late" to benefit by, because of set patterns of behavior and attitudes, and the acquired prejudices and phobias about art and society—all of which hardly trouble the young child as student of the lowest grades.

An integration of the art media for a student is uncommon in school but is the normal précis for "creative" work such as is done at Adelphi University, Garden City, New York, where (since the 1930s) the Children's Centre for Creative Arts has been directed by Grace M. Stanistreet. Her intent was to serve particular needs of children, of which most parents seemed unaware and for which normal education made little or no provision. In essence, Grace Stanistreet wanted to help each child to discover his uniqueness as the individual; his incomparability as a person. And to do so through artistic creativity and disciplines.

For such approach, conventional attitudes and orthodox meanings were redefined, as for "success" and "encouragement." At the Centre, success is not the measure by which one student, competing in a group, excels amid his peers—as failure is not his inability to maintain a group norm of "performance" in periodic examinations that test his knowledge. Encouragement is not qualified through praise, since praise, especially too easily earned, develops vanity and stifles initiative. And the Centre strives to free its students from adult concepts of creativity; from orthodox artistic modes evolved by adults; and from the "labels" society applies to the arts and artists.

In the Centre's seminars, students participate in weekly discussions with Miss Stanistreet, to share ideas, and in workshops of six week durations. For six weeks, a group of students attends classes in acting and music; another group attends classes in dance and music; a third group, a class in graphic arts. Every six weeks a new combination of workshop classes commences for each group, with different teachers, and some specialties of the program like Bruce King's Boys' Dance Class (studies in improving the body, and for expression of idea and feeling through movement as dance). Important theatrical artists (modern dancer Katherine Litz, for example) serve as guest teachers on the faculty.

Adelphi's Children's Centre's programs are designed to stimulate the will or desire to initiate expression, calling into use what already exists as feeling and experience in the individual child. He is told *what* but never *how* to create. And he is guided to recognize ways in which to refine and improve his creative impulses and their results, as artistic expressions. The students are of all ages, childhood into adolescence, and from a variety of social and economic environments, representative of several different communities and schools.

The idea governing the teaching is creative self-expression, but nothing about Adelphi's Children's Centre for Creative Arts could be considered "play," and its students are not deluded into believing that performance in art is relegated to the category of "games." Instead, a total involvement by teacher and student, an absolute intent to qualify creative impulse and performance, commit teachers and students to purposes that are of themselves serious and profound. That this climate and these conditions develop high degrees of happiness for the children is, in effect, through the artistic life, not through a contrived atmosphere for breeding sociological "culture."

Such programs may be instituted in colleges, as workshops for student teachers (who serve as teachers' aides at Adelphi's Centre) out of the normal college curricula (which generally includes experimental programs); out of church recreation; in community projects of the "recreational" type, both civic and privately supported; and, with necessary adaptations, become integral in general curricula in education, pre-school into secondary education. Public and private schools, in summer sessions of crash courses in science and mathematics, frequently have subsidiary recreational courses in arts and crafts, and these subsidiaries, under cognitive teachers, could become realistic programs in the arts—providing the programs were treated seriously, by educators, and not established as "play" instead of work.

In community and church educational-recreation lack of funds may preclude a fully staffed approach to an arts program. Teachers are recruited from social work, conventional school classrooms and as parents with experiences of growing children. These often work as volunteers (without salary) and cannot make the fullest preparation for teaching in spare time. Nevertheless, with good sense and the aid of cognitive teachers, such amateur programs can be formulated, conducted and eventually evaluated.

In an educational-recreational program children may approach several aspects of theatre arts and crafts, especially if the community or church is richly endowed with citizen resources to education, in the way of persons who practice livelihoods in the creative and performing arts. "Educational-recreation" is a term I employ for all supervised projects in which students work creatively in the arts. Undertaken during school vacation in summer, or as Saturday classes during the standard school year, such programs enlarge the child's horizons in several ways. He has interesting experiences as a social person, with adults and with his peers, and occupies a somewhat more distinguished position, as person, than he does as a student in the school classroom. The project should offer wide areas of approach, to elicit the greatest possible responses from the largest number of children, so that the program curriculum is usually varied. If a child has a greater interest in drama than in dance, or in making scenery and designing decor than in performing, his greatest interest should be allowed first expression—even while he is being coaxed to explore areas into which he has not yet ventured, as artist or craftsman. He has an altogether freer, more gregarious relationship with the adults who teach him or supervise his work, than is normal between teacher-student in school. The child as a social person is more articulate and less inhibited than the child in school, and, as a rule, the approaches made to him (for eliciting his response and developing his faculties) are better informed than at home. The teaching *per se* occurs in the child's free time (outside the classroom) and has pleasurable associations *if the approach is such as to arouse these associations for the child.* The child working as one of a group realizes that it is a group unlike the classroom one, that it is offered more freedom, more possibilities of individual expression. According to the teacher's discipline, the child abuses or uses this freedom within the group.

I use the word "discipline" advisedly, and to emphasize the character of the approach inferred here, which is within the serious and profound nature of the arts, within a climate of encouragement and tolerance, and of high adventure. By thinking always of the work as *discovery* relating to *experience*, of the education as a process of finding out for the child (and, for the teacher, of finding out *about* the children) the approach to dance and music becomes a working thesis and not a frivolous or playful one. Within such a thesis the broadest tolerance of creative impulse and extensions into performance retain freedom of experimentation and "discovery," but a very real discipline is maintained—the discipline inherent to working in art media, as amateur or as professional. Maintaining respect for an art is the teacher's obligation, and should be inculcated as an aspect of art for the student, regardless of the educational or recreational theme in which such discoveries are experienced.

In an amateur project (one instituted for adults volunteering to work in church or community recreational program) there will be wide diversity of teaching skills, but there need be no disparity in the quality of discipline predicated by the approach. Teachers will, naturally, encounter wide disparity in groups of children and in physical facilities afforded recreational projects, but they will work in the primary circumstance of approaching children outside the "basic" educational curricula, without requirement to "grade" progress in a set ratio of marks for failure and success.

Since in "recreational" projects, of all kinds, the general plan is to provide "activities" for children, a program is basically gymnastic. Extending play as games and sports into activity within the arts invariably brings us to Dance, which is both gymnastic and aesthetic. Dance, logically, is the best single basis of all creative activities for children, who learn through active, physical involvement, and respond primarily through a sensual instinct.

I prefaced this book with the statement that children approach dance and music as one, and that children, like people from ancient societies, make little or no separation between dance and music, but develop these, functionally and dramatically, as extensions of each other. Yet until now I have written primarily of approaches to music, for organization of the contents of this book and also because of the nature of dancing.

The house in which *The Child at Home* lives, and the classroom in which *The Child in School* works, are not as physically well suited, and not as aesthetically inviting to dance as the more expansive areas of the gymnasium and auditorium. Space is an extremely important factor for the dance, and space, for the child who is approached through dance, has an emotional climate which is as influential on his responses as its actual physical dimension.

The sounds of music, which he hears, and the movements in dance, which he sees, assume a different character in the auditorium to that character known only in the living room at home and the crowded, two-dimensional classroom in school. It may be only now, released in an open area, that the child consciously understands what it means to dance.

Archaeologists and biologists debate which came first: dance or music; a child does not. All children dance, including the lame of brain and body, the deaf and the mute, and the blind. The handicapped child approaches dance with fear and fascination, afraid of falling and injuring himself, yet responsive to the rhythmic impulse. Everyone who has worked with deformed and mentally impaired children knows that such children, when they are ecstatic, move in ways that they think of as dancing, however clumsy, ludicrous and aesthetically ugly the movements may actually be as dance.

In a group of so-called average children there are always some who are fearful or shy, and very often these are the most sensitive, the most naturally perceptive among their peers. Many musically gifted children lack the verbal, gestural and literary rapports of communication normal to others, and are articulate only in a musical medium, perhaps instrumentally, perhaps in dance. Lonely, timid children and children of apparently anti-social tendencies will often resist all attempts to integrate them in a group, especially in games. They will successfully foil the teacher's attempts to make them sing, by mouthing silently within the chorus. But almost all children will dance in preference to standing still within a censorious group of their peers, since movement, especially rapid movement, allows them to escape notice, such as is fastened on the stock-still figure in a dance. Eventually, all children dance, when dance frees and articulates their petrified and inchoate states, and when they form pleasurable associations with the act of dancing.

Many children are not at all competitive. Games, gymnastics and dancing all impose physical activity—but games and gymnastics are feats of skill and contest; dance is not. Dance is an art and not a sport, although containing a great deal of movement that is acrobatic. It is a mode of expression of the inner self, and of communication with the outer world. For these reasons, children dance.

When we move children from the classroom into the gymnasium or auditorium, and if we approach them musically as well as gymnastically in such an area, we are able to begin a constructive education in dance, the first principle of which is the individual concept of self-expression. Disciplined in art form, this becomes creative dance.

Dance is important when a child begins to move among his peers. In "social" dance the child works with a partner, and also works in groups or ensembles, in which he takes his place as an individual. Choosing partners for dances (and being selected as a partner) is in itself a valuable lesson; children become aware of each other and of how they move in space as two persons, instead of one. For many, many children this is the first conscious knowledge of others—of the solidity of the human body and the rhythm which is distinct in a person and gives him a great deal of his physical "personality." If a child comes from a home where he is the only one, or the only one within his age span, dancing may be the first actual experience of working with his peers.

In a class in nursery school, kindergarten or the 1st grade, a teacher can teach the fundamental fact of dance: *all dance is movement, but all movement is not dance*. From here, in an approach qualified by the group's awareness, the teacher can progress in a musical arts education. It may take a gymnastic rather than an artistic trend, by which for example, the children discover movement as pedestrian locomotion (getting from here to there); movement common to activities (in sports and games, like running, jumping); movement defined as dance (which are movements artistically related to space, time, level, direction), through rhythms, tempi and other *musical* elements.

The teacher's approach should be guided by certain principles, one being to teach the child *conscious* knowledge of elements in dance and music, many of which he actually knows, but does not yet realize. The children in a group must have enough knowledge to serve as basis for reference, and all that they find out in class is thought of as "discovery," while all that they accomplish, in the group and from individual contributions, becomes "experiences."

School classes vary in size but are usually to be described as "large." The material researched for this book varies from "ideal" classes of five children, to Music and P.E. classes of fifty to seventy children, in public schools. Groups in recreational arts programs may be even larger—a hundred, to a hundred-and-fifty, and over!

Principles of Approach

My principles of teaching are the same, regardless of the circumstances or the kinds of children, in that I approach dance and music as substances of sounds and movements. The approaches, however, are flexible, so that the most elastic uses can be made of the essential substances for all groups of children. The recreational and "children's creative center" teachers should read not only the chapter devoted to *The Child as a Social Person* but also those relating to *The Child at Home, The Child as Artist* and *The Child in School*, to understand environmental factors. Into every group come so many children, each child a unit of energy and also of knowledge and experience. It is the teacher's job to combine the units of energy for group endeavor, but to practice a sufficiently flexible plan so as to allow individual thoughts and points of view to be recognized.

"Creativity" cannot be mass-produced and, to my belief, does not emerge readily from the masses. Its potential is always within the individual and at the commencement of a creative dance and music class no one, least of all the teacher, is sure of this potential. The challenges the good teacher must set for the group of children in her care are in truth challenges for her own acumen; she must glimpse fugitive talent and persuade it to assume form figuratively and spiritually for the child and his group, and she must develop a variety of abilities so as to strengthen the group out of its weakest and timidest members.

Pilot programs described here give the teacher a pragmatic understanding of how to effect this miracle. For miracle it is, to sustain the single member in the group, to help him to grow to such stature that he develops his individual forte while contributing strength and purpose to the group, and to hold to the idea of art as "form" while working freely and as eloquently as possible within its original or truly creative sense. To achieve something of this miracle the teacher must make an approach within herself before making the approach to the children. And many teachers must first free themselves of compulsive methodologies and the accumulated prejudices with which the adult looks and listens, or brings individual emotional and intellectual responses to art forms in themselves.

Teachers are often so concerned about children's individual adjustments to the group that this concern becomes the over-riding aspect of the program, to the detriment of the artistic development. In every group, certain children as individuals emerge as leaders and this leadership may be constructive or destructive to group effort. And in all groups some individuals are overtly or secretly rejected by their peers. What educators call "sociometric" circumstances affect the program in so far as group responses and creativity are concerned, and palpable hostility (to one in the group, to the teacher herself, to some ideas propounded in the program) is inevitable, to some extent. Inexperienced teachers are puzzled when "things don't go well" in a program that, as pilot program in a seminar for teachers under cognitive teaching guidance, proceeded step by step towards a successful conclusion as "course" of lecture-demonstrations. These inexperienced teachers are apt to blame themselves for what they construe as an unsuccessful approach and a poor development of a program. On the contrary, each teacher should inaugurate and sustain every program with fullest awareness of its "sociometric" condition, qualifying her own approach and the responses elicited not strictly according to the pilot program sketched for her *but according to the particular nature of the group with which she is working.* Its human nature will qualify its artistic one.

Even in a stated "recreational" program discipline must be instituted and maintained, since chaotic circumstances are not conducive to creativity. Revolutionary ideas, original expressions of thought, true creativity, emerge from argument and debate, discussion and experimentation, but these are altogether different from riot. No good and true exercise of a musical arts program may be conducted without authority on the part of the teacher and good manners on the part of the students. Therapeutic uses of dance and music for socially maladjusted children (like therapeutic uses of the arts for the physically and mentally ill) are separate from the musical arts program described here for educational-recreation.

I make a point of telling my students that we *work* to *discover* basics of dance and music, as art media, in order to experiment and *resolve as experiences* individual and group effort. Instead of "success" I speak of "accomplishment," on the précis that to experience is to find out or know (hence: to learn) and no experience of itself can be a bad one, or a wasted effort, since what would be construed as an "unsuccessful" experience is a validly successful one in that it has proved, by failure, a point taken towards accomplishing a purpose.

With children of all ages, I am overtly conscious of the difference between the sexes. In the United States, the competition between male and female begins in the cradle, when mothers and fathers commence making comparisons as to the respective merits of girls and boys. Thereafter, the contest increases, especially when the children start school. The extraordinary majority of conventional teachers are female, and many of them, consciously and subconsciously, dislike working with boys, are afraid of "handling" boys' education and discipline, and "do not understand" how boys learn. Every child passes through phases of discovery, each of which totally preoccupies his imagination for the time being. He first discovers himself; then, his family; eventually, the world he inhabits as a person. He spends his first six or seven years working to understand the first two phases of life and brings to the third phase experiences accumulated out of the primary two. His moral sense, and to great extent his artistic sense, is essentially set by the time he meets teacher in kindergarten or 1st grade.

The relevance of father and mother, to a child, in his home environment, is an exact relevance of the individual child, according to gender, within a group. In what our culture considers normal circumstances, children recognize and define masculinity as inherent to the father and to all males; femininity as inherent to the mother and all females. When children dance they do not at first perform as artists, in the professional sense; they perform as human persons—and they are most likely, in normal circumstances, to dance like boys and girls. What this means, as applied to the musical arts program, is that a teacher must allow girls and boys to dance in ways particular to their innate responses, and to seek and find pleasurable associations in music that, we may say, has "male" and "female" characteristics.*

The relationship between parents and children, in "normal" conditions of our culture, establishes a daughter as well as a son as looking at the father as all-powerful and all-wise, as the provider of good things and the protector of the family, subtly different from the relationship established between daughters and sons for a mother, who comforts hurts, encourages endeavor, pacifies quarrels, and in general softens and sweetens the daily course of existence. When children work in dance and drama they retain their relationships to each other and to their society, as they know it at home and abroad, even while assuming distinct roles of character within a

---

* Possibly of interest to a psychology student is the fact that most little boys like Bach, who is ordered and precise, and Mozart, who as a musician was an inveterate comedian, but dislike much of Tchaikovsky, a favorite of girls, except for his ballet music, which many authorities on music consider to be that composer's best and least sentimentalized work.

plot or libretto. Only after scrupulous training, and the exertion of super-
human discipline, does a professional actor and dancer cease being himself
in order to thoroughly become an artist. The reticences and responses of
children in a musical arts program are predicated by the children's individual ideas about their characters as boys and girls more than by ideas about
dance and music.

Inasmuch as I work with collaborating teachers, I am usually able to
arrange for cooperation between P.E. teachers, male and female genders,
and my own programs for boys and girls. Introducing an overt consciousness of the difference between the sexes is not difficult for a female teacher
if she is able to enlist the cooperation of a male teacher, at the commencement of her musical arts program. This male figure may be a teacher of
dance and music, or one of physical education. His role is that of the
masculine figure to which the boys in the musical arts program relate
themselves as males, through whom the girls in the musical arts program
establish a sense of difference in the sexes. Ideally, boys should be taught
dance in boys' classes and then brought into mixed classes to work with
girls, and both should be early and continuously exposed to the male
artist, especially as cognitive (artist as classroom guest) teacher.

Freedom of choice as to how to dance (as well as what to dance) is
very soon shown in coeducational classes. When Tim's class in nursery
school (see *The Child at Home*) composed a work to Holst's *The Planets*
there was a definite masculine approach, which emphasized the feminine
approach. The children, of their own accord, chose genders for the planets,
making the Sun a boy and the Moon a girl, and choreographing movements for these that were aggressive in attack for the first; lyrical ("full
of soft rounds," explained the infant choreographer to me, with perfect
aplomb) for the latter.

When the planets coursed the "sky," on stage *the human natures* of
the dancers, male and female, were clearly manifested.

This dance work was composed, rehearsed, produced and performed
without any adult supervision whatsoever, by children of median age four-
and-one-half years.

In dances about birds, animals, insects or plant life children instinctively
adopt differences in movement, differences in characterization, to establish
differences between the sexes in the approaches to movement as dance. A
girl will elect to be "a pretty little snake," and offer a convincingly slithery
performance as one, never stating the sex of the snake but imprinting it

with a feminine gender. A boy with long legs, dancing as a grasshopper ("early on a wintry day") was arrogantly male and heroically "died" (when the wintry weather overcame him, he having improvidently failed to provide himself with a home during the summer) while girl "bumble bees," swooped about him, buzzing as they waltzed with sanctimonious sentiments concerning their industry. The children chose the theme and here, again, no adult suggested a separation of genders, nor a style of movement, and sex of character, for these children.

Noting how responsively boys dance in classes outside the conventional ballet school, to which they are often reluctantly led, one wonders why dance classes are not taught separately for boys and girls, and these brought together for special classes in partnering—and why boys, from the inception of ballet instruction, are not taught a masculine approach to movement, preferably under male teachers. Indubitably, contemporary American boys have genuine masculine concepts for dancing, want to dance, and will dance with the most pleasurable associations when they are permitted to perform what they think of as *boy's dances.*

Most of the approaches suggested for *The Child at Home* and *The Child in School* are applicable for *The Child as a Social Person.* The teacher will find that she may make the most direct approach, and usually secure the most spontaneous response, from young children. Adolescents accumulate prejudices about the arts, saying that they dislike or "do not understand" any dance and music outside the faddist styles of their immediate generation. Younger children, and children who have been approached through good creative arts programs at early ages, are more likely to initiate musical and dance experiences, in the manner described in Bruce King's demonstrations. Older children, who have not previously made constructive approaches to dance and music (and who have formed unhappy associations with certain styles in dance and music) resist initiating original or creative work, until they have been stimulated by challenges within their groups, or through responses to the teacher's approaches.

Teachers working with children from "deprived" coteries will find that there is already a rising norm in response out of spontaneity (through programs like *Head-start,* children are being approached at early ages), and experience (more children are acquiring more knowledge conducive to helping them approach dance and music). Children of Negro, Mexican-American, Puerto Rican, Filipino and other so-called "minority" groups, from "ghettos," and children of white, English-speaking American families where the norm of illiteracy is higher than average (and the mode of residence, transient) now more quickly respond to approaches at ages 9–11 than their siblings aged 13–15. These children, especially the girls, in current 4th and 5th grades seem able to learn differences in movement with more alacrity than their older siblings now in grades 7th and 8th. (Movement difference, for example, between *walk* and *run*, which is not only a matter of accelerating or decreasing speed but also a mode of movement; and between *jump* and *leap—a jump* is a movement on two feet, simultaneously, rising and descending; *a leap* is a movement on alternate feet, rising on one and descending on the other; *a hop* is a movement on the same foot, rising and descending; all such movements are within the term of "elevation" or movements off the ground, in dance terminology.)

When set to learn a dance form like the Virginia Reel, 7th grade children now master it in less than one-quarter the time required by some 9th to 12th graders.

The teacher working with younger children, therefore, can make more and more spontaneous approaches and be fairly certain of like responses.

The teacher working with older children must make more studied approaches, and more flexible approaches, and be prepared to find that apathy or prejudice in the group rejects many approaches which immediately succeed with younger children.

Older children dislike change, whereas younger children love novelty as an element of danger—the older children grow, the more set they become in their ways, and the ways of teachers and parents who influence them. The teacher who suddenly innovates or inaugurates a totally new experience (in which failure is inherent, effort is demanded, and a standard of achievement is made integral) faces hostility and alarm as part of the response. Unless the teacher knows this beforehand, she will not think to make provisions for this part of the group experience. Forewarned, she will find ways of arming herself to engage the problems within her group.

In general, older children are embarrassed to gradually develop skills and explore consecutive areas of knowledge. They do not understand and cannot actually perform the basic musical and dance exercises which younger children are then pleasantly learning, but they resent having to start at the beginning when they are already twice the age of the beginners. The teacher's requirement is to teach the older children all that the younger are learning, so that the older ones will progress thereafter at their own or at an accelerated speed of growth; her problem is to find approaches which mask the elementary character of the subject, so that the older children respond with dignity befitting their place in society.

Elementary knowledge of dance and music can be digested in a variety of ways.

The commodity all teachers most lack is time enough and to spare. For this reason, I always make a plan for myself and adapt it according to the requirements of the group. Teachers who go cold into a class, waiting to be inspired after they get there, are likely to draw desultory and faltering response, or no response. The approach is the initial step; the necessary initiative, and knowing how to make this approach is one of the teacher's main requirements.

Mine is generally to present to the children sounds in music, and movements as "discoveries" leading towards "experiences." The children know, before I join the class, that we are working with dance and music, and they assume that they know what dance and music are, although very often they have vague knowledge. Very seldom do they really know how they relate to music as singers and instrumentalists, and to movement as dancers. And it is this knowledge that we pursue as "discovery."

After we have discovered (and proved by experimentation) some fundamental attributes of music and dance, we set to work with these substances, to develop "experiences."

This general approach, "scientific" rather than "artistic," leads into a variety of other approaches, always according to the group's abilities or limitations, and its individual requirements and areas of richness.

I usually employ a series of "key" ideas, referred to in educational semantics as the "block" method, for building interest and forming an architectural plan. Such a method protects the teacher and the group against loss of time, especially in the first lesson of a series, or at the commencement of a single lesson. The "block" method can be used in two ways: by the teacher choosing to inaugurate the building of an experiment through choice, or by the teacher delegating to the group the choice of the "key" or first building block for the lesson, or the series of lessons. All such experiences fall into two main parts: what is discovered or found out (and proven) and what is drawn as conclusions (which may be points of view on an idea).

One means of approach for response, within the "block" method, is for the teacher to offer the substance of an idea, perhaps a single word, requiring the children to develop and create from that point. (See Bruce King's use of *sad* for dance, page 221.)

It is not necessarily a focal point, since a group of children will have radical ideas as individuals. The teacher will often find that the result or response is opposite to the substance of the idea offered. In many instances this divergence is the best sign of accomplishment, showing that with an initial idea the group can travel far and fast into original themes.

Ideally, a "creative" class should be one of spontaneous and original works. In practice, I realize that many children today must be impelled or triggered into original ideas, particularly when they come into the recreational dance and music class from materially rich environments. Satiated with "canned" entertainment, they innocently proffer, as their own "created" ideas, the most cynically hackneyed and bowdlerized dance and music off the television and movie screen. Children are adept imitators and frequently can be recognized in the "creative" class as assuming the personality as well as voice and mannerisms of real life singers and dancers. Mime is in itself a theatrical art, but the performer must be fully conscious that he is giving an imitation of someone else. The danger for the children and the teacher working in a "creative" class is to presume that imitation, however smooth, is a talented piece of work, and an original idea interpreted by song or dance.

An even greater danger is for the teacher to assume that the children will create dance and music as adult artists or according to conventional ideas of entertainment. If a teacher misguidedly strives for these results she will stultify the true creativity in the group and what emerges as pleasing in the conventional view will not be creativity at all but dwarfed imitations of adult performing artists: plagiarism disguised as creativity. This will be true of any age group of children, and the danger is acutest for the youngest child, who cannot distinguish between creating and copying. Unless he finds means of expressing his ideas he may become incapable of conceiving anything like an individual point of view, far less an actual idea that is original to himself and his group.

Since my teaching is not pedagogic, but is an "approach" in order to draw *creative response*, I work to call forth the most voluntary expressions from the children. (Here let me say, to pedagogic music and dance teachers, that this *basic but conscious* development for the child in no way interferes with a later or even a simultaneous study of instrumentation or voice, or of a codified dance form like ballet. On the contrary, the first and early evocative approach to dance and music makes the child the more aesthetically sensitive, the more intelligently perceptive, when he moves into pedagogic studies of music and ballet.) "Expression" is therefore part of the form; *form* is understood and recognized.

How does one describe expression to a very young child? Musical terminology should be used as much as possible, since the greater the conscious use of musical terms the more fixed the form as art. I like the most

(text continues on page 189)

INTRODUCTION TO PHOTOGRAPHS

Drama, dance and music are important elements in the development of the growing child, as food, shelter and clothing are necessary material elements of his existence. The arts should be the source of a child's education, not a superfluous frill attached for status symbol later in life.

We are a rhythmic race; our hearts beat, our blood courses, we walk and run, in rhythms. We speak and we sing. We make music. Poetry and proverb, allegory and myth, inspire abstract thought, teach moral values, inspire the mind of the growing child. Drama, dance and music illuminate the real world and the world of imagination. The child is by nature artistic, in that he strives for self-expression, yearns to create and perform. As the artist, he establishes a personal identity.

The child is also scientific, wanting to know how and why a thing is, from what source it emanates, towards what purpose. Therefore he likes to discover the technical or scientific aspect of the arts he practices; he is made secure and powerful through accomplishment. He learns techniques and rejoices in possessing knowledge of them.

A child is like an ancient Greek: loving life, fearing death, believing in magic but seeking the meaning or scientific reason for all that fills him with awe and delight. And like the ancient Greek he passionately desires to live forever. Legends and fairy tales in his nursery culture, art and religion in his maturity, help him to find himself as the human person and to relate to the worlds inhabited by the mind, the body and the spirit.

The child needs to play, for when he plays hardest, he works hardest, and what he learns is what he discovers as experiences.

For all these and a great number of other sound reasons, a child should grow in rhythm and music, poetry and literature, and should know the arts of painting and sculpture, and design. All these are contained and may be approached within the art of dancing. Of all the arts, dance most involves the person. To dance is to make a total commitment of the human self.

[188]

1. Theodore R. Brunson, an instructor in the Suzuki method of "Talent Education" at the San Diego State College Department of Music, introduces four young people to string music.

2. The miniature instruments used by Suzuki students are explained to a pupil and his mother. Parents are taught how to tune instruments and conduct lessons at home.

3 & 4. Suzuki students begin at once to play their chosen instruments.

5. In the course of study the student will change instruments
   to suit his physical growth and manual dexterity.

6. An approach to dance begins with a discovery of movement in space, in various directions, at various levels. (Bruce King with pupils.)

7. It continues into the discovery of the self; how the human body moves, its capacities and limitations; its weight in space, and how the dancer controls weight, direction, speed, et cetera.

8. Dancing is movement with meaning, with rhythmic elements. The mind is not divorced from the body when we dance. On the contrary, the dancer is both mind and body, a thinking, feeling creature. Dance is serious artistic composition.

9. Dance is action; movement with rhythmic and dramatic elements. A dance is really a series of transient images which express an idea, convey a thought, relate an episode, depict a character. The dancer writes a story or paints a picture on the air. This dance was created as *Spiderweb*.

10. Bruce King with young students in a creative dance and music class.

11. The dancer works on the floor ... (Bruce King, *Studies in Technique*)

12. In command of space, where his body moves in various directions, levels, weights and speeds ... (Bruce King, *Designs in Space*)

13. And in elevation, a command of space above the floor. *Dancing is as close as we come to natural flight*. (Bruce King, *Studies in Technique*)

14. A dance may be about a *Cloud* . . . (Bruce King, *Cloud*)

15. About a *Ghost, Calling* . . . (Bruce King, *Ghosts*)

16. A *Ghost, Exiled* . . .

17. A *Ghost, Mad* . . .

18. Or a dance might be about an enchanted Beast . . . (Bruce King and Bettina Dearborn, *Beauty and the Beast*)

19. Who was transformed into the handsome Prince he really was . . .

20. By the love of a good and beautiful Princess.

21. And dance can be solemn and ceremonial, worshipful for Divine praise. (Bruce King, *Song of Praise*)

direct approach, and the ideal that to learn, first, the right way, the approved way, is the best short cut to the ultimately greatest achievement. I therefore make use of terms like: *allegro* and *adagio* for fast and slow; *allegretto* and *andantino* for moderately fast and a little faster than *andante* (or slow) and, also: *affetuoso*: affectionately; *dolce*: sweetly and softly; *feroce* and *fuoco*, fierce and fiery; *tranquillo*: tranquil, and *vivo*: full of life, offering explanations and asking for expressions of opposites or differences in movement and expression. (The music as accompaniment is to suit.)

The usage of such terminology prevents the exercises from falling into "play" and the sweetish sentimentality of "feeling" that is the bane of adult interpretive dancing. The child is asked to express his dance intent, either before or after he dances, so that he will think of the dance in its elements of form in movement, music and emotion. Pragmatically, the children take to themselves the names and attempt the "personifications" of Adagio, Allegro, Feroce and Dolce, Fuoco and Vivo, and so on, and are judged by the group as to how well, in dance and music, they interpret these. *Yet if asked to "express" in English-language terms they become overly self-conscious!* It is only when we deliberately attempt dramatic interpretation that we speak of "feeling" or acting within dance—but all musical expression, as song and dance, is done for me *with expression*, and the children must try to achieve the fullest expression they choose to develop.

"Creative" Work By Children

The teacher must have a thesis of her own, before she can frame one for a group of children. She finds her thesis, ideally, by inquiring what precisely is a "creative" class in dance and music.

It is an exploration of sounds and movements in environment (all that the children know, think and feel and the expressions they are capable of communicating). The exploration is a conscious effort to express and within the form of the art medium such exploration is subject to failure and necessarily involves challenge. The teacher's role is to encourage the children to seek means of solving their problems through the individual and group imagination, inventiveness and abilities. The ultimate goal is accomplishment, of the teacher's theme or idea, or its corollary or successor.

In large degree, this is the basic premise for Adelphi's Creative Centre which describes two goals for children (1) the immediate goal of making the child stretch his imagination, strengthen his capacity (to look and listen), develop his ability to concentrate, and to respond to the needs of a situation (within the dance or music class); (2) the long term goal of preserving and furthering in the child the courage and ability to initiate an idea and to make use of the tools he acquires to help bring the idea to fruition.

In the creative music classes under Helen Lanfer the distinction is made for the children between such classes and those normal to the school curricula, where a rhythm band or a music appreciation class is the general mode. In the rhythm band class the teacher (a skilled musician) plays the piano while the children follow the teacher, and/or learn to play instruments. No active part in the planning of the experience is required of the child, whose activity is ordered by the adult in charge. In the music appreciation class, children hear music which the teacher analyzes. But in a purely creative music class, as in a creative dance class, the child explores, finds his way, learns to give and take, and acquires skills and knowledge through active participation.

There are many principles of creative dance, particularly as propounded in "Modern" dance forms, but comparatively few principles and methods of approach to creative dance for children. I have not, of course, observed every approach, or studied thoroughly all those approaches I have noted, since my work is not primarily to teach dance—rather, my work is within the enormous area of researching means for establishing communication between human persons, in all forms, including through artistic norms. I have therefore chosen to rely on an authority on creative dance for children, the dancer-choreographer Bruce King, instead of attempting to describe a variety of approaches to creative dance.*

My reasons for choosing Bruce King as my resource on creative dance are several. Firstly, I know his work very well, as teacher and as choreographer-dancer, and over the last decade, during which he gradually formulated his original methods, and crystallized those he inherited in dance in adaptations to the child today. I am therefore able to write freely about

---

* Of interest to the teacher are the following recommendations by Bruce King, concerning treatises on creative dance: of the 1930s, *Power of Dance* by Madeline C. Dixon and *The Rhythm Book* by Elizabeth Waterman; of the 1940s, *Articles on Creative Dance* by Blanche Evan; of the 1950s–1960s, *Creative Dance Movement* by Gladys Andrews and statements from Virginia Tanner, of the University of Utah.

King's work, especially as he has contributed his own statements to this book, to make his principles and methods abundantly clear. Also, over the period of our acquaintance I have been able to query various aspects of King's teaching, and to obtain his explanation of theory and method.

Bruce King's work is especially attractive to me because he works with *music and dance*, because he is a dancer with music training, and because he makes use of the widest representational range in traditional and contemporary music—commissioning original scores, as those by the young American composers Paul Kueter and Douglas Nordli. An example of this musical catholicity is a program to music by Nordli, Kueter, Anton Webern, Edgar Varèse, Paul Hindemith and Maurice Ravel. Yet, despite having a musician's knowledge and respect for formal music, King also uses several other forms of accompaniment when approaching dance for children, some of them quite unconventional, like the sounds typical of skipping and clapping games children play, arranged for a "musical" motif in a dance. His is the best example, among creative dance teachers, of the dancer who makes authoritative choice and appropriate uses of all kinds of music and themes for approaching children and dance and music. He is one of the rare adults who can relate, imaginatively, to the child, while maintaining a benign authority as teacher. While his principles are austere, in the ideal of dance as art, his approaches to dance and music for children are so flexible, his respect for the individual child so much a part of his work, that he is able to adapt his methods to the greatest range of dance in education. I consider him the foremost cognitive teacher in his field.

The psychological aspect of this choreographer-dancer's work is also very pertinent to my own work, in my principles for approaching children and dance and music. He is male—a man working with dance and music; a masculine artist. This is a comparatively rare personage in the artistic life of the American child today, as read what I have written on the subject of the familial and educational norms for the child at home and the child in school. A number of children, boys and girls, now have no personal relationship with an adult male, for having no father in the home, for having no social environment which includes the male adult, and through being taught, predominantly, in school and recreation by female teachers. When I am able to introduce the male artist into an approach to children and dance and music, I consider this a fortunate development for the program. Invariably, the response from the group, boys and girls together or in separate genders, proves the need for integrating more male teachers in education for the American child today, and in no phase of education more than the artistic and the gymnastic. I am therefore interested in Bruce King's creative dance from all the perspectives in which I view it, and include it to be viewed here by the teacher making an approach to dance and music for the child.

Finally, and of extreme pertinence to my readers, Bruce King is an articulate dancer-choreographer (a comparatively rare forte) who is able to intelligibly define, describe and teach his own methods and approach to creative dance. His work in dance extends to teaching methods to teachers working with children in elementary and secondary education, and into the university fine arts and humanities courses of higher education—as noted in Bibliography under *List of Sources*, Bruce King is currently developing a curriculum in creative dance for elementary teachers, under a Federal grant to education.

His thesis, as he describes it "is that children will create dances that are more beautiful than the ones adults can teach them, by rote. In my classes in creative dance, efforts are directed towards creating and developing, rather than teaching and drilling. I try to help children develop, through dancing, a medium for sincere, direct communication. Movement improvisations seem to me to be the best means of understanding dance and discovering new ways of moving; improvisation that is directed and focused so that the dancer and those who watch (the audience) learn more about the technical and expressional aspects of human movement that is dance. Children's efforts are fragmentary but when these "pieces of beauty" are recognized by the teacher, the children grow to respect them as their experiences and the experiences of others. As they acquire technical skills in dance class, their imaginative and movement expressions are developed into real dances. Children have convictions about the reality of their feelings, and the ideas they propound, combining with technical skill in demonstrating them, are often beautiful. These convictions and impulses are the core of children's dances."

On performance by children, he says: "Good performance by children is relative to their connection, physically and psychically, with the material of the dances. When they devise dance—when they compose *original* dance—they certainly understand it; their art is by no means obtuse to them and they are intelligently concerned with their work. As example of performance: taking as source an opera-ballet, Humperdinck's *Hansel and Gretel*, a group of my children composed an original work based on the piano accompaniment, as the excerpt: *The Dance of the Gingerbread Children*. They knew the story and their movement ideas were clarified and extended under my supervision. The presentation, as a lecture-demonstration for adult audience and educators, showed what children create, and how a teacher brings such creativity into focus for an audience in theatre. Here the demonstration was to support my theory that a dance created by children can be successfully communicated to an audience. My role was to analyze the problems and draw solutions to them from the children. It is essential for the teacher to have faith in the creative power of children, which is largely dependent on the teacher's faith in his or her own creative powers."

Developing that essential faith—and a sound basis on which to pragmatically support it, must be cultivated by a teacher before she attempts to conduct a program.

The best program is through the cognitive teacher like Bruce King, who in a basic teaching act defines ideas for students and thereafter helps them qualify ideas and discoveries according to standards or ethics in art. It is sufficient for an artist to perform, in the sense of theatre, but the cognitive teacher has to be a particular type of artist: one articulate and patient enough to define his work for teacher-student communication. Such an artist-teacher is the most authoritative and inspiring source; he enchants by his art, as the composer and performer; and he establishes rapport between the child and art from the human involvement of the artist and his work.

The introduction of the cognitive teacher like Bruce King into school classrooms or educational-recreation is, in my opinion, the best means of interesting children in dance and music and of sustaining the creative instincts within our mechanized society. This cognitive teacher should deal in basic ideas, and define, as lucidly as possible, the structure of his material. A group should be prepared in advance for his visit; to extent that the conventional teacher should deliberately excite the group at the prospect of the visit of the cognitive teacher. Such visits usually last an hour and in that time more response will be elicited by the artist-teacher than a conventional teacher can hope to generate in a month of classes.

The primary value of the cognitive teacher is that, as the artist, he has genuine concern for the individual and he will automatically, rather than axiomatically, treat each student as a person despite working with members of a group. On the momentum of only one visit from a cognitive teacher I have known a conventional teacher sustain group interest in a project until the accomplishment was positively successful in terms of teaching skills and expressing original thoughts. As an example of how the cognitive teacher works with large groups of children study the *Pilot Program in Dance for Children* by Bruce King.

Pilot Program in Dance for Infants and Children

Some conventional teachers, although skilled enough in rudiments of dance and music to conduct a program for young children, find themselves tongue-tied and semi-paralyzed when faced with the typically large, boisterous groups of strange children in recreational classes, especially those for culturally "deprived" children who are unaccustomed to working in art forms. This is a common experience for Bruce King, who is regularly confronted with scores of children, at once, who do not know him, and whom he can be sure of seeing only once in the "enrichment" plan of education. Within a very short time, perhaps less than one hour, he must establish communication with them and, moreover, rapport between the group and dance. Usually, the children are of both sexes and their only common denominator is a median age. Almost always, they derive from comparable economic and social environments.

An example of the cognitive teacher's work with such large groups, typical of children in educational-recreational dance and music, is this pilot program presented by King for Dance Masters of America, Syracuse, New York, February, 1966, since presented in several other places for educators and dance teachers. Here King describes the program as a demonstration for an audience; he served as accompanist as well as director of the dance and music experience, for children aged 3 and 4. The program is easily adapted from infant class to that of children aged 5–6 and older.

> To begin, I established contact with each child by asking his and her name. Next, it was necessary to establish a relationship with the audience (educators and dance teachers, students in this demonstration class). My third relationship to the group of children began as I explained the first class form.
>
> I invited the children to suggest the movement with which we would begin our dancing, so that they should initiate the dance and know, from the commencement of our association, that their ideas were to be valued and would be used. I first defined, by action, class forms: (1) the circle;

(2) the follow-the-leader pattern; (3) all moving in a circle with a leader; (4) taking a turn alone; (5) taking a turn in twos and threes.

The children, having chosen the movement, demonstrated it to clarify it for themselves and the group, and to set tempo for the accompaniment. One of the most important principles of such work is that children learn from each other. In a peer group, when one child does something it seems possible to some of the others to emulate him on one hand; more challenging to do it and do it better, for others in the group, on the other hand.

The first circle was established by walking. When it was set around two invisible poles (places which defined the size of the circle), we ran. I asked: "How else can you travel in a circle?" The children suggested these movements: by skipping, galloping, hopping and jumping, and performed them in follow-the-leader pattern. I asked: "Who can slide?" to bring the awareness of sideway movement into the lesson. We did sliding and then a child suggested the walk again. We had begun the lesson with that movement but to have refused her suggestion should have excluded her from participation in the experience—so I asked her to walk, *backwards*. The jump-turn, and the skip-turn, were some further variations of movements already performed.

Children perform many dance movements without realizing what they are doing. The teacher must relate ordinary movement to dance and must bring the movement as dance vocabulary into the child's conscious use. The basic "two-footed" patterns are walk and run, and leap, jump, hop, skip, gallop and slide. With directional and speed variations [what might be correlated in music to range of pitch and counts of beats] and with arm coordination, these basic patterns have infinite variety; and they make up the elements of allegro in ballet.

To get the children to use the spine out of the vertical and to bring attention to the use of the arms, I asked them to perform "animal" movements. They at once named several animals, from which we got ideas stated before attempting movement. The first animal chosen to inspire movement was the elephant. Because it was a too ordinary movement— walking, swinging the arms as the trunk—the children were not immediately able to develop this movement source. We had to take time to think what the elephant was like; what he did with his trunk. Someone suggested: "He drinks water." For this, the children leaned over, stretched their arms down and then towards their mouths. On another suggestion, that the elephant eats leaves from a tree, they reached up and towards their mouths.

I pointed out to them that they were making downward and upward movements, and asked them to suggest other movements that might be performed by elephants. (By making them analyse and qualify movements and movement sources, children are led from merely imitative or literal movements into *expressive* movement that eventually, assuming musical principles, become dance.)

Cat movements were the second source, to get a different quality (a feline one) of movement, and change of level.

Thirdly, I asked the children to dance as birds. They enjoyed "flying" and spontaneously invented patterns of flight, with great gusto. Then I asked them to incorporate "landings" in their dancing, for contrasting movements to flying. And, also, to balance movement with ultimate stillness. This sequence was followed by a longer one, in which the children spontaneously assumed identities as birds. Some chose the roles of mother birds. The mother bird fed her young. Each child as a mother bird set her (invisible) nest in a special place; the nests became the dancers' focal points, with irregular flights and landings to feed the young, from and back to the nests.

An improvised dance resulted—an essentially asymmetrical one with a plot as episode and a space pattern. Half the class watched the other half perform the group-created dance. Next, the first audience became performers, while the other half watched. It is as necessary to watch and see in the learning of dance as it is to listen and hear in the learning of music.

The third section of this class was more formal, as dancing. I set up a diagonal pattern, using chairs to mark the starting positions, and gave the children a point to which movement was to be directed. Concrete objects were used to define an area of space. Elements from the first part of the class, which was *rhythmic*, were put together with movements from the second, *creative* section. In this way, the dance ideas covered in the lesson were emphasized and extended.

Best results were the conscious use of the gallop combined with the conscious use of the arms from the "bird dance." The "elephant dance" movements were used as the closing exercise in the class, to stretch the lower back, and to return the children to a movement they enjoyed and found comfortable.

As the children filed out of the room, I repeated the ceremony with which the pilot program had begun. I asked each child his or her name, recognized *the person* to whom I said "goodbye," just as I had recognized each person by his or her name at the beginning of the class.

The movement patterns within this lesson shift often; in three large sections, with several changes in each section. Children should consciously experience many different kinds of movements and bring into focus every change in movement of the dance. They should learn to recognize the kind and quality of movement, and become conscious of a vocabulary for dance and music.

This pilot program demonstrates teaching that encompasses physical movement and rhythmic movement, combining imaginative challenges for the children.

Children learning to move in a large, open area, like the gymnasium and auditorium, experience a new feeling about themselves and about movement. Acoustics in music are exciting and strange to elementary students (amplification of sounds, distortion of sounds, changes in sound—as when, by grasping an instrument being played, its sound becomes less clear and bright), opening up a whole field of exploration into the resonation of music. Movement as dance may often be as exciting and strange to children, if they have not consciously performed dance before. Children, who have only consciously known dance on film, remark that they see "dance in full" when a living dancer performs, instead of a flattened image on television and movies. Sometimes, when small children are set free in an expansive place, they retreat to a corner in which to dance. Others will dance as though enclosed in a quite restricted area, moving forward and backward instead of sideways, or in large rounds. Seldom, to begin with, do they begin to dance with jump and leap and wide swings, but rather more often skim, glide and slide, low to the floor, as though shy of using too much of the enticing large space offered to them in the auditorium. A teacher often has to coax movements in a large space, when she approaches children in the auditorium.

The change of perspective is often too revolutionary for the shy child, or the child who has not consciously danced before. The obvious physical reason for the change of perspective is space, and the possibilities of direction in space. Children, as a group, encouraged by a thoughtful, skilled teacher like Bruce King, embark on the adventure of dancing (tantamount, physically and psychically, to a daring new venture into the element of space and the nature of rhythm), while they are likely to hesitate to do so as individual dancers. In the classroom at school students grow used to two dimensions of communication, teacher-student and student-teacher; and in our modern schools, of large numbers in a class, this is more often a dictatorial teacher-student communication. In a dance class, children (sometimes for the first time in their lives) discover that space exists all around them and above them, as well as in the expanse of floor beneath their bodies. Direction exists in several angles. At first, young children, in "creative" dance, make only forward movements. Encouraged and stimulated, they move backwards and sideways. Eventually, they learn the qualities of weight, level and direction in the *conscious* act of dancing.

A teacher can usually learn something about children in the first lesson, by their earliest movements. She can tell the most sanguine and outgoing from the most withdrawn—the latter holds his elbows against his sides or tightly extends his hands and forearms, he has a characteristic stiffness of the neck and upper back. Until the child responds to the teacher and to dancing it is difficult to know his potential as the dancer, whereas a good singer will almost immediately proclaim himself by the melodic nature of his voice, and his control of its pitch and volume. At the beginning, it is always wiser to work in group dance, especially to elicit creative responses, than to single out a child and ask him to dance alone, especially in a large area which dwarfs him. In good time, he will command space, as *the dancer* . . .

Work always to discover a child's best and most facile ability to dance, sing or make music. After he has exercised his easiest gift, then work to develop latent ones. As the group works, the teacher must use every difference, every contrast to point its value for the child. I never leave a movement until an alternative movement is recognized; this is most readily performed as its opposite one but several other related movements in rhythmic and musical terms should be explored and identified by the children. They will do so in idiomatic ways; the dance and music teacher should compare this with the pedagogic terminology, thus giving the child *conscious* knowledge of what he is doing in the art form.

The first day and certainly the first week that children work in a large area they find that one *moves* in different ways and singing *sounds* differently depending on the place where we dance and sing. Space, direction, also: speed, weight and acoustics, are affected.

Among the earliest things the teacher should teach is that there are (in the principles of Delsarte) three main orders of motion: *oppositions*, when any two parts of the body move in opposite directions simultaneously; *parallelisms*, two parts moving in the same direction simultaneously; *successions*, movement passing through the entire body or any part of a body which moves the whole or whole part in a fluid wavelike impulse.*

Delsarte defined zones or realms of emotion, three main ones being the space normally occupied by head, torso and legs. Shawn writes: "Sur-

---

* François Delsarte's principles for music were also applied to dance and drama. They are briefly described in my *American Modern Dancers: The Pioneers*. In *Every Little Movement*, with an introduction by Louise Gifford of Columbia University's School of Dramatic Arts, Ted Shawn explains the master's work in modern prose.

rounding the body in all directions is space . . . Almost all of our actual life and experiences takes place beneath the top of our heads, the common, natural experiences of every day." And it is in this space that children tend to work, while it is beyond this space they dance when they have original ideas of expression. The child tends to dance towards the teacher because, as Shawn points out, in front of us are the things seen best, thus better known, better understood, and feared less. Gesture in front of us thus becomes more vital; to the sides more emotional . . . whereas gestures ending behind us may be motivated by rejection ('Get thee *behind* me, Satan'), negation or fear of the unknown, unseen and inexplicable. All human beings reveal themselves through gesture—the dances children create are their most eloquent revelations about themselves. (See "stick-figure" choreography, page 200) When they sing it is the manner in which they sing, more than the song, which the teacher should note.

We move, generally, in an individual rhythm (particular to the one) and also in a typical rhythm (one fairly common to a type of person). These natural rhythms, when matched, allow an aesthetic development within a group, such as when a boy and girl are well matched as partners; or an ensemble moves, we say, "as one" although it is made up of several dancers. Children acutely sensitive to rhythms are often unhappy or awkward dancing with partners and in groups who have strong difference in rhythm; these same unhappy, clumsy dancers suddenly achieve harmony and ease when placed in another group whose rhythm is better suited to the individuals' rhythms. The same applies to singers, but is always more overt for dancers.

The very fact of difference and contrast inspires original ideas and what is called creativity in a group, since counter-rhythms in dance, and part song, or fugues, in music, allow the teacher to develop interesting combinations, all of which she must, as has been emphasized, point out to the children for their *conscious* use. Children like to know (and should know) that they are concerned with time in rhythms and vice versa, qualities of tone and pitch in music, and of space in dance.

Space, in dancing, is direction and focus, levels that rise from and descend to the floor, and dynamics which qualify movement in space. One initial lesson in movement is a simple but scientific one which the teacher can develop on the pendulum—levels, directions, speeds, rhythms of an object of certain weight and various suspensions; and/or of objects of varying weights in a single suspension.

"STICK-FIGURE" CHOREOGRAPHY: COMPOSITIONAL EXERCISE FOR DANCE AND DRAMA

normal or "human" area of movement
what the person sees and knows, familiarly:
in front, and from the face (below the head)
down to the earth or floor.
typical of movement that is robust and exuberant.

also of movement that is aggressive;
arms akimbo and feet widely paced is uttermost
gesture and stance of aggressiveness.

mysterious area of movement
the space behind the person, unseen and unknown
typical of movement that has more abstract
quality than the movement within the normal
or "human" zone.

mystic area of movement
above the corporeal being, over the "human" zone;
an area potent and ethereal, with movement and
gesture invocative of a power that is spiritual.

stick-figures by P.L.M.

all rounded movements are more lyrical than
angular ones, which are more staccato.

Exercises in Discovery of Dance

The child's first conscious discovery about dancing is how he relates to space and what movement means as travel and stillness in space (comparable to sound and silence in music). The lessons in high and low, light and heavy, loud and soft, fast and slow, and the exercises that emerge from them, are good beginnings of self-awareness. The teacher has to keep watch and remark or note (for the group as a whole) what these discoveries are, enlisting whenever possible the children's own descriptions of *what is felt, and what happens,* within a movement phrase or a musical exploration of balance or equilibrium and fall of the human body. Examples of rhythmic exercises (see the Farmingdale Project) are good as basis for the teacher's development of her own class discoveries.

Almost always, children will, of their volition, incorporate contrasts within the simplest composition and these contrasts must always be noted for them, so that they understand, from the beginning of their experiments with dance and music, that one of the disciplines of these arts is the avoidance of monotony and the development of dynamics. If and when monotony is deliberately assumed for a melancholy or comic effect, then its content and meaning must be within the dance or musical context—on purpose and not by chance. When an effect is obtained by chance, it must be analyzed and recognized.

Varieties and differences in strong or subtle contrasts offer materials for improvisational work. The child, however brilliantly he improvises, should always be urged to refine a work until it stands true and strong enough to be repeated, and also to be performed by someone other than its creator. As soon as a child creates something of worth, the best way to reward him, and to preserve his work, is to delegate him to teach it to others. Thereafter, whenever possible, write or record it to keep, to use as reference and for debate in later evaluations of the child's initial effort and other factors within the program. The tape recorder and some elementary knowledge of music and dance notation will here serve the teacher well.

Teach children that all "works" have beginning and end, and that the tonic element in music is also a tonic quality in dance—a center or focus towards which to rise and fall away from, to tense and relax.

When I work with "exceptional" children, who are deaf-mutes and emotionally disturbed, I extend this exercise until every child in the group has benefited by it. Within a group of "average" or physically, mentally and emotionally normal children (the kind of children representative of the groups described in this book) the equilibrium exercise is shorter in the course—but none the less significant. All kinds of children, and a great number of adults, are deeply affected by the atavistic fear of falling, and before children will learn to dance they must explore and experiment with this fear, from within their physical, psychical selves.

Shawn writes in *Every Little Movement*: "The *forms* of falling are infinite—the principle of falling is one." At first, the children fall in two ways, precisely reflective of their natures: with glee and boisterous enjoyment, and with hesitation and terror of harming themselves. The regulation gym mat or fair facsimile should be provided for the lessons in falling, and the children should work in bare feet (indeed, the more they dance in bare feet the better they understand movement and *levels* of movement).

I begin with free fall—falls by every child in his way; the child's natural or chosen manner of falling. Next, we work on falls from a variety of levels—sitting, stooping, kneeling, standing, all heights that do not hazard a hurtful fall but that spice the act of falling with a certain degree of daring and what the child assumes to be risks of "a bad fall." Past this phase (he has fallen and survived the fall) we begin to work on studied falls and opposites of arising; descent and ascent in all levels.

If the dance and music teacher is working with the gymnastic instructor and drama teacher in the program, these should develop understanding of movement for the children, aspects of physical movement with emotional or dramatic content or *meaning in movement*, including falling and rising movement. Music in its idea of *tonic* is the corollary of dance in its idea of equilibrium.

Working with the human person, as one works with falling, is a complex affair. Conventional teachers making use of my programs ask what "falling" has to do with dance and music. My reply is: everything, since the fall connotes the rise, and alternation in movement is synonymous with dance and music.

The child learns best and learns most happily when he perceives a fact or assimilates a thought through himself: his person. Children's bodies are infinitely aware, the senses of feeling, the perceptions we think of as emotions, the very fabric of the thought process, all are within what we consider the "bodily" creature. Children do not distinguish between feeling and thinking, which is why they express creatively in art forms with more eloquence and truth than through communication media adults accept as logical, instead of romantic. Even in their most oblique expressions through the arts children are self-revelatory.

The youngest child, like the adolescent child, has an enormous love and respect for the self, and the wonderful body he inhabits. And the child, too, has a lively, more or less scientific curiosity about himself. This love and respect, and curiosity, are the main rapport between teacher and students in a creative dance and music class. The approach then, is to discover three particular objectives: *the self*; the relationship of the self to others, i.e. *other selves*; and the physical territory: *the world*. Discovery entails finding out limitations and capacities, modes of communication (between persons, and also between places as in traveling from one point to another, or moving from a "key" idea to the other ideas). Discovery is also finding out how we think and feel; *what happens*, mentally, physically, during such communication. Ergo: discovery is something like falling and discovering how many ways there may be to fall and, as the opposite of the fall, how to rise. Applying the principle of falling and rising to music and dance, the teacher moves the child into dance and music with the same curiosity that the child innately feels about himself.

Discovering movement sources should extend from how one and also all in general (persons in a group) fall and rise—and how we bow and *what bowing says or means*. In daily course, we give very little thought to our backs, presenting our fronts as our obvious selves—but the back is an eloquent portion of the body and presents us as we truly are, behind the mask of the face and the gestures of the hands. An erect spine and buoyant gait exude confidence and well-being; as the bowed back, with the bent head, is a universal sign of suffering and defeat. Therefore, in my classes, right after we have learned that *falling and rising sounds* are like pitch in music, and that *falling and rising movements are part of dance*, we begin to discover *expression*, as through the means of the human bow.

If I correlate the dance and music class with a class in art *per se*, then clay and other malleable materials, as well as drawing, painting and soap sculpture, provide ample means of elaborating on this lesson. I make great use of pipe-cleaners, which can be manipulated by very young children, and with the drawings of "stick figures" which are anonymous (they have no faces) and can be sexless (but can also be put into masculine and feminine shapes of attire). With pipe-cleaners and stick-figures children rapidly learn to artistically perceive form. They learn the elements of chore ography, in that what they model or draw lies either within or without the capacities of the human dancer.

This is an essential discovery for the child who creates dance, especially when he works with dance *and music*. Music is a larger, freer dimension than dance and the composer can work on several levels simultaneously, although many or all these "levels" may be divergent—for an explanation of this nature of music, see *Enjoying Opera* pages 74–75. Dance is bounded by certain laws, one being gravity, or the pull of the earth or floor, from which the greatest dancer can only jump so high, and over which the fleetest runner can only speed so fast, and no more. The pitch of sound can rise above the hearing of the human ear. This is one of several differences between dance and music and the child needs to discover these differences in order to work within both art media. Often, a creative child will mentally make a dance-and-music piece that is best suited for a mutant performer—he then discovers that there are no seven-footed dancers available to perform his composition. What does the teacher do in such an instance, when the radical composer is subject to censure or ridicule among his peers? She gives him opportunity and time to solve his problem, scoring the point for the group that problems exist to be resolved in life as in art.

In one instance where a child in my class had, indeed, composed a piece for a seven-legged rhythm, she resolved her problem by requiring a right or left dancer to alternately dance on one leg. It was an eccentric dance but not to say beyond the norm of modern dance, where eccentricity is currently a vogue.

The conventions of art as well as the unconventional ideas in art have to be discovered by the child, for him to have a workmanlike grasp of his medium. But, as is surely obvious, the wider the approach within all the arts, the richer the child's ultimate knowledge. For this practical reason I urge the integration of dance and music with painting, drawing and modelling classes, and consider all these classes (in dance, music and arts of color and design) *de rigueur* for drama classes. Fortunate, therefore, is the teacher who singly executes a wholly integrated "creative arts" class for a group, with sufficient experience to approach all the arts. As fortunate is the teacher who collaborates with other teachers working within an integrated "creative arts center," and in these circumstances the children benefit most, since they enlarge their associations with the adult world through an assembly of teachers.

Understanding and sympathetic though I am, of the many problems teachers encounter, I nevertheless feel that too often they waste their energies and opportunities by complaining about the materials and facilities they are given. A more constructive and practical idea is to look at dance and music *per se* as the substances or materials, and let the children within the group discover, experimentally or creatively, the materials. *To begin*: fall and rise. To continue: *bow*, and explore all methods and meanings of bowing. Learn to look and listen, to move, and to explore and distinguish what one hears, sees and feels.

Agnes de Mille, an original choreographer whose structural dance is based on ballet and modern dance forms as well as folk dance forms, begins all her classes with running and walking, because adults forget how to run and assume ways or manners that are not natural. Bruce King, in his creative dance classes for boys, always asks for diagonal crossings of a room, travel between two farthest points, in a variety of movements: skip, hop, gallop, and so on, to distinguish individual sense of movements.

Helen Lanfer's music workshops, primarily to educate teachers to teach music, require *learning to listen*, with one exercise based on listening to how many sounds can be made with the clapped hands . . . and how many of such sounds, put together, might make a "composition." This idea, utilized for children in a music class, is a discovery that may be made into an experience, by the premise that *if you can explain (or recognize) the sounds, you may use them.* (See the Farmingdale Project, *Exploratory Experiences*, in *Appendix*, and *Sound Sources*.)

"Discovery" of a drum, for instance, includes how many different sounds can be produced from one drum, and its various parts, and the musical possibilities of any one or any combinations of instruments are infinite. But first the child must know something about rhythm and pitch, and the rudimentary attributes already described. It is when he *consciously* puts together loud and soft; high and low; fast and slow sounds that he begins to compose music.

And it is when he begins to move *conscious* of the weight of his body, of the parts of his body, in relation to the time in which he moves, the space in which he travels, the rhythmic tenor of these movements, that he begins to compose dance.

"Creative" work in dance and music, however, is not wholly and always "free" to the extent where it owns no relationship with a known form. It often is necessary to approach children with a formal concept of dancing, before they will work towards discovering original or individual versions. Many "free" exponents of dance and music courses for children disagree with this principle, but I have learned that it is sometimes necessary, to motivate a group to creative work.

Students learn quickly at any age when they know *how to look* and *how to listen.* American education spends millions of dollars on "remedial reading," acknowledges illiteracy among students who are "problem readers" (and seem apt to be shunted into special schools, colleges and crafts for "non-readers"—an appalling solution!) and struggles to devise formulas for learning that are "new" and "easy." Memory is the grave factor in learning—how quickly or how slowly the student "takes in" what he is taught depends on how well he can hear and see, and remember what he has heard and seen. While educators fail to recognize that children have to be taught how to look and how to listen, before they can command research in libraries and laboratories, the student flounders about in a wasteland where the expensive audio-visual materials offered him are useless.

The first job for the teacher is to discover if the children, as a whole class, know how to look and listen. Can they see and recognize what they see? Can they hear and identify the sounds heard? There are "shapes" that are integral to dance and music, images shaped in movement, and organized sounds, and intervals of silence and sounds. Verdi wrote of "the shape of sounds" as a reality.

The second job for the teacher is to discover how much the children know about themselves, *their physical selves*, in the dimensions of time and space. Beyond knowing right from left, here are some of the primary things I teach for dancing: what are up and down; what are high and low; what is *reaching?*—or stretching. What are backwards and forwards, and can we move backwards and forwards in a straight line? a slanting line? a curved line (like a round or turn)? and in what other ways, such as sliding, gliding, running, walking, crawling, and so on, do we move backwards and forwards? What about a movement that is neither backward nor forward, but *sideways?* How many ways are there in which we can reach by some *kind* of movement? (for instance, standing or sitting or lying still and *stretching*), and by a *whole* movement? (the full act of moving the body from one place to another, as by sliding, gliding, running, walking, crawling).

How does your body allow you to *move?* How many parts of you are "hinged" and can be bent? where: backwards? forwards? sideways?— and (for the various degrees of bending) how high or how low? how fast or how slow? What about a turn or twist? How does your body twist and how far, in which direction? Are there, for instance, movements that are two twists in themselves, as when one twists *sideways* and *downwards?* or *sideways* and *upwards?* How tightly will the body curl, like a worm, so that it is furled shut (like closed petals of a flower) and then unfurled or uncoiled (worm or flower according to the animal or vegetable choice of teacher and child!) and *how slowly*, or *how quickly?*—and in how much space: a *little* space? or a *great* space?

We have here moved the child consciously into *time and space*, the elements in which he has lived from birth, but which he seldom acknowledges or understands and that no one has yet told him he *uses*. The student must know time and space before he can work as an athlete or an artist, for in both the gymnastic and the artistic life he commands (and is subject to) time and space.

What about speed in movement: how fast is fast and how slow is slow?—what are *possible* degrees of fast and slow? What is *soon*, as to now, a little later, sometime, then, but *soon* as differentiated from a *long time ago* and *a far time away to come*. What are present, past and future? When we dance, we are here, there and moving in all the ways we have examined above—always seen as *being here* which is a long or a short *time* ago and also a far or a near *space* divided *as here from there.* How do we reach *here* from *there?*—through what kind, or what combinations of kinds of movements? (to which the teacher must add all those she can lay tongue to—wriggling, weaving in side-stepping, counter movements of to-and-fro and side-to-side, combinations added to the basic movements of backwards, forwards and so on). And how much *time* does it take for us to reach from here to there, in the various kinds of movements used for the reaching? When we are *here,* we are at a *point of arrival* that, when we move to *there,* becomes a *point of departure*; i.e.: we are doing two things at once and two things are happening together.

Teach the children a clear idea of *time and space* and some of the infinite means of moving and *not moving* (as *stillness* and as *silence*) but of remaining *alive.* It is extremely important for the teacher to clarify and to ascertain that the entire group understands silence and stillness for what they are, since many children believe these to be a form of being dead; inert, and without thought and feeling. A knowledge of silence and of stillness leads naturally into an inquiry into emotion. I repeat the movements that have now become consciously known to the children and require them, individually and as a group, to express the emotion connected with movement. In composing a dance about space-craft, we had the following discussion:

ME: "What is the *highest* high?"

BOY: "A missile shot into outer space!"

ME: "What sort of movement does that require?"

BOY: "A *high, fast,* "up" movement, *very* straight!"

ME: "Then make a high, fast, upward, very straight movement and tell us what you feel. Let us all watch to see what will happen."

Feet move together, legs straighten, arms are raised and palms placed together; the body collects its full force, the face shows the intensity of the emotion, the child launches himself, like a rocket, as high, fast and straight *up* as he can. He says (in his own words) that he is exhilarated beyond belief, and unable to restfully and in full control return to his non-rocket state, he rushes about the room, prances, leaps, curvets, whoops and must be captured, returned to the group, asked to attend to the next demonstration: what is the *lowest* low? If it is *deep in the ground,* the child becomes a mole and burrows or is a worm or snake and slithers; if it is *deep in the sea or lake,* the child dives and swims. We qualify and observe the differences in emotions and movements, since to leap into the air, to dig into the ground, and to dive into water are all different. To the elements of time and space we have added a conscious knowledge of how we move, or *feel* we move, in air, earth and water.

The children, of course, do not really know what it is to fly as a rocket flies—but they think, they feel they know. So it is not essential that the children shall have actually experienced diving and swimming in water—it is sufficient to this moment that they know, or think they know what it is to dive and swim. The same applies to delving in the earth—and emerging from the earth, which is a demonstration of a very *low, slow* movement illustrated by a child. Here the requirement of the dance was to incorporate low and slow in one movement. The composition was a dance about "growing out of the ground up into the air."

GIRL: I am inside the ground, low, low down—as low as "lowest."

From a seated position she falls back on her heels, assumes, quite instinctively, the foetal pose, hands clasped and tucked under her chin, eyes closed, face drawn down to the drawn-up knees, the spine curved at its tightest arc, the bare toes rolled inward as far as they will go. A quite breathless pause— no one breathes, for all the children in the group catch their breaths and many of them close hands into fists, pull their lips in between their teeth; a few shut their eyes and then open them quickly when they discover they cannot see the low, slow movement.

From the foetal pose the girl opens herself full length on the ground, prolonging the "low" movement, and as slowly as she can control the timing of the movement, and then "grows" from seed to tree, complete with waving branches (arms and hands and fluttering fingers), on highest tiptoe to complete the contrasting movements of low and slow, which are high and quick. She later choreographed a group work about dying in winter and coming to life in spring, for a religious Easter concert.

I always require contrasting movements in a group, so that children will know *differences* in movements. Sometimes, two children work together, or two groups, for the contrasting; sometimes one child performs, consecutively, the opposites of values in timing, weight, direction.

We work with music, sometimes with music whose time the child asks for—time in music as fast and slow being the element children most readily *consciously* realize. At other times the child "blocks out" the movement and then repeats the movement within music, often requesting a change in music because the first choice, or the teacher's choice is rejected as being not quite right.

My elementary training, as a very young child, was under a teacher whose précis for approaching dance and music was adapted from the Montessori methods of teaching. My fellow students and I therefore learned from an approach made overtly and precisely to our senses, and responded in a physical manner to both dance and music.

In such concepts, music is felt, imagined and seen through movement, and dance is constructed and created as a visual or corporeal part of music, or of the elements of music. Movement in response to all musical stimulus, before initiating movement within dance form, is, I believe, the crucial elementary education of a dancer.

Using the tonic property of music as definition, the dancer employs energy and the relinquishing of energy—quite naturally, this force is related to gravity, but gravity in dance is dependent on the dancer's will. From my own training, and from my extensive uses of it in working with children for thirty years, I am convinced that physical movements act more powerfully on the total organism than any other medium, because they draw direct responses from the human instincts. Only by these means does a child fully understand concepts related to time and rhythm in music and dance.

Musical terms are difficult to translate into precise verbal equivalents; more so than dance terminology, since dance can be visually illustrated as movement. By using the inherent relationship of movements with musical elements to music *per se*, actions and sounds as one become the base of approach to dance and music.

Such training entails study under a dancer who is a musician, but appears to be feasible in some aspects of dance if inaugurated under a music teacher, as evidenced in the Farmingdale Project, which conducted a pilot program for developing musicianship through rhythmic studies in music and movement.

This approach was developed from ideas originated by Dalcroze, who proposed that physical movement be combined with music for the most effective development of musicianship—a subject approached, in his time, through isolated aural and rhythmic experiences. The Farmingdale Project's program was designed to assist students in discovering their musical resources through experiences with a variety of musical elements, some isolated, some in synthesis.

The student's body assumes the role of a musical instrument, experiencing musical stimulus combined in hearing, thought and action. "Movement, the source of physical rhythm, is itself the means for rhythmic awareness. In experiences unencumbered by instrumental or vocal techniques students learn to transform something abstract into something with life and meaning."—In essence, the précis here is the same as that described for my own training.

Movements were analyzed: those used in ordinary life being steps, gestures and swinging movements. Musically, such movements alter chiefly through the degrees of weight (body weight) deployed, and the manner in which the body is used—levels and directions, relative in space, are other factors to consider. These three types of movement (step, gesture, and swinging the body or part and parts of the body) are interchangeable: each may assume a leading or take on a supporting function. Thus, they may be used to represent various musical equivalents, in time and space, considered as movements equivalent to aural effects in time.

The *step*, in particular, is flexible in both time and motion, it is capable of almost any temporal effect, from the most simple metrical succession of equal units to the most rhythmical designs.*

The Farmingdale Project brilliantly organized experiences of this kind in the musical elements of rhythm, melody and harmony. Class activities emerging from this pilot program were initiated by asking the students to jump vertically and return to the floor-spot from which they jumped. The action was linked to a musical motive represented by three consecutive notes of equal length, followed by one staccato chord—the landing from the jump was required to coincide and finish with the chord. The first was played on the piano at a different tempo each time, without prior warning to the students. *Report*: "This experience resulted in the realization that they could determine, by hearing and thinking, simultaneously, whether a movement represented a rhythmic goal, or a preparatory function. The effects of rhythmic structure, experienced with a single movement, provided an essential preparation for tempo. Even more important, the experience led the students to *think while acting in musical time*."

---

* Such studies should have greatest significance for dance teachers, since the 20th century or neoclassical ballet has a pronounced musical nature, rather than the dramatic one of its older tradition as *ballet d'action,* or story ballet. The choreographic inventions of Massine, Nijinska, Balanchine and others are often symphonic and Balanchine still tirelessly explores the musical elements of dance. His *Serenade,* with the music of Tchaikovsky's *Serenade in C major for String Orchestra,* "tells its story musically and choreographically, without any extraneous narrative," and serves to illustrate the thesis of musical movement, described here. His *Symphony in C,* to Bizet's *Symphony in C major,* is another example, and perhaps the best one is his *Symphonie Concertante,* to Mozart's *Sinfonia Concertante in E-flat major, for Violin and Viola* (K.364), in which two ballerinas correspond to the solo instruments: viola and violin, with an uncanny and bewitching fidelity. A great body of work from this choreographer has come to be called "Balanchine Ballet" and is controversial as a "Balanchine system," since he must actually make the human dancer into a *musical* instrument. Such training, however, is not merely a personal choreographic idiosyncrasy and the "musical" dancer should in fact be formed in the classroom, in order to perform within 20th century aesthetics of the art.

This class of students, 6th through 8th Grades, were not trained musicians or dancers and, up to this point, the Project's pilot program's use of music and movement had been sporadic, a combination of stops and starts, lacking the integrating principle essential to musical flow or continuity. The same example was used to introduce varieties of tempo in a context of undetermined meter. Thus, in the second, a series of steps beginning on the ictus (the beat, as of a pulse) was continued four steps after the playing ceased, regardless of the prevailing meter.

Each of the seven examples' new tempi demands a different type of movement determined by speed plus energy.

Sustaining one of the units of pace was achieved by combining skips, leaps and claps.

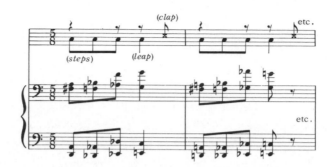

Three short steps were followed (on the 4th beat) by a leap high enough to keep the body in the air until the following ictus. This ability to control height and level of leap, *within musical elements* of time and rhythm, was further developed by shifting the temporal location of the ictus.

Here the air-borne clap becomes the ictus and the descent or landing after the leap is less significant. These completely opposed motifs were fitted into a musical phrase, adding a resting point.

The original motif was then modified by contrasting or expanding one or both of the musical cells.

The effect is mastered in these stages: (1) Measure 1 repeated until signal to change to measure 2, continued into signal, to return to measure 1—but if a third signal is given the change would be to measure 3, see above. (2) The same sequence, except that measure 2 or 3 is performed only once before returning to measure 1. (3) Measure 1 is repeated until signal to change to measure 4, which is repeated until next signal. The movement on the dotted quarter becomes a lunge, not a skip. (4) The same sequence is repeated, except that measure 4 is performed only once.

After mastering this series of exercises, the Farmingdale Project noted, students were able to recognize these elements in a phrase of music.

The experience was realized in movement and then notated as music. (The example was then "orchestrated," using a few percussion instruments. A carry-over into singing was evident in performance of a canon by Hindemith and the speaking chorus of the *Geographical Fugue* by Toch, by the 31 students from Grades 6th through 8th who participated in the Farmingdale Project.)

Such formal musical methods, combining with movement as exploratory or introductory principles for dance, may be applied for younger students, with more primitive instruments than the piano making improvisational music.

In the San Diego Project, children in Grade 2nd (median age 7) began by exploring "sounds we hear in the early morning," which could be imitated on the classroom "orchestra," with these results:

SOUNDS	INSTRUMENTS
Alarm clock	Triangle
Bird	Light bells on stick
Little brother playing	Tambourine
Scraping shoes	Sand blocks
Mother sweeping porch	Sand blocks
Footsteps in the hall	Drum
Church bells	Triangle
Two barking dogs	Drum and voices

After developing the précis for composition out of the San Diego Project for a dance-and-music creative class of 6 and 7 year old children, I suggested they compose a work on an *early morning* theme, and on completion of the music tape-recorded it for the dance score. Over a six week period, working for 55 minutes three times a week, sixty children composed the music and choreographed dancing for a full-scale work *they* titled: *Early Morning and Children's Night-time.* The class divided into committees and one committee undertook to define and explain the work; the reason for "children's" night-time sounds, movements and moods was "because children's night-time comes earlier and looks and sounds, and smells and feels different from grown-ups' night-time." This work, when completed, was theatrically sound enough to be presented in assemblies for schools in the district; the performances held the attention and earned the enthusiastic responses of other students, from kindergarten through 5th Grade.

Such an acid test is proof positive of the worth of a created work in dance and music, since children in the elementary grades are seldom diplomatic in their relationships with their peers. On the contrary, such audiences are hypercritical of children's compositions, and so entirely honest in their criticism that they will not put up, as the audience, with shoddy work. They will not applaud anything or anyone they do not like, or which fails to communicate and earn response.

This same group (following the pilot program of the San Diego Project) learned to count music and relate it to dance movement through stamping and clapping experiments with rhythmic response to patterns, from the exercises of counting meters in 7 and 4 on page 155.

Changing meter, by use of five resonator bells and also by piano accompaniment, in the notes d,f,g,a,c, inspired the composition of simple songs, which were used for song-and-dance "action" works, of themes that related an incident or episode for *early morning* and *night-time*. They became extraordinarily adept at learning to shift movement in meter. To be noted: the San Diego Project's pilot program taught young students examples of changing meters (2 and 3) by singing such songs as *Little Bird, Go Through My Window*, from grade school music text book *Music Through The Day*.

Groups of my students tried dancing to various meters, alternated for familiar, simple songs like *Twinkle, Twinkle Little Star* and *Did You Ever See A Lassie?* in 2/3, 4/4, 2/4 and 5/4 meters.

In expanding it for my own work, I evaluated the 2nd Grade experiences of the San Diego Project as among the greatest accomplishments of a class of students median age 7. The teacher was exceptionally well suited to working in this kind of project, being the young mother of pre-school children as well as a teacher trained in the necessary techniques of approach. In addition, she happened to be the wife of the composer-consultant for the project, and, quite unintentionally, an atmosphere of great warmth and happy ease permeated the entire experience in the classroom. Speaking to some of the children thereafter, one gained the impression that the experience in toto had been a memorable childhood experience, and one in which the children had won confidence to make approaches of their own to dance and music.

"What did you learn in that class?" I asked a child; who replied, distinctly and precisely: "I found out that I am really just mad about music."

He had made acquaintance with Brubeck and Partch, and liked them very much, describing Partch as "just about the wildest guy there is" but adding that Partch was "very easy to understand; all you need to do is listen and he tells you what he is getting at in the music." This child had become very interested in the outré musical styles of his age, and offered me a newspaper clipping for my files concerning a "futuristic" piano specially built in London for a science-fiction film which purportedly enables a pianist to blend the sounds of the piano with those of woodwinds, strings and percussion instruments, as a one-man symphony orchestra. At the time, this was the most coveted possession of the child who, according to his parents, had evidenced not the slightest interest in music and music-making until his experiences in the San Diego Project's pilot program—which was basically a project to explore approaches and teaching techniques through contemporary music in the elementary and junior high school grades. Moreover, another new development was that the child had become an omnivorous reader—of everything to do with "new" music, and of quite a bit about music, in general.

It is comparatively easy to correlate a dance experience with one in music.

As a group of children explores kinds of movements, and distinguishes them with *conscious* knowledge of how they control these movements by their bodies (within space, time, and so on) the teacher should ask each child to put together various movements as experiments. *From these experiments and the emotion within the action comes created dance. Moreover, the child is fully conscious that he is creating dance, and when the dance is within music then he is consciously working with dance and music.*

My principles are to lead the child to conscious knowledge of the substances of music and dance, and thereafter to invite him to experiment with these, because as he experiments with *conscious knowledge*, he quickly and easily acquires *conscious use* of the art form and its basic terminology. Ergo: the child learns to work towards the ideal of creating form in art: a masterwork, or masterpiece.

The teacher of any subject will at once realize the nobility of this concept for the child, who is enlarged within himself through accomplishment, and who is measured within his peer group by achievement. To play at dance and music is witless and eventually tedious; to *work* at it is to accomplish and, eventually, to achieve.

This book does not allow space to develop principles for an entire course (which entails a philosophy for the teacher, and means to teach the child conscious recognition and control of various parts of the body; of basic expressions in gestures and movements; degrees of movements, and content or *meaning* within context, or *form*). However, what I write here and in *The Child in School*, with some references to *The Child as Artist*, should give the reader a plain but workmanlike theory for developing the individual program.

The ethics of this program should qualify the work as being of an *artistic* substance, despite the obvious twin natures of its gymnastic and scientific substance. All physical movement as dance must be qualified as being substance within dance arts; all acoustical and other scientific observations about music must be qualified as pertaining to systems of creating organized sound which is not noise *per se* but is Music.

The teacher working with dance and music must never deviate from these ethics if the children are to recognize them and accept them as their own.

When a group meets regularly, the teacher soon sees a levelling off which is in part a rising up—the forward, ruder children are contained within the group either as constructive leaders or as an aggressive, active element, while at the same time the shy and quieter children are discovered and thereby discover themselves as being of worth in having a particular talent or adeptness.

A means of accelerating this process is to ask the chief fault-finder to work constructively to repair or correct a work he considers poor—and to stand in the judgment of his peers as having bettered or worsened the original. After every original or created work, the group should discuss it as to its form, content and degree of success of communication or interpretation. The discussion should begin with the loudest and more restless children, who are compelled to let off steam, and proceed to the quietest and slowest children, to give them time to form their opinions—sometimes, on the basis of the comments that precede theirs, to organize ideas of distinct worth.

When a work is poor or bad, the children must decide by discussion and reconstruction how to change it for the better, while maintaining the original idea. This attempt must be made even if the idea is not feasible within its context, since in the reconstruction better or different ideas will certainly evolve. The teacher's objective is to develop a fruitful experience in itself, regardless of how the experiment begins . . . any point of arrival at a failure is also the point of departure towards a success.

Having discovered his relationship to time and space, a discovery of Self, the discovery of others is the next development for the child in dance. He does this through dancing in a group, dancing as a partner, and also by *consciously* looking at others dancing—eventually, by arranging movements for another child or several children, as when he teaches something he has composed.

Discovering others, awareness of another's solid body and personality, is very necessary for the child. Without this discovery, he may never be able to understand that outside himself there exist persons as real as himself, like to him in many ways, yet so unlike as to be different, to be "one of a kind," as *he* is one of a kind.

Everything a child *knows* he first *learns*, and a child learns rapidly (he has a tremendous rate of physical and mental growth in his earliest years) and does not inform us, day by day, or hour by hour, what he has gradually come to know. Much of this first knowledge is distorted, because the child takes the literal but not the meaningful statement as fact, and unless we can correct miscomprehensions communication breaks down between parent or teacher and child. The only means of knowing that the child has misunderstood is to get him to express or explain what he assumes he understands; therefore the more he responds and in the most expressive ways, the more we learn about him. Often he cannot *tell* us what he will dance, sing, act and draw for us.

Some miscomprehensions are ludicrous to the adult but terrifying for the child, like a little girl who (cast to dance Woe) revealed that "holding your head in your hands" seemed horrible to her, because she had heard of someone who did this, and assumed that the poor woman lifted her head off its neck and sat in a chair, holding the severed head in her lap! (Then there is the little boy who shuddered to hear an adult reading aloud, about a man who "threw his eyes around the room and out the window.") "Woe," in this instance, realized, through the dance we were creating, that to hold one's head is to sink into melancholy, to turn away from the world in grief, to nurse one's great misery in private. She learned a new word, a new dance, and corrected a horrid misunderstanding in the same day.

In our mechanized society, the awareness of the I and You appears to be lessening, and many groups of adults are attempting to cultivate this awareness through self-improvement cults based on modern dance forms and calisthenics, and aspects of Zen Buddhism. Children gain this awareness without cult, by dancing together. Every child dances in a special way because every human creature moves in his own rhythms, as has been explained. Dance sharpens the perceptions or awareness of this human difference, particularly when children dance together and in the part-performer, part-audience ways I have described.

Anne moves heavily, even when she attempts, consciously, to move lightly—she moves lightly as Anne, but always more heavily than Barbara, who is a light-footed, delicately moving creature by nature. Yet they dance with the same skill and concentration, performing the same steps in the same time.

Bodies are different, as when Caroline discovers (a thing she never knew until now) that she has tight, hard muscles and cannot stretch or perform the looping movements that are so easy for Diana, a child with prehensile toes and sinewy limbs who, with ease, coils and uncoils like a pretty little serpent. However, Diana cannot dance with the force and drama of the intense Caroline, who seems to have been packed tautly into her vibrant skin.

Boys who leap with fine elevation, bouncing like thistledown on the ground, almost touching their fingertips to the "flies" on stage, may turn out to be poor partners, better suited to solo roles.

In the invariable differences there are always compensations, as when a child has the poorest possible body for *the dancer* but turns this frustration into good account as *a choreographer, a teacher, a designer, a singer* or *musician,* or some other valuable and meaningful kind of person.

In the musical arts program there is time enough, a space and a place, and opportunity, for the child to seek and find himself—and find others, too.

In dancing and acting, the child purges himself of a great deal of anger and fear—emotions destructive to himself and others. For therapy, such dance and drama are good in themselves as medicine, but even the angry, frightened child can eventually learn to turn the release through dance and music into a formal or structured piece of work. When the teacher succeeds in teaching objective ideas then the child can put his secret feelings (sometimes, so secret that they are unrealized by himself) to work within the form of the dance, or the mood of the music, or the theme of the song he composes. I have found that one way of teaching such objectivity is to ask a child to compose a piece, to tell me what he "thinks up" as his idea and then to draw or write it (as a libretto or sketched outline of a dance). I then ask the child to "show" or dance it his way; next, to observe how another child or group of children "perform" his work. Almost always, the observation (when he has supervised it) of his work, frees the child from its original personal knot. He dances the anger, fear or hate out of his system and is then able to judge the dance *in a form* as it stands on other dancers.

Since there is not the anxiety over graded marks and urgency to succeed so as to be promoted, as exists in school, children in recreational creative classes give and take criticism with an aplomb many adults might envy. They are quick to spy faults but equally quick and eager to praise perfection.

"I just can't make my turns in time!" Ellen mourns, distressed and disgusted.

"Never mind," consoles Frank, who can turn like a top and whirl like a dervish. "You can hold a high note and I can't—my voice breaks!" However, he tries to sing!

Without rue, they laugh at each other for their failures, secure in the pride of their accomplishments. Even the thin-skinned take constructive criticism because it is directed not against the child himself but towards the form of the thing he has composed or performed. And in any group which works together there is gradually but palpably an increase of perfection and a decrease of failure, since children rapidly learn how to excel at their best (what is called "areas of richness") and the teacher naturally encourages each child to work at what he most enjoys and does best. But she must do more, even for the child who accomplishes or "succeeds." Encouragement and praise are not enough; she must lead the student into ever more daring and difficult areas as "achievement," and instill in him pure love of the pursuit of excellence.

Pilot Program in Creative Work

Once the group has achieved an environment (either by showing that individuals can contribute experiences of their own, or have developed them from the preliminary "discoveries" with the teacher in the class) a realization of "creative" work should be made.

This is, of course, best done under the cognitive teacher like Bruce King and no better guide or pilot program exists for the conventional and vocational teacher than from within the work of the artist-teacher. As example of the principles, methods, resources, developments and results of a "creative" experience Bruce King writes:

> In my creative dance classes for children my main thesis is: Dance should be meaningful to those who do and see it. This is not a new idea and can be found in the notebooks of Isadora Duncan, written before 1904, and many books on educational dance published in this century. One of my particular areas of interest is helping children develop their own dance idiom and helping them to feel a respect for this idiom. The child's idiom is the movement that provides an appropriate medium for the expression of his experience and imagination. Though all improvisational movement is expressive of the person moving, it may express a desire to please adults or the timid attempt to imitate adult dancing. Instead, I try to establish an atmosphere wherein more meaningful and original expression emerges.
>
> In one class, for example, a child did a "father dance" with the stimulation of one prop: a papier-mâché hat. This dance consisted of putting on the hat, picking up something (an imaginary brief-case or lunch-box), opening and closing imaginary doors, tipping the hat (to an imagined passerby on the street), and taking larger and more definite steps than were usual to the child. This dance developed from a pantomimic base without logical sequence, beginning or end. Yet the child's impression of the father and the father's activities was recalled and communicated to others—a dance with immediate and absolute meaning for the dancer and his audience. *Nothing was second-hand*. The dance was limited only by the concept and facility of the dancer. Dance techniques could not make it better. Further investigation and planning could make it more valuable artistically, but that will come later in the class. The essence has been experienced.
>
> In order to discover what is meaningful to children one must go beyond the general desires to make cowboy or flower dances. I keep probing to find out *what else* do cowboys do, beyond galloping in a circle, or drawing an imaginary gun that goes *bang*. Flowers, for example, not only grow but also wake up and go to sleep, and exist in a garden where they are parts of a world relating to butterflies, bees, caterpillars, worms—and the weather. So,

in this class, a child as a flower died, because a caterpillar ate too many of her leaves. But then the caterpillar became a butterfly . . .

Such dances, based on the knowledge and thought of children, have an honesty and immediacy that give them real beauty. The summarization of feelings becomes an event in the child's life that has importance at the moment of the dance, and is a step forward in total growth for the children in the group.

The transitory dances that encourage such growth do not look like television dance, or what some adults think "a dance" should be. The movement forms become more appropriate as the ideas reflect more clearly for the children who create them. The success of the movements in small and large forms rests upon the degree of appropriateness (appropriateness that reveals an honest intention fulfilled).

As the rightness of a leaf in nature makes it beautiful *and a leaf,* the rightness of a dance fragment brings the same kind of beauty and definition to the expression of children.

Children are not artists in the adult sense but they can and will find forms to convey their ideas. In the effort to convey, they discover the satisfactions of human communication.

In one class we were working with moods under two headings: *happy* and *sad*. The room was large enough for all the children to experiment at the same time and while they were exploring the *sad* mood I noticed that Madeline was moving with conviction and developing a motif. She held her arm up to shade her eyes and kept looking up, with her torso in many angles —standing, leaning back, kneeling, finally lying down. It was clear that she had a definite idea and that it had special meaning for her.

When the group completed this mood, I asked Madeline if she would do an improvisation for us. She wanted to and got up and began to dance. She stated and developed her motif quite beautifully. We who watched responded to the line of the movement and the dynamic structure that evolved. All of us were aware of the emotion that poured through her dancing. When the dance was over, I asked: "Does this dance have a story?" Madeline replied: "I was a little girl who was waiting to be taken out to play in the park. I was looking to see if the sun kept shining, because if it did they would come and take me out." I told her that it was a beautiful dance and we went on to the next child.

I thought that since this had been a *sad* dance the sun had probably not come out (she may have been lying down in despair) and I felt sorry that I had stirred an unhappy memory, but after class Madeline came to me, glowing, and said: "Oh, I had a wonderful morning!" Whatever the emotion of the actual experience, the experience of the dance had been a good and happy one.

Though the child is not expected to be an artist, the teacher should be. To be effective, the teacher must be convinced and courageous—with a point of view that is defendable. I feel that I have the responsibility of increasing the children's knowledge of dance as an art form.

"Creative dance" is more than skipping about. It is concerned with communication. But how? Movement can communicate specifics, yet dance is essentially an abstract medium that expresses an area that eludes us in everyday speech, feeling, atmosphere, attitudes.

Margaret's solo improvisation of a bird teaching its young to fly caught the imagination of a group of seven-year-olds. They worked on this dance idea once a week for a month. Margaret's flying, watching and swooping down to aid her imaginary fledgling inspired a girl to take the second role (the fledgling). Others preferred to dance roles of mother-birds. To give more children an opportunity to dance, these mothers added fledglings of their own, resulting in a group dance.

The feeding of the fledglings in their nests became a prelude to the main theme. Elizabeth showed how the legs would shake, as the young birds stood on the edge of the nest to try their first flight. This suggestion became a set movement used in the dance as it was repeated and developed. Elizabeth was rewarded for a successful contribution—the use of her idea by all who danced the roles of fledglings. When the young birds had learned to fly, each built his own nest, ending the dance quietly as all settled into their new homes.

This class of little girls danced out their ideas with tenderness, concern, responsibility, courage and industry. The children made a remarkably positive statement in dance. Artistically, the dance developed by the group is beyond the conception of one child. The children performed this work with an understanding that could not have been superimposed by an adult.

Creative dance is moving, improvising, exploring, deciding, doing, with meaning. The individual is strengthened by group participation—the whole group assumes responsibility for developing a single role in a group dance. As the group accumulates a rich reserve of ideas, the individual becomes aware that this is his resource, which he may use or ignore. As a result, the individual has the strength and courage to take a suggestion from the pool of ideas, and make it uniquely his.

Technical skills are developed in my classes to add to individual and group achievement. A technical problem arose in the first meeting with a group of eight-year-old children. They were coming across the floor in follow-the-leader pattern. Each child had his turn to be the leader, suggesting the movement to be done. One said: *skip.* Immediately, Donald stepped out of line to complain: "But I can't skip." Without changing the rhythm I was playing, I replied: "Then, gallop. You can gallop with this rhythm."

He galloped and we got through the movement without Donald suffering needless discouragement.

When one child in a group cannot skip, he is much too obvious and easily embarrassed. It was necessary for me then and there to reshape the materials of this lesson to meet the needs of this one child. And when a boy insisted he could only use one foot, I suggested that the boys hop a movement on one foot, then suggested: "Now do it on the other foot" for those who could and would. When a slide was done, the group was asked to do it on one side, then the other.

At our third meeting, we talked about right and left, instead of "this side" and "the other side." The group worked on this problem, which I selected so that Donald would have time to practice, that would prepare him for skipping movements. During the improvisation periods, Donald's ideas were used whenever possible, demonstrating to Donald and the group that his ideas were valuable.

In the fourth class, when the children came to the follow-the-leader pattern I said: "Usually, you choose the movements we do across the room. Today is my turn." I chose movements the group had already performed, at previous sessions, but arranged them so that they built towards the skip. When it was time to skip it fell (as planned) to Donald's turn to lead. He began: "But I can't skip . . . " "Keep trying!" I urged, without changing the rhythm. The boy changed from galloping to skipping and after everyone had crossed the room I said: "Donald, do you know you were skipping?"—"Yes!" he said.—"Good!" I replied. "Now, everyone do it again."—The children followed my direction, dancing with greater satisfaction and confidence because everyone could perform the movement pattern.

If I had taken Donald by the hand the first day and said: "Look, this is how you skip," he should have been stopped cold from trying to learn how to skip. Instead, he was given time and opportunity to learn, as everyone went forward at individual paces, reaching together greater skills. Now the group was further improved by Donald as a stronger member.

Letting children create their own dances gives them opportunity to express thoughts they cannot put into words. Some dances mature after obvious thought. I could see that Fred, aged seven, had been thinking of a dance all week. When he began, he entered calmly and sat on the floor—watching. Then he arose and backed away, reversing his first action. Instantly, he became the seated victim—receiving the blow, jumping up, then rolling over to lie in stillness. The solo, though brief, was complete. Fred's awareness of violence was expressed—released—through the construction and performance of his dance. It was too far advanced as a composition for the group to deal with. Yet the group and the teacher learned something by seeing it.

Children should be made aware of the seeing and doing aspects of dance, as of the hearing and doing aspects of music. The first task in a creative dance class is to open the children's view to "seeing" life and meaning in terms of *movement*. Their dancing is more significant if it is built from life experiences than from "dances" they have observed. Many adults who see children imitating dances from television marvel at their ability to reproduce dances exactly as they are observed. But not all adult dancing is appropriate for children to study or significant for them to perform. *And the television audience does not see children's creative dance but dancing performed by children imitating adults dancing.*

As parents often encourage this kind of dance imitation, children come into creative dance classes with a totally erroneous idea of "creating" and their "second-hand" dances have to be coped with and overcome before they can "see" meaning in dance and in their own living and activities. It is not easy for the teacher, but it must be accomplished before any real progress is made.

Eventually, as children learn to "see" truth they become selective and will choose from their environments or their feelings movements that are spontaneous improvisations with which to communicate effectively to an audience. When this point is reached, the teacher works in a continual refining process. I try to help children define the problems to be solved in their original ideas, pointing out the successful solutions when these are made, if the children do not recognize them. I stimulate discussions for many possible solutions of a problem in a group project, and I often select the focus. Improvisation, to a degree, requires focus.

When children make individual responses to an approach they often need help in voicing their thoughts, and this approach can take the aspect of questioning. A class was concerned with solo improvisations of dance and music and Richard volunteered to dance. Since I was the accompanist, I asked what kind of dance he would do, and what kind of music I should play. Richard shrugged, unable or unwilling to state. "What is the dance about?" I asked, since all activities have purpose and meaning, however unconventional. "A giraffe," said Richard. "Shall I play the drum or the piano for the giraffe dance?" I asked. "Well, it's got a lot of leaves on it," he explained. So I played the piano, (which has lots of keys) instead of the drum.

As a teacher, I expect their best efforts from the children and I accept only what I know to be the best at every stage of the individual and group development. There is emphasis on spontaneity, for it is honest, but there is equal concern in my classes for quality. The quality of a response is meaningful.

And as a teacher, I expect a great deal of myself and am willing to put myself into the situations the children find themselves in, when they are discovering and experimenting. When I feel there is good reason I will dance with or for a class. This may be to help a child discover his own capacity through participation with an adult. Or I will do an improvisation to make a point, and then discuss its successful or unsuccessful aspects.

In one class of twelve-year-olds the children were trying to develop a dance about a friend. They had agreed that "a friend comforts you when you are in trouble." To work this out in terms of movement and music, they began a dance which placed one child as a stranger in a playground, and a group "playing" at a game, and ignoring the stranger. The stranger tried to attract the group by interrupting the game. At the third attempt, the stranger fell down. The group left the playground area, but one dancer returned, to help the fallen stranger to her feet and comfort her. Then these two exited together.

I was not satisfied with this dance, which only accomplished telling a story or communicating an incident. The children agreed that it was not very interesting for an audience. I was concerned that the main idea (the idea of *comforting*) was lost in the social aspects of the scene.

During the experiment Nancy, the younger sister of one of the twelve-year-olds in the class, was brought into the studio to watch and wait. She sat quietly observing us for ten minutes. I wanted a dancer to help me develop the final duet (the one who falls and the one who comes to comfort her) and I said: "Who will try this part with me?" Nancy raised her hand. The group decided that it would be good for her to work with me, and that she should be the one who had fallen down. She walked to the center of the floor, lay down, and curled herself up on the floor. When I entered, she did not move. I stood over her and finally I bent and lifted her head. Here was the key to the dance. Nancy moved when I touched her, and only moved with my physical help. I was free to develop the movement ideas I came upon in trying to comfort her. It was a long time before Nancy rose to her feet. Then we two, adult and child, began a slow exit. The dance was finished.

The sensitivity and concentration of the little girl sustained her role, and inspired me. My knowledge of movement and improvisation sustained the child's imagination. We two were able to dance the duet to demonstrate to the class that the movement and the emotional ideas of this dance could be interestingly and clearly communicated. The dance, in its final duet, had done more than tell a story.

When appropriateness or truth in movement, and discipline in communication are achieved, the child has in fact begun to develop his vocabulary or techniques in dance. The more fluent and powerful these techniques, the more concisely the child can repeat them and teach them to others, the greater his artistic capacity. It is through appropriateness, discipline and technique that final judgments can be made in a creative dance class, and this thesis is far away from the assumption that children aimlessly run and jump about when they are creating dance. As it is erroneous to assume that in experimenting with conventional and unconventional organizations of sounds a child in a creative music class is simply making noises. The very experimentation with noise is in itself a musical technique, and when the child in my class choreographed a dance for a seven-legged dancer I took care to tell the derisive group (and provide it with experiences in listening to prove this statement) that whereas composers had conventionally worked in the standard scale before him, Arnold Schönberg had chosen to break the rules of tonality and to work in a chromatic scale wherein twelve (not seven) tones became a new and revolutionary precept for music.

At the point which only the individual teacher can distinguish for a particular group, all creative arts classes should discuss the breaking of rules in arts media, the revolutions and reforms. Many children need to be metaphorically freed from conventional thought patterns. It was only after Jane had been reassured by Schönberg's revolt in music that she dared produce her 7-legged dance work.

As we note from examples here, children begin creative work in dance by relating movement to real experiences, while early creative forms of music may be more abstract, as sheer experimentation with sound. Abstract qualities in dance are impossible to convey in words but the child should be led to understand these very early in his studies of dance and music. Eccentric and comically antic, grotesque and macabre ideas are likely to emerge in dance, and to be echoed or inspired by unconventional musical sounds. Going beyond this experimentation with "non-reality" the teacher must lead the child to an awareness of poetic thought and allegory, to enlarge his concepts as the artist and quicken his awareness as a member of the theatre audience. Most often, the child today requires knowledge of a palpable shape or technical insight before he frees himself from canned stereotypes of dance, enough to attempt genuinely original work.

A primary lesson by the teacher should show the idea of "pure music," a symphony as being music of itself, without literal connotation or accompaniment of word or action. And relating this idea to dance, the child should know that "pure dance" is one of the contemporary forms of the art, developed to such extent that it stands as dance without *meaning* in a literal sense, without a story or characterization.

The differences between fact and fantasy should be *consciously* explored, so that the child understands "dream" and "reality" to have reflections as abstractions and realizations in art. And he should be left free to develop his own tastes for these, rather than directed to an "appreciation" of one genre more than of another. Correlated with lessons in painting, where "abstract" techniques are visual, these lessons in dance and music will give the child a fundamental understanding, without bias, about impressionistic art forms.

The creative arts class should not be wholly an "activity" class. Children need a place and a time to dream in, and in our contemporary society a child often has no place or time to dream at home or in school. He should know theatre.

The Child in Theatre

Theatrical participation is of two kinds: working within theatre arts, as composer, performer or technician; sharing the arts and crafts of theatre vicariously, by looking and listening. *Both kinds of participation are true experiences.* The first kind is experienced by the child as amateur but this same child may also experience a professional aspect of theatre, as audience.

"Children's theatre" is a broad term descriptive of theatrical performances by and for children, or specifically for children (by adults), and it is an experience I consider of great worth to the child in our contemporary society. Earlier in these pages I commented on the paradox that although children are allowed to share adult entertainment as movies and television programs, they are not so generally encouraged to share "adult art." Yet, when we consider the child in theatre, we must qualify what of its adult art should be included in the child's experience, and especially as first or early experiences.

I believe, for example, that the initial approach to Shakespeare and opera should be made with direct relationship to theatrical productions of dramas and operas, since Shakespeare wrote his plays to be acted and opera is conceived as a *performing* art. I have found that when young children experience *Julius Caesar* or *The Tempest* in first-class performances *as theatre* they are more likely to want to read or to hear readings of the plays in camera. And that when the right approach, combined with the most pleasurable associations for the child, is made to opera, young audiences become opera buffs without consciousness of the "cultural" status this title implies for their elders. These attitudes apply equally to dance and music for young audiences.

My first requirement of theatre for a child is that the production should be first-class, as a matter of course, however modest in scale, or simple in theme. Second-rate "professional" productions simply will not do, in theatre arts for the child. Better a good amateur performance than a shoddy or careless so-called "professional" one contemptuously undertaken for an audience of young persons—among whom there will not be present a critic to flail the second-rate production in the next day's newspapers. Regrettably, a great deal of matinee youth concerts fall into the category of the second-rate, in the hands of conductors and orchestras incapable of believing that young persons can discriminate between the mediocre and the first-rate.

And many adults carelessly introduce children to theatre through poor media, as by incompetent amateur performers. If a performance is bad, it will hardly arouse good response. Spare no expense, take the greatest care, in introducing the arts to your child because half his standards, or aesthetic tastes will come from his first loves. (If he studies an art form, observe the same purpose in selecting his teachers; the other half of his standards will come from his first masters.)

I should not introduce a child to an art medium through "pop" and "non-art" works of the current mode, which are faddist in contemporary society. In recent years, I have attended concerts in which pianists "performed" by twirling on revolving stools between four keyboards and "playing" the keys with bare feet and feet shod in tennis shoes. Some of these pianists also destroyed a piano as they played, by dismantling it, or treated the piano as a fetishist object (sprinkling leaves and flowers into its insides, painting the white keys red and the black keys white, for instance). Others maltreated other instruments in similar ways. The occasions of mayhem were described as "modern music" concerts, were almost invariably matinees, and were attended by children and adolescents. All whose responses I was able to determine experienced these concerts with fascination or amusement, but obviously the fascination was horrified and the hilarity nervous, because the children felt guilty of sharing in wilful destruction. In such "experiences," the young audience understands itself to be the witness of an extraordinary adult rite though expected to recognize the occasion as a *musical* experience.

Children can be prim, not to say strict, in theatre, as adults are more likely to be in church. "Happenings" mystify and sometimes frighten them, although these may be first-rate artistic satires or considered as musical and dramatic works of merit. The symposiums that "create anew" through destruction, as when a picture is ceremoniously burned in an art gallery showing, to "recreate" it as ashes, bewilder a child. So does a dance work in which the performers dance against frames of film spliced at random, and set on fire, in the "violence in art" fad which is described, quite seriously, as "aesthetic of a total experience, soliciting from the audience a total response." A child may remain indifferent to drama which might appal an adult, who identifies with it, because he cannot relate to an inexperienced catastrophe. Yet he will be greatly shocked by the destruction of a piano, which he has been reared to respect as property not to be violated.

Cruel if "true" satire, and the theatre of the 'destructivist' art theme now in vogue, should, in my opinion, be excluded from the experiences of children and adolescents. The most avant-garde music may be acceptable and even inspiring for young persons, but theatre, which is audio-visual in dance and drama, is a more intense experience than the purely musical experience. In an early approach to theatre, the principle should be to provide artistic experiences to which the child will respond and from which he will benefit in his education—bearing in mind that "education" does not stop short of the school classroom but extends into every waking (and, perhaps, the dreaming) experiences of the child. Theatre is a very natural extension of the child's secret world, in which reality and fantasy are conjoined. These two worlds are much closer than most adults know. For the child, the theatre experience is a confirmation or realization of the secret world of imagination, the animate and corporeal matter of what is contained in books as stories and related in the verses of songs. He expects exactitude for familiar characters and plots, and may be greatly disturbed when these appear altered.*

Children are often bored, but they do not tire of the familiar and beloved plots and characters of the nursery, providing these are related, sung and danced, and enacted, with verity. They are a gimlet-eyed and critical audience, pouncing on the slightest discrepancy onstage from the known "facts" of a story, and they do not accept changes from the original. Fidelity to what they think of as "the truth" about *Alice* and other familiar nursery characters is what they demand, over sophistication of staging techniques.

However, children will agreeably accept and intelligently analyze new works in theatre, providing they approach these with an emotional preparation for what will be new and perhaps strange. "Abstract" dance, for instance, is generally translated by children in the audience to dance with positive meaning and, often, dramatic context. The child does not approach "cerebral" dance, or dance devoid of literal relationship to a plot and characterization,

---

* A great outcry arose from children in 1966, when a television "satire" of *Alice* proved to be far removed from Lewis Carroll's original—and, it must be noted, fell far short of any artistic merit.

with an intellectualized idea of movement. Instead, he sees the movement and hears the music as a visual and aural experience, and if no program notes are read to him, or printed for him to read, he is free to "make up" for himself "what this dance is all about." I have frequently read for an illiterate child only the name of a dance work or a dramatic skit, in the theatre before the performance, and later had revealed to me what the dance or the drama was about as themes, plots and characterizations never dreamed of by the choreographer and dancers, or the playwright and actors.

Yet while a child may, in the audience, feel and think independently and perhaps in an opposite direction to the communication the composers and performers of the work intend to achieve, he is alert to the honesty of the work, and perceives far more about its worth than he is generally credited with doing. His attention must be captivated; next: he must be convinced of the *truth* of his theatrical experience.

Trained, gifted artists are capable of creating illusion and sustaining the nature of poetry, the epic quality of the hero, the atmospheres of daemon and faerie—and they must work diligently as accomplished craftsmen in the disciplines of their media. Such artists work for adults and for children without conscious approach to these as types of audiences, only with consciousness of them as audiences.

As to choice of a bill of fare this is largely determined by the availability of theatre in the child's geographical area. But if the choice is various, the adult need not be bored; he can select programs which he will share with enthusiasm and pleasure equal to his child's. Here, for example, is a dance program by Bruce King:

BRUCE KING's *Concert of Solo Dances:**

Studies in Technique	Paul Kueter
1. Floor	2. Vertical
Design with Poles	Percussion
Running Figure	Douglas Nordli
Lament	Paul Kueter

* This program was presented at Harkaway Theatre, Bennett College, Millbrook, New York, December 1, 1965, with *Ghosts* in première, commissioned by Bennett College. Its construction of works and intervals is a good one for an experience in theatre for the child and young adolescent. Note that the arrangement of each of the three sections of the program allows for a natural entrance and exit for any one, or any two sections of the program, so that a child likely to be exhausted by the whole program might attend one or two parts, without feeling (or, even, knowing) that other parts of the program were on view. An adult might

Ghosts . . . . Anton Webern

1. Falling	4. Exiled
2. Calling	5. Lost
3. Mad	6. Adrift

Cloud . . . . Maurice Ravel

Five Short Dances . . . . Paul Hindemith

1. March	4. Very Quiet
2. Pastoral	5. Scherzando
3. Anger	

Themes . . . . Edgar Varèse

| 1. Desert | 2. Sky | 3. City |

In analysis, from the child's perspective, let us examine what we have here. This is not a child's program, in the sense of being a theatrical entertainment planned for children; it is a dance program, in which the adult and "young" or "student" audience strata may very easily be integrated.

Studies in Technique is a technical concept of dance movement. *Design with Poles* involves another artistic concept (one out of design) with movement in dance and with sound as a percussive type of music. *Running Figure* is a universal motif. *Lament* is a recognizable emotion. There is an interval, for rest and refreshment, essential to an audience and especially to a young audience—and the portion of a theatrical program marked *Intermission* is a part of the program; a vital, integral part. It also allows a tactful leave-taking from a program which in its entirety might exhaust a young child of limited concentration span or the physical ability to sit comparatively still for long periods. The adult should use every *Intermission* to good influence for the child at the theatrical performance, taking care that the rest and refreshment period is not fatiguing or distracting, so that the continuation of the program occurs after a pause, not an interruption.

The Bruce King program used here as example continues, after the first

---

thus approach this experience by introducing the child gradually, through few dance works at a time, by choosing the intermissions and works which constitute any of the three complete sections of the Harkaway Theatre bill. On film, every dance work here might become part of an integrated concert program, in the form it was produced at Bennett College, or stand by itself, unrelated to other works, as whole experiences for audiences, some in dance techniques and aesthetics, some in aesthetic communication.

interval, with *Ghosts* and *Cloud*, two works of particular interest for the young audience. The terror of the supernatural is atavistic but for children it is also a delicious thrill which they invite and sometimes invent. And, too, all children at some phase of development experience great fear of death, as being totally extinguished and "separated from people who know who I am." The loss of identity, the passionate revolt against annihilation, causes some of them to create private ghosts, not to terrorize the night time but to reassure them that beyond death beings are still sentient and moving. Bruce King's *Ghosts*, created for adult audiences, thus becomes a good choice of a work in a program for the young audience.

The ghosts danced are *Falling, Calling, Mad, Exiled, Lost* and *Adrift*, and the *Lost* ghost, who carries a valise apparently made of some astral whitish substance, is lost in a railroad station, "the worst of all places to be lost," a child earnestly informed me, "because you are among millions of people who don't know you!" A child has no difficulty whatever grasping the significance of adult dance, or "appreciating" the quality of adult music.

He is quickly aware of symbolism in art, as in Bruce King's *Cloud*, and relates instantly and entirely to the concepts of such a work. A work like King's *Themes*, of *Desert, Sky* and *City*, is equally lucid for him.

In programs specifically developed for children with literal content, folk lore and fairy tales should take conspicious character. The best themes are those which pit forces of Good and Evil against each other, but not in blatantly preachy styles. Good and Evil have connotations as Beauty and Beastliness, or as heroic deeds opposed to tyrannical might. Not for nothing have stories like *Beauty and the Beast* and *Jack, the Giant-Killer* survived for infinite number of generations, among uncountable societies of peoples.

R. S. Lee, M.A., B. Litt., D. Phil, Chaplain of Nuffield College, Oxford, and Fellow and Chaplain of St. Catherine's College, Oxford, points out that fairy tale and myth are essentially reassuring for the growing child, making supportable the almost unendurable primal fears of childhood. The idea of the father as God and the concept of himself and his father in what psychologists call "the Oedipus complex," cause a boy to believe that he is in danger of being destroyed by an omnipotent father, jealous rival for the affection and attention of the boy's mother. "One of his fantasies at this stage," writes Dr. Lee in his psychological treatise *Your Growing Child and Religion*, "is that his father will eat him up." In the ancient Greek myths Chronos devoured his children, one of the several incontrovertible proofs of myth being the earliest form of psychological definition of the human condition. Fairy stories like *Jack, the Giant-Killer*, are favorites of young children because they do not sound in the least improbable; on the contrary, they are reassuring. Dr. Lee remarks: "The giant eats up little boys, but the hero (Jack) outwits him and slays him instead. That is what the boy wants to do to his father." And this, Dr. Lee adds, is not the description of a depraved childish imagination but only part of normal development, without which a boy should remain emotionally infantile, permanently attached to his mother. This normal development continues far past the fairy-tale stage; logically, into theatre experiences (and also through literature and other arts) for the child.

Beauty and the Beast has great empathy for both girls and boys, since it perfectly underscores the Occidental ideal of the sexes: that Woman shall be a tender ministering angel, fearless and gentle, overcoming evil (or supplanting ugliness) by her feminine beauty of person, and converting the worst in Man (his "beastliness") to the noblest (a royal or princely estate being symbolical of nobility). Bruce King's *Beauty and the Beast* ballet becomes, for young audiences, far, far more than dance performance; it is a moving and memorable experience in theatre.* The child today needs many more such theatrical experiences, to grow on.

In such perspectives, of theatre as an extension of the child's world, and a world which he inarticulately inhabits, often in utter secrecy within his parental world, we take our children to theatre not for shallow entertainment but for the same magical and healing properties mankind sought in theatre, when it was first conceived and produced.

A wholly changed idea of theatre is slowly evolving in the culture of English-speaking peoples, with a gradual but distinct development of theatre arts in education. *Why* theatre is; from what intensely human requirement it evolved out of ceremony (for animals had rites before mankind: as in the dances of birds and beasts), is the reason for theatre now, as it was for theatre in its dim beginnings. In accepting the need for "theatre experiences" for the child we recognize the nature of theatre, and in adopting certain aspects of theatre in education we are belatedly realizing the values of theatre arts in the civilized condition we call our "culture."

The child in theatre, playing (meaning: *working*) at its techniques in an amateurish and overtly pleasurable way, or the child sharing theatre out of the audience, is totally involved, wholly committed, in manner unlike any

---

* Bruce King's works include *Children's Suite* to Ravel's *Ma Mère l'Oye*, of which *Beauty and the Beast* is a part. Currently, filming of some of King demonstrations and dances is in progress; already available, as described in Appendix II, are recordings for his dance and music education.

adult's concept, except the adult who is a gifted and dedicated theatrical artist. The average parent and teacher must evaluate theatre before he can understand what it means, or should mean, to the child.

Theatre, we may say authoritatively, is a laboratory for research; for searching and finding all thoughts and actions of the human person, discovering all of our past and attempting to fathom our future. In theatre, we stop time in its tracks and return to any era in history, there to assay another time and place, a distant society with its own ideas and behavior, its manners and mores, turns of speech and way of dress; its mode of movement, as in the dancing; its voice, as in its song; even something of its material or physical possessions, through the music made by the instruments of that particular place and time. But theatre is more than a laboratory for researching history via graphic and lively arts, since theatre offers us a mysterious and convenient means of discovering our inner selves, as we recognize these selves and then advance towards or flee from them as subtly masked and mimicking images from the race. The child is more courageous although more fearful than the adult and he is less terrified and repulsed than enchanted and illuminated in theatre. He goes there to see what is put on view, to look and to listen to what shall be shown and heard. He goes, unconsciously, in the state of one awaiting revelation.

In theatre, through dance, drama and music, the child learns about himself and finds empathy, between his own time and place and the past with its real and symbolical racial images. He is, in a phrase, made more secure as a human person, out of allegory and myth, absorbed by osmosis through the eloquent and vivid media we call "performing arts." The valuable lessons he learns here could not be taught by better means than the artistic ones, for it is to these that he instinctively responds in a sensual perception. He feels more than he thinks, for the healthy young child, as described by William James, one of the greatest of American psychologists, is a pagan.

The Child in Church

He goes to church, therefore, as he goes to theatre, curious to experience what he shall discover through his senses, eager to be made to feel—whereby he is, eventually, compelled to think. He goes to church as a child, and not as an adult. He does not worship as an adult, and is incapable of praying as adults are counselled to pray: for a state of grace, instead of for largesse from a benign and powerful "parent." Most adults forget, conveniently, how they consciously prayed as children: to obtain favor, receive material gifts, or be saved from impending disaster. When children consciously pray, they pray as pagans and that propounds the grave consideration (by psychologists who are also men of religion, like Dr. Lee) as to whether the child should ever be taught to pray, except to call from a Deity blessings on all loved (and unlovable) creatures. A child may be taught to praise God, by singing, dancing and making music in His honor and name, but it is impossible to teach a child to worship an unseen, imponderable and unknown divinity. How then, better to approach the child in church than as we approach him at home, in school and at play: with music!

Dr. Lee says, in *Churchgoing and Prayer*, Chapter 13 of his book: *Your Growing Child and Religion*, that children from about the age of three begin to need group activities, presenting an opportunity for beginning religious training. Its aim and function, he believes, should be to make religion interesting and enjoyable for infants and young children, and to make Sunday school and similar religious instruction of the happiest associations for the child.

It is easy enough to interest the child in religion, or, rather, the outward signs and appurtenances of religion. In chapel, church, synagogue and other places of worship there is an altogether *extra*-ordinary atmosphere, compared to that of the ordinary home, school and other places of daily existence. Such novelties as the architecture and decor and furnishings of church, and of the pious attitudes and conduct of congregations communicating through prayer, are bound to intrigue the child. Having caught his interest by what, at the risk of seeming sacrilegious, one must consider the theatrical quality of religion, it is usually easy to teach the child an etiquette or set of manners particular to being in church. But this is not to say that one has made him religious. The best we may hope to achieve, if we are ourselves religious, is to make religion a good, normal *and happy* aspect of life, as early as possible, for the child.

In an environment in which religion is a normal element, the child responds and will behave as though church were part of life, although something particular in it—rather as he thinks of theatre, to which he may be taken on a school holiday like Saturday, as he is usually taken to church on the Sabbath day of his parents' religious denomination. Certain things in religion will attract and intrigue him, and they are likely to be those aural and visual (and tactile and olfactory) aspects of religion to which his senses respond. Children confide that they like "the look" and perhaps the "smell of church," (hot wax, flowers, polished wood, the clothes congregations usually dress in). Church can be an entrancing "show" of itself, and when the ritual, so solemnly undertaken by adults, is amplified by music, it becomes, most often, a genuinely thrilling experience for the child. But it would be hypocritical to delude ourselves that the child experiences a religious thrill, when he in truth approaches the pomp and circumstance of organized worship with the irresistible delight and awe of a savage—or a little child innocent of hypocrisy, with faith in miracles and trust in omens. It has always seemed to me the greatest adult folly, and the gravest loss of innocence for the child, to attempt to divorce sweetness and gaiety from religion and assume a rigid pattern of subservient fear of the wrath of a placatable God. The child, Heaven help him, already fears the wrath of father and mother, and teacher, and all other adults who rule his world; a giant world in which he is a pygmy and, in addition, without "rights" as he knows them, no income and no property which may not be confiscated "for his own good," powerless even to change his mode of life and place of residence, since, if he runs off, he will be brought back in disgrace. To please adults, he must placate them by assuming *their* ways and suppressing his. As sheer self-preservation, he seeks and finds a place for dreaming, and a place in which to superimpose a life on his own terms; normally, this respite is play-time, a facsimile of theatre, the imaginative realm; sometimes, it is in art. In both theatre and in church (which originated from one source, and that one the theatre) the child's approach to art and to religion is through universal human responses, of the senses, and not the intellect or the "Soul."

He is attracted to experiences which he seeks out or discovers out of curiosity, another word for interest, and in church he is motivated by this curiosity, not by abstract concepts of Divinity. If his eager interest is stimulated, within the utmost pleasurable associations for him, the child grows to love God and enjoy his religion in the same way that, in school, he grows to love knowledge and enjoy the learning process. The cardinal principles of teaching a child are to keep him curious about making discoveries for himself, and happy in the assimilation of experiences, and it is these same principles that the parent and the religious teacher must work in, when attempting an approach to the child in church.

For adults who think of religion as a duty, and an onerous one which intrudes on, and to an extent suppresses, a happy human state in ordinary life, this approach to the child in church will appear wrong and, perhaps, sacrilegious. For those adults who look on religion as spiritual refreshment and joy, and on worship and praise of a Divine Being as the most spontaneous and the happiest act of the human person, the approach will be valid, since it is the approach the child freely and naturally makes when he is introduced to religion. If the child is to enjoy his religion, to such extent that it will become meaningful and satisfying in later life, he must be allowed to enjoy it on his terms, within his tastes.

Drama, in story-telling, and music, are general to church, as they are to school and theatre. With dance, drama and music provide the best means of illustrating or defining ideas for the child. Dr. Lee says it is almost irrelevant what children are taught as religious instruction, so long as they are kept interested and made happy, and not bored—"because boredom is a terrible enemy to children, and it is not unknown to be bored in church!"

Every religion, romantic in its history, is tremendously exciting rather than boring, if only the materials of religion (its rituals and lore) are imaginatively presented, and the child approached through these with genuine respect of his intelligence and emotions. Into adolescence, children do not clearly distinguish between emotion and thought. Thinking for the child is largely through images created by the imagination or through sensual experiences (what he can see, hear, touch, smell and taste), not by logical deduction and inference. Only comparatively few adult mentalities consciously and continually think by means of purely abstract ideas. We must allow a child to approach God on human, not divine, terms.

The Book of every religion which a child approaches today contains the most dramatic material for interesting a child in his religion, and of granting him an awareness (which is, in fact, a human necessity) of his close relationship with his (really, his parents' or guardians') God. The stories out of the Bible, which are those that English-speaking children generally know as their religious lore, are as much theatre in artistic essence as theatre based on antique Greek mythology. Accepted by the pious as gospel truth, the Bible is also as deeply imprinted with moral as the great fables.

Every teacher, secular and religious, should be, or should work to become, a superb storyteller, and the art of storytelling should be more assiduously studied and cultivated by writers of books to educate and to entertain children. This art, whether practiced orally or in literature, should be embellished with a wealth of detail, since children have omnivorous curiosity for detail, and pore over the sifted sand to find the meaning of the ants' industry in building their marvellous ant-heap.

In literature, song and "action" dance, what children love and cherish may be essentially simple in theme but it is always embroidered meticulously with detail—*ad tedium*, to the adult! For it is only by accumulating grains of sand and identifying details, that the child is able to relate himself, a minute creature, to the large and whole significance of an episode, a character, a person, a life. Adults who have sung to children and told stories to them, especially when they make up songs and stories for the particular child, know the questions imperiously asked: *What happened then, right after such-and-such and before so-and-so? What happened before, in between, and after?* with which the thread of a narrative must sew, with tiny stitches, the fabric of the thing told or sung. Dance-games are preserved as rituals by children.

In dance and music, as though with moving sculpture and illumined paint, storytellers as dancers and singers create the visual and aural detail by which the child both feels and thinks his way into the heart of the matter, the center of the story, the root meaning of the dance and the song. An approach to religion through drama, dance and music is therefore a most feasible one, since through action, or participating as a witness to the action, the child translates what he feels into what he thinks about the world, and the God whom he is taught made it, and him.

"Participation in the [Bible] story is the valuable part," says Dr. Lee, and adds that the story must be left to point its own moral. He warns the conventionally religious that Bible stories are apt to intrigue young persons from aspects that seem less creditable than a religious lesson. Usually, a story about the Good Samaritan will result in more interest being shown about the thieves than about the Samaritan and the victim, and Moses will elicit more enthusiasm for the doughty way the patriarch slaughtered the disagreeable Egyptians than for the exodus of God's chosen out of bondage. The only obligation of the religious teacher supervising the dramatized action, or telling the stories (according to Dr. Lee) is not to make the children feel ashamed or wrong in their natural interest and enthusiasm—and to cultivate enough acumen to make characterizations and the events concerning the "good" or moral parts of the Bible as dramatically entertaining as the "bad" or immoral ones. He urges more singing and dancing games in church, treating the child in church as a social person.

The problem then arises as to what the children shall sing!

Unfortunately, a great number of "children's hymns" are intolerably banal, musically and in verse, while almost nothing is composed as sacred music for the adolescent—a phenomenon, in an era during which the adolescent is rigidly segregated by advertising and salesmanship (with his own faddist "pop" music, clothes, and coiffures) separating him from the pre-teen and post-teen strata of the population. But adolescents in my phase of that maturity were as enervated by the sickly sentimental sacred music relegated to them as are my children and their contemporaries today . . .

The infant, child and young adolescent, especially, need stirring new sacred music for a contemporary approach to religion, and, I believe, the churches should develop dance arts beyond the secular uses for recreation, the better to arouse responses of the child to religion. Sacred music, in itself, could breed better religious tolerance.

When our daughter was very small, she would frequently ask to be allowed to attend a church with a friend of another religious denomination, "to hear the music and see the service." She thought of the music and the ritual as one, or as closely related, and would remark, quite often, that she preferred to attend a certain church of our faith for its choir. She went to church with a pagan enthusiasm for music and ceremony, but, it may be noted, she went to church of her volition and with the most pleasurable associations for religion. It was this child and her catholic friendship for children of several other religious denominations, who taught me to appreciate the Psalms for children as the best single approach to God.

One of her genuine discoveries in childhood was that Christians and Jews shared religious ideals and the Psalms. She said: "We sing the same Psalms," for to this child the Psalms were made to be sung. She did not speak of them as prayer and she did not say "We pray the same," but that "We *sing* the same . . ."*

In as much as the Psalms are common to several faiths and denominations, they might (with an acceptable English translation) become a shared, and common act of thanksgiving and praise to the Divine Being, as he is known and worshipped by Jews, Greek Orthodox, Protestant and Roman Catholic children.

Nothing in these religions is better suited as a musical experience for the child. 73 out of the 150 Psalms are accredited to David, the shepherd boy who as poet and musician became a hero and warrior-king. There is

---

* The Psalms were originated to be sung and were sung several times daily, to the accompaniment of an instrument like an Irish harp, by the early Christians. Moreover, they were joyously sung. James in his epistle comments: *Is any among you afflicted? Let him pray.* But he remarks: *Is any merry? Let him sing Psalms.* And *Seven times a day do I praise thee*, is embodied in the Psalms, an approach to God as a benign authority.

hardly a more interesting Biblical character for children than the boy David, and he not only sang and played upon his harp, but also danced—and with all his might. As for the Psalms, they are remarkably well suited to childish choirs, being short in structure, simple in theme, and poetic in imagery. When they touch on ordinary things they refer to sheep and shepherds, beasts of the field and fowls of the air, of mountains and valleys. In them we find night and day, rain and thunder. They tell, too, of the proud and of the meek who are put-upon by the tyrannical, and in such concrete terms as a child readily understands, and draws inference for his contemporary state and deductions for his contemporary world.

To a child living in the Mojave desert of Arizona, who told me the meaning in the Psalms of the singer who thirsts for God as the parched earth thirsts for rain, no other statement in our language could have held more meaning and greater verity, for the spirit yearning towards a Divine Being. She knew the texture, sight and smell of parched earth and the miracle of its flowering after rain. Before she was emotionally mature enough to love God, she *understood*, implicitly, what such an experience would mean . . .

A brilliant high school student, in a mood of great depression about the contemporary world and his estate in it, was crushed by the sense of the largeness and inevitability of conditions beyond his control and his insect-like inconsequence in society. But he found in the Psalms, as through a "sign" or personal revelation, that as a human being he had been made only "a little lower than the angels," made to hold dominion over the works of Divine hands, by a Being who had placed all things under his feet. Before this young man's conception of the Psalms' significance, Julian Huxley had pointed out the Psalms' theological statement of an astonishingly scientific truth: that man, biologically, is unique.

If a child were to have only one approach to God, what better way to offer it than through singing and dancing the Psalms?*

The child is there offered a moral code, to love the law, deal in justice with his neighbor, keep his word, befriend the poor, bridle an unruly tongue. He is given assurance of boundless love: *When my father and mother forsake me, then the Lord will take me up*; reassured in his fears: *The Lord is my light and my salvation; whom shall I fear?* and given a promise of immortality: *I will dwell in the house of the Lord forever*. Let him smart with a sense of injustice and water his couch with his tears; he has only to

---

* Dancing and singing, together, is the ancient human means of thanksgiving and praise, for which consult the Bible to find the several recorded instances.

cry out of the depths, to make his voice heard, and know that *If thou markest iniquities, who shall stand them?*

The adult must consciously approach the Psalms from the child's perspective, as I advised him to approach a simple song like *Cool Water*, in *The Child at Home*, in order to understand the significance of the verse. Emotionally, the themes of the Psalms are complex, being of life and death, good and evil, justice and mercy. Aesthetically, their language and the images conjured, are the most beautiful imaginable for the context as thought and statement. Their greatness may lie in the fact that while dealing with ordinary things, many of them corporeal, the Psalms express the feelings of the human spirit. "There is no movement of the spirit which is not reflected here as in a mirror," wrote Calvin. "All the sorrows, troubles, fears, doubts, hopes, pain, perplexities, stormy outbursts by which the hearts of men are tossed have been depicted here to the very life." And, Calvin should have added, here are contained also the great human joys: promise of salvation and assurance of immortality.

Recently published hymnals reprint the Psalms, restoring them to congregational singing. They have been maintained in the repertories of trained choirs. Only in church and church-school do children now learn the Psalms. The ban on religion in American public schools has come at a time when reading Scriptures aloud, in a familial sharing of them, is a habit long extinct in our society. Many young persons practice their religions devoutly but only in church. They have not the time and inclination for reading books or singing sacred music outside of church. Their religion is within their environment but kept separate from daily affairs. It falls to the churches, in our contemporary society, to provide occasions that feature religious dance and music in the life of a child.

One way to do this is to commission works of religious themes and to have them performed and produced in conditions that make them dynamic for young audiences. *The child should participate in an artistic religious life as well as know religious dogma and ritual.* As example, the Psalms should not only be sung by rote in church but should be discovered as a dramatic musical and poetic experience. It was not an American church but Chichester Cathedral in England which commissioned Leonard Bernstein to compose his oratorio on Psalms 108, 100, 23, 131, 2 and 133.*

Other composers, Kodaly and Stravinsky among them, have employed the Psalms but what is needed is a thrilling contemporary ballet-oratorio for

* Sung in Hebrew and receiving an American première by the New York Philharmonic Orchestra with the Camerata Singers in New York.

young congregations. As participant and audience, the child is particularly responsive to "action" song and dance but he is seldom encouraged to express his religious nature by these means. Reluctance to permit this, on the part of his elders, is from the notion that "performance" of sacred themes may be sacrilegious—a notion that should be dispelled by observing the ethnic or religiously inspired dancing of so-called "primitive" peoples. The Mormon Tongans, as one example, perform an "action" song and dance relating the founding of their church; seen on an American tour arranged by impresario Sol Hurok, this theatrical presentation enhanced rather than diminished the evocative quality of the song and dance. The child's church, today, like his school, should explore every channel or approach through which to move him. I use the word "move" in the literal sense of *change*, or of *activation*, physically and mentally; of gaining new insight through altered perspectives. The school and church must seek to move its scholars and worshippers; otherwise, these are moved only by less academic, less spiritual sources.

Many religious teachers believe that the churches, where ritual is a normal aspect of sacred drama, should approach young congregations with theatrical tension and climax, and that Sunday school classes and similar religious instruction should extensively employ audio-visual facilities in general use in schools. Those who disapprove of theatrical techniques for religious teaching are ignorant of the profound sources of theatre and prejudiced against theatre *per se* as a frivolity. Audio-visual aids, themselves innocuous, dehumanize religion, unless carefully used.

Acquiring physical facilities for audio-visual approaches do not ensure children's responses to their uses. The child responds to the insight gained and the imaginative stimulus from such aids, but they must be used within a human and not a mechanistic approach. All that I have written concerning the child at home and in school, or at play, applies equally to the child in church. Architecture alters for house, school, recreation hall and church but all these physical facilities contain a total environment for the child. However, a more fervent and less pragmatic approach is to be made to the child in church, than that possible for the teacher in school or the recreational supervisor, and responses that embarrass a child in practical or frivolous circumstances (school work or group play), are permissible for the child within a religious environment, according to childhood mores. We should make the most of his fervent response, to encourage self-expression and communication for the child.

Subject matter now taboo in schools is not only permissible for the religious teacher; it is required, as in comparative studies of religions. Mrs. F—, a conventional teacher, who conducts social studies (Civics) courses for students in junior high school, and also teaches Sunday school classes of young adolescents, relates her experiences within a polyglot cultural and social environment:

In the school district where I work the normal curriculum allows only a circumscribed approach to sociology and none, whatever, to religion. Although the urban educational area, bounded by suburban areas which share the high schools and junior colleges, are populated by various ethnic and religious groups, I am disallowed the introduction in my classes of "cultures" emergent from ethnic groups like Negroes and Polish, and religious groups such as Jews and Roman Catholics, all of these represented within the student body of my school. I am required to concern myself and my students with the culture of only one strata of the contemporary United States: the Caucasian, Protestant, white-collar, English-speaking group to which I belong—and which I believe needs to be known and understood by other ethnic, religious, and socio-economic groups, as much as my group needs to know and understand cultures differing from our own.

But what I am forbidden to teach in school, I am encouraged to teach out of my church, and with collaboration from other religious denominations represented through the churches in our area. Junior and senior high school children have (or should have) already become familiar with the Bible and continuing Sunday school teaching based only on the Book bores them. For six years, I have extended the basic religious instruction of our church to studies of dance and music, concentrating on the musical cultures inherent to students in the public school where I teach. Sunday school is attended by the Caucasian, Protestant, English-speaking children of white-collar workers in our area. In my classes, for the first time in their lives, these children (now in their teens) become conscious of humanity's essential and universal pattern of worshipping God through various approaches, out of various cultures, and in tenets of a variety of faiths.

They learn that the differences in societies and the differences in religion make some people and some faiths strange to others, but that what is *different from* is not, by its nature, inimical to their society and their faith! This conscious knowledge has had a very far-reaching effect in our immediate area of the country, where socio-economic stratas further subdivide the children into ethnic and religious groups, warring in gangs against each other as Jew-baiters and Roman Catholic-baiters as well as anti-Negro and anti-Polish gangs—or, reversely, gangs from these ethnic and religious groups against children of Caucasian, Protestant parentage.

The foundation of my work in our church, emanating from a lecture course under Olga Maynard in 1960, is the study of root sources of dance and music and the derivative influences of immigrant cultures and arts in contemporary America.

For example, within *Roots of Jazz* we study the Negro as he has lived, worshipped and contributed to dance and music in the north and south American hemisphere—whereby we discover that the minstrel show, the Spiritual, jazz and other dance-music of Negro origin or inspiration in the United States is not precisely that contributed by the emigré Negro to the Latin American cultures.

When I inaugurated this course of study (which is developed to extensions into reading about religions in which a society of people are largely represented as worshippers) I invited professional Negro artists to dance and sing for audiences of my church—and presented the performances through my Sunday school class. The children actively worked to make this presentation: selling tickets, ushering, and even attending to the back-stage chores. They were made responsible for the performances and accepted the responsibility with enthusiasm. The proceeds of those initial performances (which were of jazz) became the root fund of our dance and music banking account, from which we have continued to engage and present dance and music theatre representative of several cultures, some of the performances being of a "sacred" character, but not, by any means, always of this character.

Eventually, with collaboration between my church and their churches, we introduced students from peer groups (chronological age) in other religious denominations as guests at our Sunday school classes, for description and discussion of tenets and rituals as forms of religious worship. On these occasions, members of the choir of the visiting students performed for the class, by singing sacred works representative of various church feasts. Thus, at the Jewish celebration of Hannukah we entertained Jewish students in our Sunday school, and these related the significance of the feast. Eventually, when we inaugurated reciprocal visits to other churches, members of my Sunday school class performed traditional Christmas carols for students of faiths which do not celebrate the birth of Jesus Christ.

Note that I have used the words *performance* and *performed*, since there is utterly no attempt at proselytizing. And since sacred music is only one part of the dance and music studies and performances, it would be wholly incorrect to assume that our purpose is to share church music, exclusively.

Our purpose is to provide young persons with some knowledge of and a tolerance for other societies than their own, whose emigré arts and religious beliefs subdivide the American culture into multi-cultures. This "multi-culture" in American life is established and underscored by a preface, at the start of the Sunday school year, with discussion on "indigenous" American culture, exclusively that of the American Indian.

All our local churches have united in "musical culture" for their junior parishioners, and in the six years that I have developed the dance and music courses out of my Sunday school classes, the senior high schools and junior colleges to which the junior high school students of our area graduate have noted academic and social changes in their students.

Academically, students who participate in the dance and music courses are better prepared to study the social sciences in higher education. Socially, they are far less antagonistic to ethnic and religious groups other than their own. For one instance, when I began to work six years ago, night-time football games had been banned, because of gang fights between separate ethnic and religious groups, and the Polish students who continued their education into secondary school and college grades were victimized by "hazing" by students outside their ethnic and religious groups. Terms of opprobrium concerning their Polish antecedents and religious faith were used to stigmatize these students even in the elementary school grades. Faculties in local schools note a lessening of these rabid anti-social tendencies, especially in senior high school.

One of the notable results of our dance and music studies was a teen-age craze for the polka, originated in dance and music classes out of church recreation hall. The Polish society in our town had, until then, danced only for its own people; now, they danced in exhibition or performance for audiences in our church recreational hall (an auditorium with stage facilities); finally, to satisfy the demand for learning the polka, we instituted lessons in the dance, taught by accomplished Polish performers. I considered it a triumph for the dance and music course when a polka troupe began dancing well enough to be featured weekly on a local television program, and to go on short tours within our state, not because of the proficiency of the Polish Roman Catholic youngsters in the troupe—but because a number of the dancers and some of the orchestra were not of Polish antecedents nor of the Roman Catholic faith, but were by antecedents Scotch-Irish, Russian, German, and by religion Protestant and Jewish!

Dance and music, in our area, levelled the very barriers that antecedent nationality and religion had raised between boys and girls, who despised, out of ignorance, religions that were strange to them, and had no recognition of the characteristic multi-culture from which their own national heritage *as Americans* derives.

Not just incidentally, my students learn a great deal about world dance and music, also!

The individual Sunday school teacher, or worker with young persons in social and recreational projects emanating out of a religious base, will seldom have such ideal opportunities of establishing a dance and music program as this inspired teacher has had. The rewarding results and already evident worth of her work are in large part attributable to the influences within an entire area, and the collaboration of churches with each other, for the ultimate good of their young parishioners. Still, Mrs. F— offers a valuable example to other religious teachers and, positively, to dance and music teachers who participate in the social and recreational work of their churches.

The simplest approach may have far-reaching effects when one works with dance and music, and especially when these are dramatized into "action" dance and music for children. Recently, an influx of Cuban refugees into a small town precipitated a social crisis among the young parishioners of a Roman Catholic parish, whose large parochial school at once noted difficulties in the academic and social aspects of education. The Cuban children could not speak English, or spoke it haltingly, and did not understand the student idiom, plus suffering a natural bewilderment about the educational terminology for classwork. Much older than their classmates, they were physically awkward as well as academically laggard, and became the butt of their companions, half in jest—but very soon, in earnest cruelty. The Cuban children seemed alien to their American companions even when they prayed in church, since some of their rituals were subtly different from those of American Catholicism. Against all efforts of the sisters (the teaching order of nuns) and lay teachers, the school divided itself into cliques; inevitably, one clique physically pitted itself against the other with resultant warfare.

At Christmas, in choosing the annual school play, the music teacher, a lay teacher, determined to find a Spanish-spoken drama, one with music and opportunities for pageantry and dancing. I recommended to her Ariel Ramirez's *Missa Criolla*, Creole Mass, a folk composition for soloists, choir and orchestra. The teacher did not know Spanish and had very sparse facilities for presenting her sung dramatization of the birth of the Christ. For one thing, she had no orchestra or choir and was dependent on recorded music. She therefore used a taped recording of the *Missa Criolla*, as it is recorded by the Philips Connoisseur Collection, PCC 619.

Obtaining the help of bi-lingual Cuban parents of some of the children, the American sisters and lay teachers produced an amateur dance pageant to the *Missa Criolla*, in which both Cuban and English-speaking American students participated. The dramatization was by dance-mime, and the children were well rehearsed in gestures and facial expressions suited to the plot and characterization of the "play." To explain the drama, the lay teacher read the verse of the *Missa Criolla* in English translation, and bilingual parents of Cuban students read the Spanish version several times over. The children, from 6th through 8th Grades, were interested in the story, which is related in the Spanish liturgical text in use in Latin American Catholicism, and contains idiomatic phrases of the Latin American peasant. The Christ-child, according to the *Criolla,* eats honey and receives as gifts, from the shepherds who pay homage, sweet basil and cedar, thyme and laurel. The Wise Men include "black Balthazar" (to the surprise and pleasure of the Negro children in the program) and among their precious gifts is a poncho of alpaca. Parents contributed ponchos, honey, basil and thyme; teachers conducted "field trips" in search of an alpaca goat (and the feel of his hair live and woven into cloth), and of cedar and laurel wood. The children saw, smelled, touched and tasted all physical evidence of the homely little world of the Latin American peasant Christ-child, as preparation for performing their amateur *Criolla.*

Certain portions of the *Criolla* proved particularly attractive for both the Spanish and the English-speaking students, like the verse, from the Shepherds' song, in which one Julio Romero is asked for a song with a guitar. A shy and sullen boy whose name was Julio Romero was made, against his will, into a popular hero—a condition on which he softened and shone and soon thrived in his academic and social life. Presently, he was teaching new-found Americano friends to play the guitar and they were helping him to learn English and acclimate to a new society.

The *Criolla's* music, even more than its verse, enchanted the students (and, it may be noted, the audience of parents and guests who saw the dance-mime pageant performed by them). This music is made on regional instruments of Latin America conjoined with a harpsichord (which the composer chose because of its traditional role for the leading voice). Thus, for percussion there are two drums, a battery, a gong, and native instruments called *tumbadora, cocos* and *cascabeles.* In total, they make irresistible rhythms that harmonize with the choral part and more traditional (European) orchestral instrumentation. The combination of religious liturgy and folkloric art is especially evocative for the simple, familiar story of the birth of the Child to poor country people. More to the point for the purpose of the teacher who adapted it for her students, it was at once so strange yet familiar (so true and yet so far from orthodox English hymns and carols) that it enthralled the sophisticated American children even while dignifying their Cuban schoolmates.

What the composer has accomplished is a matchless contemporary *and humanized* musical work on the sacred theme, one to which very simple audiences, including those made up of children, relate in very personal terms. And, also, a work which the church is able to respect and promote for its artistry and for its conception of the peculiar and particular attributes of a society (in this case, a Spanish-speaking, lower-class society), whose customs and terms of speech as well as whose music are the basis of the composition. Perhaps no better example exists of the inherent dynamism of current Catholic ecumenism and the words of Pope Paul (*Ecclesiam Suam*) "We have to do with all that is human."*

It was clearly their involvement with the human aspects of the *Missa Criolla* that united the two alien groups of students of the parochial school, not only in a Christmas concert but, continuing out of that, as intermingling societies—so that the school has introduced Spanish classes into the curriculum, on demand, and is developing a course in Pan-American cultures that, in certain respects, is closer to the junior college curricula than the average junior high school's.

This same *human* involvement which marked the Christmas concert showed itself as what might be considered a human relationship to animal, rather than supernatural influences, when at Easter the students of another school voted against dramatization of the Crucifixion and Resurrection but staged, instead, a dance with chorus and orchestration of St. Patrick's song of the deer, taking the deer as a symbol of life, and rebirth in the spring of a year.

This amateur "Deer" production was inspired by a contemporary composition: *Discovery and Praises* by Conrad Susa, and the children were frankly interested in this work because it was new ("of our own times, and by an American composer") and because it had been commissioned for performance by a choir in which children participated.†

* The literature for the *Missa Criolla* points out that "The Church must cry as man cries . . . through its fidelity to Christ, must laugh with him who laughs. She became Greek with the Greeks and Roman with the Romans. She must continue so . . ."
† The cantata *Discovery and Praises*, now in process of publication, was commissioned for St. George's Episcopal Church, Nashville, Tennessee, by its organist and choirmaster, Gregory Colson. The premiere was Easter, 1966, by the Nashville Symphony Orchestra, under the composer's direction.

EXAMPLE FROM *The Deer*

The descriptions of two forms of approaches through dance and music, out of a religious source, are not pilot programs but merely indications of programs that may be developed by religious and lay teachers, and within the social-cum-recreational aspects of religion. Churches are not generally organized for social studies, or arts appreciation courses, but enterprising teachers within the church can develop such programs, for children, and, of course, for older parishioners.

In the case of Mrs. F—'s program, one commendable development was the bringing together of older and younger folk, in agreeable circumstances, when retired persons were recruited to help teach the patterns of old folk dances and the music and verse of folk songs. This project extended to inviting old people from a house for the indigent to visit the church community hall and play and sing for audiences, and, in turn, carried the young parishioners from their music classes to perform for audiences in houses of the aged, in orphanages, and in hospitals.

As Mrs. Kreger remarked in *The Child at Home*, religious dance on television, in general, is good. I have said: it may be the best use television has yet made of dance. But the occasional and fragmentary television religious dance dramas are not enough to sustain religious dance and music, or dynamic enough to arouse response in children and adolescents. It is the church and the church-school which must provide leadership for its parishioners in religious drama, dance and music.

We know, if we accept the evidence summed up in this book, that children sing and dance spontaneously, that they do so for joy, and also out of more poignant emotions as when they are grieved, lonely, forlorn and deeply troubled. We know that the child who sings, dances and makes music does these things for a true purpose, not for an abstract or intellectual approach to an aesthetic. *Every artistic involvement for the child is functional and the child as artist makes the most personal undertaking as the human person.*

In a religious environment, where his teachers confidently approach him with themes of the spirit, that is supernatural, and out of universal responses human creatures make towards an invisible but sought-for Divinity, there is the most persuasive influence on the child, to dance and sing with his whole heart, and his whole self. Since God is the supremest being he is capable of imagining, the child recognizes divine worship as an important act, and, if he is led to love and trust God, he will discharge the occasions of his worship familiarly, but no less profoundly; with gaiety as well as with solemnity. When the child approaches God with the confidence that *he*, in return, is loved and trusted to be his best and most beautiful self, he responds by offering himself with noblest deportment, most eloquent expression and greatest sincerity.

Then, is it not here, as the child dances and sings in church in praise of the Author of his being, that we shall know the child as he truly is—or, more wondrously, tenderly, and revealingly, as the child believes himself to be?

Appendices

Appendix I

THIS APPENDIX or outgrowth of references made to the material compiled in the 1966 Contemporary Music Report 3, is chiefly for the information of music teachers. *Pilot Projects in Experiments in Musical Creativity* were conducted in Baltimore, Maryland; San Diego, California; and Farmingdale, New York, all in elementary and junior high school. The Projects are considered as being exploratory and experimental; they were conducted in cooperation with the school systems in which the pilot programs were put into operation.

Although the scope and content of the three Projects included contemporary music and creative experiences in improvisation and composition, they were designed to serve somewhat different objectives.

The Projects in Baltimore and San Diego were organized to provide an inservice seminar for music teachers in conjunction with pilot classes at selected grade levels in different types of schools. The seminars met each week, were conducted by a composer-consultant, and involved the study and analysis of contemporary music and assignments in musical composition using various contemporary techniques. The pilot classes, taught by teachers participating in the seminar, served as laboratory groups for experimentation with techniques and materials presented in the seminar. Weekly reports were made to the seminar by the pilot class teachers.

The objectives of these projects (in Baltimore and San Diego) were to find suitable approaches for the presentation of contemporary music to children at several grade levels; experiment with techniques for providing creative music experiences for children; identify contemporary music suitable for use with students at the several grade levels; provide a new dimension in creative experiences through the use of contemporary music; and also to provide in-service education for teachers.

Background of the Baltimore Project

For many years music teachers in the Baltimore City Schools had experimented with creative approaches to music education. The creative interpretation of songs, dances and instrumental music were aspects of music programs in most elementary classrooms and for about 15 years (prior to 1964) the music and conventional classroom teachers encouraged the composition of simple songs as part of the normal classroom music experiences. However, methodology and ensuing results were frequently of questionable musical value. Improvisation had been rarely encouraged within the school music program . . . it was assumed that improvisation could become an important means of identifying and fostering creative and musical talent.

Thirty trained music teachers, working as elementary resource music teachers, participated in the seminars, which were planned to emphasize the basic elements of music; melody, harmony, rhythm, presented in the following sequence:

1. MELODY	2. HARMONY	3. RHYTHM
Scales:	Bitonality	Irregular meters
modal	Triads plus major or	Changing meters
whole tone	minor thirds	Unusual use of accent
pentatonic	Added 9th and 11ths	Polyrhythms
artificial	Added 6ths	Syncopation
Tone rows	Polychords	
Other sound sources	Use of 2nds	
(electronic music)	Chords of 4ths	
	Clusters	

Musical examples selected for analysis were chosen from sources familiar and readily available in the school system: *Music for Living Series,* publ. by Silver Burdett Company; and the RCA *Adventures in Music Series* of recordings.

BALTIMORE PROJECT'S MUSICAL EXAMPLES FROM "MUSIC FOR LIVING" SERIES

Book 1	57	In the Farmyard	chromaticism, change of note values
	80	Bell Buoys	harmonic surprise near end, does not end on tonic
	86	Pounding Waves	interesting accompaniment, natural minor scale
Book 2	6	Leaky Faucet	conventional—with sound effects
	16	Firefly	some harmonic surprises
	18	Bouncing Rabbits	use of rests, ostinato accompaniment delaying of tonic to end

Book 3   60 The Foghorn   modal accompaniment
         106 Stars   dissonant, atmospheric accompaniment elon-
                                   gated final note of phrase, easy melody

Book 4   78 Africa   good accompaniment—chord clusters melody
                                   uses major and minor, short-short-long
                                   rhythm
         95 Our History Sings   modal
        106 Freight Boats   good rhythm and harmonization

Book 5   59 Wheat Fields   modal, interesting harmony

Book 6   28 Rain in Autumn   changing meter, occasional raised 2nd
        124 Viking Song   interesting accompaniment, natural minor
                                   melody
        134 Night Journey   modal, changing meter, dissonant accompani-
                                   ment

AND FROM RCA "ADVENTURES IN MUSIC" SERIES (RECORDINGS).

Grade 1   47 Kabalevsky, "Pantomine"   ostinato in bass
                        from *The Comedians*   chromatic succession
                    Prokofiev, "March"
                        from *Summer Day Suite*
                    Thomson, "Walking Song"
                        from *Arcadian Songs
                        and Dances*

Grade 2   44 Milhaud, "Laranjeires"   repeated rhythms,
                        from *Saudades do Brazil*   dissonance,
                    Bartok, "Jack-in-the-Box"   harmonization interest
                        from *Mikrokosmos Suite* unusual ending,
                        No. 2   bitonality

Grade 3, Vol. 2 12 Bartok, "Bear Dance"   repeated note, chords—
                         from *Hungarian Sketches*   dissonant to re-
                     Thomson, "The Alligator and   peated note
                         the Coon"   percussive
                         from *Arcadian Songs
                         and Dances*

Grade 4, Vol. 2 12 Milhaud, "Copacabana"   rhythms, tango, maxixe
                         from *Saudades do Brazil* bi-tonality
                     Kodaly, "Entrance of the   dissonance—chords
                         Emperor and His Court"   moving away from
                         from *Hary Janos Suite*   each other

Grade 4, Vol. 2 (Cont.)		Menotti, "Shepherds Dance" from *Amahl and the Night Visitors*	
Grade 4, Vol. 1	78	Ginastera, "Wheat Dance" from *Estancia*	interesting rhythmic effect—shifting accent
Grade 5, Vol. 1		Gould, *American Salute*	
Grade 5, Vol. 2	37	Copland, "Hoe-Down" from *Rodeo*	accent on off-beat kind of ostinato
	22	Bartok, "An Evening in the Village" from *Hungarian Sketches*	sudden change of tonality
Grade 6, Vol. 1	70	Copland, "Street in a Frontier Town" from *Billy the Kid*	
Grade 6, Vol. 2		Walton, "Valse" from *Façade Suite*	
	12	Guarnieri, "Brazilian Dance" from *Three Dances for Orchestra*	rhythmic patterns— several occurring simultaneously

SEMINAR ASSIGNMENTS Composition assignments were made in the following order:

1. Compose a modal melody, setting a short poem.
2. Experiment with original rhythm scores for classroom percussion instruments.
3. Experiment with harmonization of a familiar folk tune, using contemporary techniques.
4. Experiment with other sound sources (kitchen utensils, glasses, homemade instruments).
5. Compose and perform tone-row compositions for classroom instruments.
6. Compose and improvise using irregular compound meter.
7. Compose a song (with accompaniment, employing musical ideas explored during the semester).

Throughout the seminars the topic of improvisation was mentioned in connection with nearly every idea discussed. The music teachers found the following suggestions to be helpful:

1. The music teacher or a student may conduct several players in a session of improvisation.

2. Establish a basic beat played by a percussion instrument as background for improvisation by one or more members of the class.
3. Introduce a repeated rhythmic pattern as a background for improvisation.
4. Initial improvisations employing pitch may be limited to an artificial scale, pentatonic scale, whole-tone scale, etc.
5. Insist upon the children listening to and evaluating their effort.
6. Suggest that the instruments "have a conversation."
7. Ask children to "play your instrument when you have something to say."
8. Avoid monotony by adding and subtracting instruments.
9. Create interest by changing meter.
10. Use a variety of means to introduce the element of surprise.

An opaque projector was utilized in the seminar to observe musical scores and compositions. Its use also enabled members of the group to perform and study each other's original compositions. Tape recorders were used extensively in recording original compositions and improvisations by teachers and pupils.

PILOT CLASSES   Four schools representing a cross-section of types in the community were chosen as sites for pilot classes. A brief description of each will serve to indicate the range and scope of the schools which were involved.

1. An inner city school, located in a crowded section of the city, with a low socio-economic level

    Pilot classes: Kindergarten and first grade

2. A school, located in an old section of the city, with an average socio-economic level

    Pilot classes: A first-grade class and a combination first- and second-grade class

3. A school, located in a residential area, with an above-average socio-economic level

    Pilot classes: Third and fourth grades

4. A suburban area-type school, with a high socio-economic level

    Pilot classes: Fifth and sixth grades

CONTEMPORARY MUSIC—BRIEF LISTING

Baltimore Project's Recommendations For Classroom Work and Private Study

COMPOSER	TITLE	RECORDING
Rhythm		
Barber	Commando March	Columbia OL 5230
Bartók	Dance Suite	Columbia CL 920
Bartók	Roumanian Dances	Austin 6240
Bernstein	Candide Overture	Mercury MG 50132
Bernstein	Fancy Free (Danzon)	Mercury MG 50183
Bernstein	West Side Story	Mercury MG 50079

COMPOSER	TITLE	RECORDING
Copland	El Salón México	RCA Victor LM 1928
Hanson	Merry Mount Suite (Children's Dance)	Mercury MG 50175
Honegger	Pacific 231	London LL 9119
Khachaturian	Masquerade	Capitol P 8530
Khachaturian	Sabre Dance	Capitol P 8530
Milhaud	Creation of the Earth	Columbia CL 920
Milhaud	Saudades do Brazil	Vanguard 1023
Persichetti	Divertimento	Mercury MG 50079
Stravinsky	The Firebird (Infernal Dance)	Columbia ML 5728
Stravinsky	The Rite of Spring	Columbia ML 5719
Villa-Lobos	The Little Train of the Caipira	Columbia CL 798
(Cage, Cowell, etc.)	Concert Percussion for Orchestra	Time 58000
. . . .	Music of Bali	Period SPL 1613
Brubeck	Time Out	Columbia CL 1397
Brubeck	Time Further Out	Columbia CL 1690

Melody

Barber	Adagio for Strings	Philips 500001
Bartók	Concerto for Orchestra	Columbia ML 5471
Britten	Young Person's Guide to the Orchestra	Columbia ML 5183
Hanson	Merry Mount Suite	Mercury MG 50175
Hindemith	Mathis der Maler	Columbia ML 4816
Orff	Carmina Burana	Angel 35415
. . . .	Music of Bali	Period SPL1613

Long Melodic Lines

Barber	Adagio for Strings	Philips 500001
Bartók	Concerto for Orchestra	Columbia ML 5471
Hindemith	Mathis der Maler	Columbia ML 4816
Shostakovich	Symphony No. 5	Everest 6010
Villa-Lobos	Bachianas Brasileiras	Capitol L 8043

Harmony

Bartók	Sonata for Two Pianos and Percussion	Vox 9600
Schuller	Seven Studies after Paul Klee	Mercury MG 50282
Shostakovich	Symphony No. 5	Everest 6010
Stravinsky	Octet for Winds	Columbia ML 4964
Villa-Lobos	Bachianas Brasileiras No. 2	Capitol L 8043

COMPOSER	TITLE	RECORDING

Form

Bartók	Concerto for Orchestra	Columbia ML 5471
Bloch	Concerto Grosso For String Orchestra with Piano Obbligato	Mercury MG 50223
Britten	Young Person's Guide to the Orchestra	Columbia ML 5183
Hindemith	Mathis der Maler	Columbia ML 4816
Kabalevsky	The Comedians	Capitol P 8530
Khachaturian	Masquerade	Capitol P 8530
Milhaud	Suite Française	Mercury MG 50173
Milhaud	Suite Provençale	RCA Victor LD 2625

Percussion

Antheil	Ballet Mécanique	Columbia ML 4956
Bartók	Sonata for Two Pianos and Percussion	Vox 9600
(Cage, Cowell, etc.)	Concert Percussion for Orchestra	Time 58000
. . . .	Music of Bali	Period SPL 1613

Improvisations

Brubeck	Dialogues for Jazz Combo and Orchestra	Columbia CL 1466
Foss	Time Cycle (Soprano and improvisation ensemble)	Columbia ML 5680

Twelve-Tone

Berg, Schönberg, Křenek	Piano music (Glenn Gould, pianist)	Columbia ML 5336
Berg, Schönberg, Webern	Orchestra works	Columbia ML 5616
Webern	The Complete Music (Robert Craft, conductor)	Columbia K4L 232

Electronic Music and Musique Concrète

Powell	Electronic Setting	Son Nova 1
Stockhausen	Gesang der Jünglinge	Deutsche Grammophon 138811
Ussachevsky	Piece for Tape Recorder	CRI 112
Varèse	Poème Electronique	Columbia ML 5478
(Babbitt, Luening, etc.)	Columbia-Princeton Electronic Music Center	Columbia ML 5966
(Cage, Cowell, etc.)	Sounds of New Music	Folkways FX 6160

Background of the San Diego Project

This Project was developed out of concern for the limited emphasis given to contemporary music as part of the music curriculum in most elementary and junior high schools. The purpose of the Project was to explore possibilities for teaching contemporary music in elementary and junior high schools.

Twenty-eight music supervisors and classroom teachers participated in the seminar, which was conducted in a lecture-demonstration format by the composer-consultant, Dr. David Ward-Steinman. Reports of the activities of the pilot classes during the previous week were presented to the seminar each week by pilot-class teachers.

The seminar content was organized to focus on the elements of rhythm, melody and harmony as used by contemporary composers, and the formal structure of music was considered in relation to the compositions studied.

SOME CONTEMPORARY MUSIC USED IN THE SEMINAR

COMPOSER	TITLE	RECORDING
Antheil	Ballet Mécanique	Columbia ML 4956
Babbitt	Composition for Four Instruments	Son Nova CRL 138
Bartók	Sonata for Two Pianos and Percussion	Vox 9600
Bartók	Mikrokosmos, Vol. III	Columbia ML 5084
Boulez	Le Marteau sans Maître	Columbia ML 5275
Britten	Peter Grimes: 4 Sea Interludes and Passacaglia	London 6179
Britten	Serenade for Tenor, Horn, and Strings	London 5358
Brubeck	The Riddle	Columbia CL 1454
Brubeck	Time Out	Columbia CL 1397
Brubeck	Time Further Out	Columbia CL 1690
Cage	Amores for Prepared Piano and Percussion	Time 58000
Chanler	Epitaphs	Columbia ML 5598
Copland	Appalachian Spring	Victor LM 2401
Copland	Billy the Kid	Columbia ML 5157
Copland	Symphony No. 3	Everest 6018
. . . .	Dancers of Bali	Columbia ML 4618
Debussy	Estampes for Piano	Columbia ML 4979
Dello Joio	Sonata No. 3 for Piano	Concert Disc 1217
Dello Joio	Variations, Chaconne, and Finale	Columbia ML 5263
Diamond	World of Paul Klee	CRI 140
Hanson	The Composer and His Orchestra	Mercury MG 50175
Harrison	Four Strict Songs for 8 Baritones and Orchestra	Louisville 58-2
Hindemith	Mathis der Maler	Columbia ML 4816

COMPOSER	TITLE	RECORDING
Hindemith	Trauermusik for Viola and Strings	Epic LC 3356
Honegger	Pacific 231	Westminster 18486
Honegger	Rugby	Westminster 18486
. . . .	Invitation to Music	Folkways FT 3603
Ives	Hallowe'en	Cambridge 804
Ives	Three Places in New England	Mercury MG 50149
Luening-Ussachevsky	Poem in Cycles and Bells	CRI 112
McPhee	Tabuh-Tabuhan	Mercury MG 50103
Milhaud	Les Choëphores	Columbia ML 5796
Milhaud	La Muse Ménagère	SPA 12
Milhaud	Saudades do Brazil	Vanguard 1023
Mossolov	Iron Foundry	Folkways 6160
Partch	The Wayward: U.S. Highball	Gate 5 Records, Issue B
Piston	Symphony No. 4	Columbia ML 4992
Prokofiev	Lieutenant Kije Suite	Columbia ML 5101
Rogers	Leaves from the Tale of Pinocchio	Mercury MG 50114
Rogers	Three Japanese Dances	Mercury MG 50173
Schuller	Concertino for Jazz Quartet and Orchestra	Atlantic 1359
Schuller	Seven Studies on themes of Paul Klee	Mercury MG 50282
Smith	Concerto for Clarinet and Combo	Contemporary 6001
Stravinsky	Agon	Columbia ML 5215
Stravinsky	Firebird Suite	Columbia ML 4882
Stravinsky	Le Sacre du Printemps	Columbia ML 4882

RHYTHM IN CONTEMPORARY MUSIC

1. The first important use of rhythm as a structural element was in Stravinsky's *The Rite of Spring.*

See also: Ives, *First Piano Sonata:* 4th movement

2. Syncopation
   1. Syncopation is achieved through a variety of techniques: change of accent, change of meter, etc.

Bartók, *Piano Concerto No. 3:* 3rd movement

cross rhythm and cross accent

Britten, *Peter Grimes:* 4 Sea Interludes: "Sunday Morning"

Piston, *Symphony No. 4:*
2nd movement — meter change
4th movement — accent, not meter change

2. Syncopation is an
   important element of
   jazz which has
   strongly influenced
   concert music.

3. Rhythmic Drive	Antheil, *Ballet Mécanique*	score calls for 2 airplane engines
	Orff, *Catulli Carmina*	
	Prokofiev, *Scythian Suite,* op. 20	
	Stravinsky, *The Rite of Spring:*	
4. Unusual meters (It is difficult to find recorded examples sufficiently repetitive and slow enough for easy analysis.)	Brubeck, *Time Further Out:*	7/4 meter
	Unsquare Dance	
	Far More Blue	5/4 meter
	Brubeck, *Time Changes:*	
	Unisphere	10/4 meter
	Riegger, *New Dance*	predominantly 7/4 meter
	Tchaikovsky, *Symphony No. 6:*	5/4 meter
	2nd movement	
5. Changing meter	Bartók, *Mikrokosmos,* Vol. V, No. 126	2/4, 3/4, 3/8, 5/8, repeated 5 times
1. The purpose of changing meters is to attempt to bar music according to the natural phrase lengths.	Brubeck, *Time Out:* Three to Get Ready	after introduction, 3/4, 3/4, 4/4, 4/4, repeated throughout
	Stravinsky, *The Rite of Spring:* "Danse Sacrale"	rapidly changing meter
6. Apparently free rhythms (no fixed meter)	Harrison, *Suite for Violin, Piano, and Small Orchestra:*	
1. Unmetered music is an Oriental or Eastern concept for the most part, and is not common in Western music.	1st movement	

7. Polyrhythm	Siegmeister recording, *Invitation to Music: Rhythm and beat*	good introduction to rhythm

MELODY IN CONTEMPORARY MUSIC

1. Scale sources (various divisions of the octave) are:	Debussy, *Dance of Puck*	Dorian
	Debussy, *String Quartet:* beginning	Phrygian
1. Early church modes	Debussy, *The Sunken Cathedral*	Mixolydian
1. Church modes are rarely used consistently by contemporary composers, although they were rather thoroughly explored by Debussy and others.	Ravel, *Daphnis and Chloë:* "Daybreak" theme	Aeolian
2. Gapped scales	recording, *Dancers of Bali*	
1. Scales employing selected notes from major or minor scales.	Bartók, *Mikrokosmos,* Vol. IV, No. 109, "From the Island of Bali"	2 pentatonic scales, one against the other
2. Pentatonic scales date back at least to 2000 B.C.	Debussy, *Pagodes*	
(1) Pentatonic scales often consist of intervals of 3 whole steps, 1 step-and-a-half, followed by another whole step.	Harrison, *4 Strict Songs for 8 Baritones and Orchestra*	all pentatonic, not tuned to tempered scale; use of re-tuned strings, piano and harp; also trombone and percussion
	Harrison, *Suite for Violin, Piano, and Orchestra*	
(2) The Balinese and Javanese pentatonic scale (*slendro*) contains	McPhee, *Tabuh-Tabuhan*	
	Partch, *2 Studies on Ancient Greek Scales*	one pentatonic with Phrygian references

5 equidistant steps. Music for the *gamelon* (Javanese xylophone) has influenced a number of contemporary composers.

Poulenc, *Sonata for Piano, 4 hands:* 2nd movement

Rogers, *3 Japanese Dances:* No. 1

Stravinsky, *The Rite of Spring:* "Spring Rounds"   clarinet melody

3. The whole-tone scale was used most frequently by Debussy and, to a lesser extent, Ravel. It is not used frequently by contemporary composers.

Debussy, *Preludes, Book 1:* "Voiles"

Hanson, *For the First Time:* "Mists"   most concentrated use of whole-tone scale by Debussy

   1. There are two possible whole-tone scales, one starting on C, the other on C♯ for example

   2. An early example of whole-tone scale is in Mozart's *A Musical Joke* (in the violin cadenza) as a scale that goes awry.

4. Contemporary composers who are writing tonally generally select material freely from many scales or keys.

2. Harmonic sources

   1. Tertian: harmonic structures based on thirds

Britten, *Peter Grimes: Four Sea Interludes*   long clarinet lines in thirds

	Copland, *Appalachian Spring*	A-major triads with E-major triads super-imposed
	Harrison, *Mass:* Gloria	
2. Quartal and quintal: harmonic structures based on fourths and fifths	Hindemith, *Mathis der Maler*	
	Piston, *Symphony No. 4:* 1st movement	
3. Development of melodic material is accomplished through octave displacements.	Copland, *Piano Variations*	quasi-serial
	Copland, *Symphony No. 3*	
	Dello Joio, *Piano Sonata No. 3:* 1st movement, variation I	
1. Though not completely new (it is found in Bach), it is an important contemporary technique.	Prokofiev, *"Classical" Symphony:* subordinate theme of 1st movement.	
2. Octave displacement accounts for the jaggedness in much 20th-century music		

4. Serial music
   1. The twelve-tone system
      1. The twelve-tone system (or "technique") was first developed around 1923–4 by Schönberg in an attempt to create a new system of musical organization to replace the existing tonal system, which he then considered to have been exhausted.

2. The "equal" use of all 12 tones applies only to the early periods after the formulation of the theory. Serial composers now use any group of the 12 tones as a "series" or "basic set" such as a hexachord (6 notes) that inverts (or is otherwise permuted) to produce a complementary hexachord completing the total chromatic; the hexachords may be further segmented and the segments may function autonomously, if desired.

2. Serial music is no more "mathematical" or "contrived" than the principles of 16th-century counterpoint. Characteristics of serial music include:

1. Automatic octave displacement or octave equivalance —the row presupposes any tone in any octave.

2. A row or series is available in 48 forms: original, retrograde, inversion, retrograde-inversion, and 11 transpositions of each; i.e. 4 prime forms that can be stated at any of the 12 pitches of the chromatic scale.

3. Extensive use of octave displacement, fragmentation, and rarefaction; (e.g., pointillism, *Klangfarbenmelodie*).

	Babbitt, *Composition for Four Instruments*	rarefied pointillism, serial treatment of rhythm and dynamics as well as pitches.
	Berg, *Violin Concerto:* 1st movement	clear statement of basic series after introduction
	Boulez, *Le Marteau sans Maître*	
	Diamond, *The World of Paul Klee*	compare with Schuller work, below; compare both with Klee paintings
	Schönberg, *String Quartet No. 4:* 3rd movement	unison statement of a 12-tone series
	Schuller, 7 *Studies on Themes of Paul Klee:* "The Twittering Machine"	
	"The Little Blue Devil"	an example of "third Stream" music
	Stravinsky, *Agon*	uses 3 series of 12 notes each, 2 series of 6 notes each, and "free" material

	Webern, *Symphony, Op. 21:* 2nd movement	opening theme is a 12-tone series
3. In "free" serial music the order of the tones is not determined in advance or rigidly followed.	Bartok, *String Quartet No. 3* Bartok, *String Quartet No. 4* Scriabin, "Mystic Chord" compositions	

HARMONY IN CONTEMPORARY MUSIC

1. Harmony is created by three or more sounds heard together; it is the vertical combination of musical elements.		
2. Contemporary (as opposed to traditional) harmonizations of folk tunes can be felt or recognized without being analyzed.	Harris, *Folk-Song Symphony* Harris, "Streets of Laredo" and "Wayfaring Stranger" in *American Ballads for Piano* Hindemith, "Old Hundredth" in *Trauermusik* Ward-Steinman, "Twinkle, Twinkle, Little Star" and "Happy Birthday" harmonization	written for this Project pub. Lee Roberts Music Publications, Inc. N.Y. [Rbt. Pace Series] as *Improvisations of Children's Songs.* Includes "Frère Jacques"
3. Some contemporary composers create compositions in which the harmony is based on a	Bartok, *Concerto for Orchestra:* 2nd movement, "Pairs at Play"	each pair of instruments scored in parallel motion at a different interval;

single interval or part
of a scale.

e.g., bassoons in
6ths, oboes in 3rds.
clarinets in 7ths

Bartok, *Mikrokosmos:*
Vol. V, No. 129,
"Alternating
Thirds"
Vol. V, No. 131,
"Fourths"
Vol. V, No. 132,
"Major Seconds,
Broken and To-
gether"
Vol. V, No. 136,
"Whole-Tone
Scale"

Bartok, *Mikrokosmos:*
Vol. V, No. 137,
"Unison"
Vol. VI, No. 144,
"Minor Seconds,
Major Sevenths"

Hanson, *For the First
Time:* "Bells"   perfect fifths

4. Polyharmonic or poly-   Honegger, *King David:*   also implies polytonality
chordal music simul-   Brass fanfare (No.
taneously employs   3A)
chords or triads with   Milhaud, *Les Choë-*
different "roots," fre-   *phores:* 2nd move-
quently from two or   ment, "Libation"
more keys, combined in   Stravinsky, *The Rite of*   Eb 7th superimposed
various ways. (The   *Spring:* "Dance of   on Fb major chord
lowest note generally   the Adolescents"
functions as the root.)
1. An early use in "The
Petrouchka chord"
(Stravinsky): C ma-
jor and F♯ major
combined.
2. The most systematic
exploration and use

of polychords has
been by Milhaud.

5. Bitonal or polytonal
harmony is the simul-
taneous sounding of
two or more keys or
tonalities that can be
analyzed separately
(even though the ear
tends to relate them
and to hear only one
root or tonality at a
time).

Britten, *A Ceremony of
Carols:* "There is
No Rose"

voices and harp bass
line in F, upper
parts move into D
and A over osti-
nato bass in F

Honegger, *King David:*
March (No. 5)

A rare example of poly-
tonality—3 keys
are used: A bass
ostinato, trumpets
in E major, horns
in D minor

Ives, *3 Places in New
England:* 2nd
movement, "Gen-
eral Putnam's
Camp"

simulates Ives' memory
of 2 bands playing
simultaneously in
different keys

Milhaud, *Saudades do
Brazil*

various movements
were analyzed har-
monically

Prokofiev, *Lt. Kije
Suite:* "The Burial
of Kije"

polytonal middle sec-
tion

6. Pandiatonic harmony is
a richer, more complex
use of tone material
which cannot always be
broken down into sim-
ple chords; it is a free
chromatic enrichment
of essentially diatonic
harmony.
   1. Tone clusters are the
   simultaneous sound-
   ing of several adja-
   cent notes.
      1. A cluster effect is
      produced when
      several notes of

Cowell, *Advertisement*

one triad are su-
perimposed on an
adjacent triad;
e.g., C major and
D major.

2. Early experiment-
ers with tone
clusters were Co-
well and Ives.

7. Quartal and quintal harmony is based on a preponderance of intervals of fourths and fifths.	Bartok, *Piano Concerto No. 2:* 2nd movement	primarily quintal
	Milhaud, *Saudades do Brazil* "Laranjeiras" (No. 11)	quintal and quartal
	Many examples by Hindemith and Piston	

JAZZ AND "THIRD-STREAM" MUSIC

1. Improvisation, prevalent during the Baroque and Classical periods, has been reintroduced into concert performance.		
2. Jazz forms have been extended into rhapsodies, free forms, etc. by Kenton, Ellington, Herman, Smith, et al.	Bill Smith (on Brubeck record), *The Riddle*	extended jazz composition utilizing improvisation
	Smith, *Concerto for Clarinet and Combo*	full-scale "classic" concerto in formal structure, but written in jazz idiom
3. "Third Stream" music was named by Gunther Schuller	Schuller, *Concertino for Jazz Quartet and Orchestra*	
1. "Third-stream" attempts to combine the freedom of jazz with technical inno-	Schuller, *Conversations for Jazz Quartet and String Quartet*	controlled improvisations in both groups

vations of contempo-
rary concert music.
2. The feeling of jazz is
retained, but the
greater resources of
the contemporary
idiom are available.

ELECTRONIC MUSIC

1. The first electronic
music dates from about
1948.

2. The French school:
Musique concrète
  1. Live or real sound
  sources are manipu-
  lated electronically.
  2. It is also known in
  the U.S.A. as "tape-
  recorder music."
  3. Proponents are:
  Boulez, Schaeffer,
  Henry.

3. The German School:
Electronic music
  1. Only synthetic (electronically generated)
  sounds are used.
  2. Techniques include:
  playing the tape at
  different speeds, play-
  ing the tape back-
  wards, cutting and
  splicing, loop ostina-
  tos, filtering, echo
  effects.
  3. Proponents are:
  Stockhausen, Eimart,
  Pousseur.

4. No distinction is made between the schools in the U.S.A. Centers for creating electronic music in the U.S.A. are located at:
   1. Columbia-Princeton (combined facilities): Luening and Ussachevsky (Columbia); Sessions and Babbitt (Princeton)
   2. Yale: Powell
   3. Illinois: Hiller
   4. San Fernando Valley State College, California.
   5. San Francisco Tape Music Center
   6. University of Michigan

recording, *Columbia-Princeton Electronic Music Center*

Berio, *Circles* (poem by e e cummings)

Henry, *Vocalise* from recording, *2nd Panorama of Musique Concrète* (Ducretet-Thompson)

Luening-Ussachevsky, *Poem in Cycles and Bells*

language broken into vowels, consonants, letters, etc., imitation of electronic technique

human voice sings "ah"

orchestra and tape recorder

CHANCE (ALEATORY) MUSIC*

1. Composers of chance music include: Berio, Cage, Stockhausen.

The Farmingdale Project differed from the others, in that it was designed to demonstrate two types of creative teaching. The students in the Baltimore and San Diego Projects were "average." In contrast, those in the Farmingdale Project were thirty-one musically talented children, students of Grades 6, 7 and 8. They worked in the Farmingdale Project for a six-week period during summer, outside the normal school-year.

Objectives of the Farmingdale Project were to demonstrate experimental techniques in musical composition, using 20th century idioms; and to demonstrate the development of musical resources through rhythmics, singing, improv-

---

* "Aleatory" or indeterminate and 'by chance' compositions of dance and music are a contemporary mode and the term derives from the Latin *alea*: a game of dice. Proponents of the mode practice a reversal or distortion of conventional movement in dance and rules in music. The compositional form speculates on intuitive potentials.

isation, and composition. While previous activities of this type have been focused on creative experiences with traditional musical styles and materials, the emphasis in Farmingdale was on contemporary music.

The background and purpose of the project were based on the Farmingdale schools' previous experimentation with approaches to studying music based on the thesis that student involvement in total musical experience (composition, performance, and listening) provides greater motivation and results in more musical learning than the traditional or standard program for music education in the public school.

Experimentation was focused on learning through discovery and creative experience, using 20th century musical composition techniques as a point of departure. The underlying philosophy of this experiment was based on the spiral curriculum approach to conceptual teaching and learning advocated by Jerome Bruner. Previous experimentation had been limited, in classes conducted during the school year. The summer pilot program of six weeks duration provided opportunity for more extensive study, and exploration of the interrelationship between creative experiences in composition and the development of musical resources, through training in rhythmic studies and movement.

CREATIVE EXPERIENCE USING 20TH-CENTURY MUSIC TECHNIQUES

An outline of the subject
    1. Discussion of music as sound
    2. Discussion of form in music
    3. Twentieth-century techniques
        Natural vocal sounds
        Twelve-tone row
        Setting natural speech patterns
        Pandiatonic harmony
        Triadic harmony
        Symmetrical chords

    4. Instrumentation and sonorities
        Percussive gadgets
        Improvisation on all instruments
        Small ensembles
        Tunable percussion
        Brass choirs
        Open woodwinds
        Nasal type instruments
        Piano
        Voice
        Electronic instruments

EXPLORATORY EXPERIENCES

1. Groups of 3, 4, and 5 children created vocal compositions using unorthodox sounds, such as shouts, whoops, clicks, and grunts, and devising their own system of notation. After rehearsal, a performance for the class was followed by discussion and critique regarding general concepts of composition.

2. The groups then were assigned to approximate the vocal sounds by using their instruments in normal and unusual ways (back of the violin, brass instrument mouthpieces, etc.).

3. Students were asked to bring an object from their room at home and to explore various sounds which could be produced with this object as a basis for experimental composition using new or unusual sources of sound. The "instruments" brought to class included a wastebasket (drum), perfume bottle and bobbie pins, machine-gun shell and spiral bound notebook, Morse-code oscillator, and night table lamp.

4. Following a study of intervals, the construction of the 12-tone row was introduced, including presentation of retrograde, inversion, and retrograde inversion. After a row had been determined, several instrumentalists experimented with improvisation for the class. The students were assigned to construct a tone row, using the several devices already introduced, and to shape an instrumental piece to be performed in class the following day.

5. The students were assigned to take a page from a newspaper, determine rhythmic values of the natural speech patterns, and set these rhythms to pitches to be sung by the class.

6. Triad construction was introduced to be used for accompaniment on the piano or with a combination of instruments.

7. The use of open woodwind sonorities (piccolo, flute, and clarinet) employing triadic or bitonal devices was presented as the introduction to instrumental sonorities. Students were encouraged to employ all the devices previously studied, but were free to select any system of pitch organization already introduced. At this point special emphasis was given to the importance of presenting accurate scores written in concert pitch. Copying details were carefully observed to insure accurate and correct notation.

8. Nasal sonorities included oboes, bassoons in certain registers, and brass with some mutes.

9. Stringed instrument sonorities were introduced with the use of symmetrical chord structures. Performance of these pieces was perhaps the most difficult, owing to the limited technical proficiency of the performers. However, the challenge contributed to substantial improvement in performance.

10. Recordings of compositions by Stravinsky, Berg, Webern, Schönberg, Milhaud, Honegger, Dello Joio, Ives, and Varèse were introduced in the third week. The class discussed each composition with respect to the use of sonorities, harmonic devices, and other similar matters.

11. An explanation of the organization of traditional and modified scales was followed by an assignment to use one of these scales (or an original scale) as the basis for a piano piece.

12. Brass-instrument sonorities groupings, including both conical and cylindrical, were the basis for an assignment in pandiatonic harmony.

The Farmingdale Project—Developing Musicianship Through Rhythmic Studies

The approach is according to theories originated by Dalcroze, on the principle that physical movement can be combined with musical sound for the development of musicianship.

Rhythmic Experiences: A six-week program was designed to encourage students* to discover their own musical resources through experiences with musical elements, isolated and in synthesis. It was discovered that through such experiences musical concepts were made vivid, and music assumed the form of a "native language," in which the students were able to think, imagine, construct and create. The relationship of (dance) actions to musical sounds was emphasized, with the body assuming the role of a musical instrument, moving in response to various types of musical stimulus—experienced by combining listening to music, and thinking and acting *in* music. Movement, the source of musical rhythm, is itself the means for rhythmic awareness, and through it students are able to translate something abstract into something physically real and visually meaningful.

The movements advocated in this pilot program are those used in daily life: steps, gestures, and swinging movements. For musical purposes, they differ from ordinary or pedestrian locomotion in respect to the amount of the total body weight deployed, and the manner in which the body is used. These three main types of movements are freely interchangeable, each may assume a dominant or supporting character, according to the decisive musical element. The step, in particular, is flexible in time and motion, and in level and direction and weight, and in rhythmic studies it may be considered as equivalent in movement to aural effects in time, from simple metrical successions of equal units to the most complex rhythmical designs.

These exercises were conducted through the main musical elements of Rhythm, Melody, and Harmony, organized in sequences.

RHYTHM   Students thought of their bodies as a type of instrument, in an exercise demanding complete coordination, with disassociation of their limbs. They were challenged in the capacity to hear others in ensemble playing and singing, and to imagine and produce contrasting rhythmic patterns simultaneously in improvising and composing.

* 31 students from Grades 6 through 8.

1. Reproduce in movement the flow and energy of sounds played on the piano. "Follow" musical changes produced on the piano with respect to speed and energy. Observe and reproduce the sense of climax on the musical context heard.

2. Lengthen beats by changes in values of pitches and rests, and through fluctuation of musical flow.

3. Divide beats into simple subdivisions. Produce basic simple patterns.

(♫ , ♬♬ , ♩♬ , ♬♩ , etc.)

4. Combine basic simple patterns into more complex groups.

(♩ ♩ , ♩. ♬♬ , ♩ ♩ ♩♩♩ , etc.)

5. Examine and experience metric shapes: time-signatures, recurrent patterns, etc.

6. Divide beats into more complex subdivisions: compound subdivisions. Produce basic compound patterns.

(♩. , ♫♩ , ♩ ♪ , ♪ ♩ , ♩. ♫ , ♫ ♩. , etc.)

7. Combine basic compound patterns into more complex groupings in appropriate meters.

(♫♩ ♩. , ♩. ♩. ♩. ♫♩ , ♫♩.♩ ♩. ♩♩. ♪♩ | , etc.)

8. Exercise in diminution and augmentation of patterns.

9. Produce and play ostinato patterns against free improvisation on the piano.

10. Reverse the above procedure: students' free improvisation against piano ostinato.

11. Develop facilities in polyrhythms and contrasting patterns produced by hands and feet or voice and hands. Prepare scores.

12. Study complementary rhythms and syncopations.

13. Exercise patterns in contrast to a prevailing meter.

4/4 ♩ ♫♫♩ | ♫♫♩ ♫ | ♩.♫♩ ♫♫♩ etc.

14. Exercise in distortion of patterns.

♩ ♫ becomes ♪♩♫ or ♩. ♫ etc.

15. Study the relationships between 3/4 and 6/8; 3/2, 6/4, and 12/8; 15/8 and 3/

16. Exercise in independent subdivision of the same beat: 2 against 3, 3 against 2, etc.

MELODY   Attention was then focused on pitch through solo singing, unison singing, and part singing. The musical material ranged from intervallic exercises to
polyphonic motets. Improvisations, individually and in groups, and conducting
were also included.

Every musical example was heard and sung until it was recognized as a
tangible sonority. As in rhythmic experiences, the approach was from doing to
knowing. Above all, the emphasis was given to developing an awareness of intervals as the building stones of music. The instruction and exercises were developed around the following topics.

1. Ingredients of melody pre-existent in speech:
   stress, timbre, movement-repose.
2. The typical linear quality of melody.
   Step-wise motion: rise and fall
   Melodic curves of speech
   Half-steps, modes, scales

Translate speech-mel-
ody into staff nota-
tion.

3. Motion by skips
   Easy skips in generally step-wise motion
4. Use of a chain of seconds in composing and
   sight reading
   How a chain of seconds produces motion

Note the tendency in
speech to use skips
when calling some-
one. Experiment
and notate skips
in speech.

5. Steps and skips in plain chant and Renaissance music
   Steps and skips, if they are the only tone
   or the first tone of a series on a syllable,
   produce emphasis by change of direction.
   Melisma produces emphasis by prolonga-
   tion.

Using these devices, in-
vent melodies on
given text.

6. Intervals—the shape and "feel" of intervals
   The meaning of an ascending interval dif-
   fers from the same descending interval
   Roots
   The distance between the root and its com-
   plement
   Inversions of intervals (a fourth becomes
   a fifth, etc)
7. Tension in intervals
   The order of gradation of tension
   The overtone series—the family of intervals
   The role of intervals as basic materials of
   music
   The binding force of intervals

8. The combination of intervals:
   Major and minor triads
   Triad inversions and seventh-chord inversions
9. Feeling harmonic cells and fields in a melodic
   succession
   The effect of harmonic cells and fields in
   halting the flow of harmonic rhythm
10. Combining harmonic cells and fields with the
    chain of seconds
    How each of these two forces acts upon
    tones, endowing them with metrical and
    rhythmical shapes, independent of exter-
    nal rhythm
11. Non-harmonic tones: Organize the class as a
    Neighboring tones, passing tones, etc.   3 or 4 part chorus
12. The harmonic tension of intervals maintained
    in chords
    The order of gradation of chords according
    to this principle of harmonic tension
13. Roots of intervals and the resulting roots of
    chords
14. Tonal centers
    Harmonic cells and fields during a succes-
    sion of chord-roots; (the tonal center in
    the one tone that more or less predomi-
    nates after such a succession)
    Tonality as harmony spread out melodic-
    ally in time*
15. Ternary tunes (ABA) leading to lyric forms
    Binary tunes (AB) leading to sonata forms

Summary and Future Implications of the 1966 Report reads:

It should be emphasized that the Pilot Projects were exploratory and experimental in design and not intended to suggest an organized pattern of instruction. It should also be understood that inclusion of contemporary music is
intended to supplement and expand the present music curriculum in American
elementary education [not intended to supplant it, or to cancel the approaches
through traditional or "standard" music.]

The development of these Pilot Programs came about from the realization
that, in general, "creative experiences" have been emphasized in music only in
the primary grades, and, in many instances, were limited to activities that were

* To quote Milton, "Harmony is Melody, writ Large."

entertaining rather than educational [the children were approached in play, not as working in music.] In addition, emphasis on creative experiences in music has usually decreased in the public schools at each succeeding level of higher grades, with little or no emphasis on creativity in the intermediate grades or in junior high school.

It should be noted, too, that although the *Contemporary Music Project* is interested in identifying and developing the creative talent of students who appear gifted in music, it is also vitally concerned with the application of a "creative" approach in teaching music to *all* children.

Current systems in musical education seem to favor students in high school grades and to neglect those in the primary grades. I urge music teachers to work as much as possible with infants and young children as well as older students. The learning process is not yet thoroughly explored and, I have reason to believe, is greatly underestimated in young children. Remember, however, that the most admirable approach is one which inspires the child to make good associations with the subject.

Music teachers are already familiar with problems of how to teach a cohesive program to the transient students of today's schools. This and the other problem of the school "drop-out" will become increasingly difficult to solve and the Music faculty of a school must devise the best means of teaching as much as possible in the shortest period. The Contemporary Music Project in Washington, D.C. recently initiated college pilot programs in "Comprehensive Musicianship," a two-year course of total musical studies, including composition, history, performance and theory. Instruction is through scores and recordings; no textbooks are used in class. The programs in effect in 1967 were at the University of Arizona, Tucson, and the California State Colleges at Hayward, San Diego and San José. "Comprehensive Musicianship" is a course of study for college students but could not certain of its principles be adapted for music education in the elementary and secondary grades?

Appendix II

As has been said, the conventional teacher without extensive training in dance and music may, with proper preparation and the correct approach, attempt work in dance and music for the child, and especially the pre-school child or the student in elementary education.

I believe that before approaching dance and music, however, the conventional teacher must have a period of training under a cognitive teacher, not only in methodology but also in the philosophy or attitude requisite for this work.

It is all too obvious that our current school system in the elementary grades, and into high school grades, is lamentably lacking in sufficient opportunities for the average student to discover and develop original ideas, or for his teacher to provide opportunities that might encourage the child to attempt creative work. Through working in dance and music and their sister arts, such opportunities present themselves as infinite and may be contained within normal education, either in class work or in the supervised recreation that is, in fact, recreational-education.

The conventional teacher, as well as the teacher in a Music faculty, must seek and find all practical ways of approaches to the child, and should work as closely as possible with the artist-teacher or cognitive teacher to develop methods of approach distinctive to herself and the children she teaches. Seminar studies under cognitive teachers in dance and music are an excellent preparation for "creative teaching acts" but such seminars must also encompass a philosophic insight into an approach to the child, and studies of the values of the arts in education, and how these values are applicable in education.

Unfortunately, only a very few cognitive teachers of dance and music are fully qualified to conduct such all encompassing seminars. The conventional teacher, too, relies on written and recorded data today, rather than on the human relationship of teacher-student—and here, again, there are few books or records which do more than generalise on the principles of an approach to children and dance and music.

Teachers have to evolve approaches that are at the same time encouraging and challenging, but most conventional teachers do not know how to begin to work with dance and music, and especially with very young children. I have therefore included in this book, as *Appendix II*, a *Pilot Program in Dance and music for Pre-School Children*, drawn from one of the best recordings extant: *Dance Music for Pre-School Children*, LP 407, S & R Records, New York, directed by choreographer-teacher Bruce King, music composed and played by Douglas Nordli.

This recording was produced in 1963 and remains the best basic work of its kind that I know—and I know it well and have put it to uses far beyond those defined for it by King and Nordli, who intended it for pre-school children. It is primarily for the infant, but may also be used for the child in kindergarten and the primary grades, providing the teacher alters her approach to suit the requirements of the group.

Bruce King is producing a series of recordings, with instructions for initiating dance movement, to music specifically composed for the movement. Besides the *Dance Music for Pre-School Children* (1963) the list includes:

> *Music for Modern Dance—Rhythmic Progressions*, HLP 4009, Hoctor Records, Directed by Bruce King, Piano Improvisation by Paul Kueter (1966)
>
> *Modern Dance—Music and Materials for Technique*, KLP 4010, Kimbo Records, Directed by Bruce King, Piano Improvisations by Paul Kueter (1966)
>
> *Methods and Materials for Modern Dance Technique*, Kimbo Records (1966), this with *Teacher's Manual* of instructions written by Bruce King.

In advocating King's principles and methods of approach to children I am most sympathetic to his stated ideal: "As a dancer, I work to achieve masterworks. As a teacher, I encourage students to seek and find methods of self-expression and communication, true and original to the individual, and I work with students to help them refine and construct their ideas and expressions in forms which, in art medium, strive to accomplish masterpieces."

Pilot Program in Dance and Music

Initiating dance for children as a teacher, be confident, be joyful, be sincere, be patient, be scrupulous in allowing the child freedom to think and express as well as freedom to move. Approach dance and music simultaneously, with conscious use of the music as well as of the movement. Begin by establishing a climate of joyousness, a human intimacy, an artistic intent. Find a preliminary movement in which all the children will participate, such as a circling movement, in which all the dancers move simultaneously. After a pleasant, preliminary "round" or two to music, work begins!

Treat working in dance and music as the serious and noble pursuit of self-expression and communication. Respect the children with whom you work *as persons*. They will respond with dignity as well as with eloquent expression and original ideas.

Remember that one listens and hears best when one pays closest attention, aurally. Therefore, make your music right for the acoustics of the dancing-place, not only in quality as music but also in volume as sound. Don't let the sound overwhelm the children and make them nervously over-stimulated or frightened. Keep the volume of the phonograph or tape-recorder low, and don't emphasize the bass.

Concern yourself only with a few essentials but in these, establish your authority. Never mind if a child, to begin with, favors one foot or one side over the other; in time he will acquire strength and skill to use both. Do not carp if one stubborn child wants to repeat only one pattern in dance over and over, instead of passing on to another; he may be seeking an extension of an idea as well as a movement from this source. Know that when executing a movement in dance, within music, it is most important to discover and use the rhythm. And as children respond spontaneously to rhythm half your work is accomplished in making them into dancers, before you even begin!

Choose the music for each dance with the greatest care for its appropriateness to the pattern and the capacities of the children to whom you are teaching the pattern. In a beginners' class for infants and young children, use music of the quality and suitability of *Dance Music for Pre-School Children*, LP 407, S & R Records, composed by Douglas Nordli specifically for Bruce King's dance directions. Says King: "Music cannot be too good for children, because they need only the best. Music for children may be too loud, or too long, or too complicated in rhythms, too complex in form. But provided the teacher works with music of excellence, she can find the right music for every dance, and each group of students."

Naturally, the soundest and most suitable choice of music is the music which, as on the LP 407 S & R recording, has been composed for children, and with which the cognitive teacher has developed rhythmic patterns as dance.

This record is marked off into "bands" with written directions by Bruce King. Side I offers eight basic patterns, plus a polka pattern, and each pattern is planned by King within music and movement, as one, and to define qualities of movement, and changes in music and movement.

The first four bands' music by Nordli are in 4/4 meter. King establishes the movement patterns as follows:

A run—to release inhibitions and to inspire the children with the joy of moving. This is continued into changes in *the quality of the run*; *run lightly* and *run lightly on the half-toe* (the dancer's term for being on tip-toe, heels off the floor); *run fast*, more a change of energy than a change of tempo.

A walk—in which form is established for the class, first in a circle, then in diagonals, et cetera, continuing into a *March*, a different walking quality (also, says King, a movement for fun, to stimulate the children's enjoyment of movement and movement patterns).

The jump, first as a *jump down*. (The teacher must insist that a jump is performed on both feet, to ensure that this movement does not become a hop or a gallop. The pilot program, as directed by King, ensures a conscious use of dance movement for the teacher and the student, providing the teacher makes explicit uses of the changes in quality and pattern of the movements.) Then, the *jump up*, which at first may prove too technically demanding for children, in which case omit, until the class develops better control.

The hop. Know that each child will have a preferred leg to hop on, and will accordingly favor a left-hop or a right-hop. After a preliminary hop in each child's choice, establish a *left-hop* and a *right-hop*, in unison. This will take time to achieve in group movement, as children have to be encouraged to use the weaker leg or the one they least favor for hopping; strength and skill have to be developed sufficiently by each child to hop on both feet, equally, before the class is prepared to follow directions for varieties of hops and jumps. When the children have mastered the hop, pass into a more complex pattern like the *step-hop*; first, through one step and three hops (all in the 4/4 meter established in the music). For this, the right foot goes step-hop, hop, hop; and then the left foot goes step-hop, hop, hop. The music and movement patterns then change, to 3/4 meter, and the right foot goes step-hop, hop; then the left foot step-hop, hop. *The teacher must make the children conscious of the change in meter, so that they appreciate their use of changing rhythms and qualities of movement as they dance.*

King now develops more complicated patterns within changes of meter from 6/8 into 2/4 and back into the 4/4 meter which is developed for the first patterns, Nordli's music, of course, continuing the changes, some of them alternately, as follows:

The gallop, in 6/8 meter. King finds it usual for young children to move easily in this rhythm, by dragging one foot behind the other, a movement related to the *chaussé* in ballet. Some will immediately turn this into a proper gallop and lead the others into it. If no child conceives the proper galloping movement, the teacher must initiate it for the class to follow.

The gallop UP, a gallop that lifts the dancer off the floor, a movement preparatory to *step-leap*, which is more complicated, still in 6/8 meter.

The skip, in 2/4 meter. Some children will have difficulty at first in distinguishing the quality of this movement, even after it is initiated by the teacher.

In that event, offer them the music for the *Slide* (Band 8 Side I on LP 407), which is 6/8 meter. Return to the patterns of jumping and hopping, which are preparatory for skipping; then encourage the slow "skippers" to try the skip in 2/4 meter, until they become proficient in skipping. The class is now ready to accomplish a skip with a turn.

The skip-turn, in 6/8 meter. King says: "Now the children really feel that they are dancing!" A turn is exhilarating (it has an element of danger, since the dancer must sustain equilibrium without stumbling and falling), and the teacher should allow each child to turn to the side he favors, which will be the direction the child chooses because he feels more confident of his strength and control in it—this being left or right. In the beginning of the skip-and-turn movement, it is sufficient to allow the children to turn to "this side" and "that side," as they usually describe left and right or vice versa. After they have performed the movement in their preferred direction (to the "side" each child favors as his choice), develop a reversal movement by leading each child into changing the direction he first chose, to perform its direct opposite in left-right movement. When this has been mastered, begin to consciously distinguish for the children LEFT and RIGHT, and demand that they henceforth name them as forms of direction instead of the babyish "this side" and "that side," when they are working in dance.

Turning, in 4/4 meter. For this pattern, King encourages "any continuous spinning movement a child elects to perform, in positions such as sitting, standing, lying and rolling, et cetera." The exhilarating turning pattern is fine for letting off physical "steam" in a class and it is a hugely enjoyable movement pattern for small children. At first, they may wish to do this free-style, unconscious of the music. Eventually, the teacher must make them conscious of the rhythm, which they discover through the music and the movement, in 4/4 meter.

The slide, in 6/8 meter. King develops three changes of movement, with correlating qualities of movement. The slide is *sideward* (again, a movement related to the ballet *chaussé*), and is a mode of movement which clarifies Left-Right directions. Demonstrate it as a sideways traveling movement, developed into the quite complex slide-turn-hop pattern which follows. As defined in the music, four slides in 6/8 meter use a *half-turn* performed with *a hop every 4 slides*; and two slides in 6/8 meter, with a *half-turn*, and *a hop every two slides*.

Use the two sideway slides, next, *in a forward traveling movement*. When the class has mastered this change of movement and direction, the children will have learned the simple steps of the polka. Presto! they can now dance a "real dance," as they often think of a dance form, and will do so to the engaging air, in 2/4 meter by Nordli, Band 9 of the LP 407.

When I make use of the King-Nordli recording *Dance Music for Pre-*

School Children, at this stage of the class-work we recapitulate what we have learned, the children taking turns to demonstrate each of the patterns mastered in the run, walk, jump, hop, hop-step, gallop, skip, turn and slide, and the varieties or changes in these basic movements. As one or more child demonstrates, the others take turns to identify. I am thereby assured, after this session, of the entire class having *conscious* knowledge of the movement patterns, a most necessary preparation for the student dancer. We also identify the musical meters.

This stage of the class-work may be extended to several other factors, primarily for understanding dance and music, but also in development of purest comprehension out of lessons in "looking and listening." Some of my methods are:

Print in large letters, on a blackboard, the term for each dance movement and musical meter, as these are investigated and the music heard, the movements performed. For pre-school children, prepare mimeographed papers at terminal point of Band 8, on which, in bold lettering, such terminology is simply stated, with a "stick figure" drawing as illustration of the dance movement. (Refer to examples of "stick-figure choreography" in *The Child as a Social Person*.) The children should have these papers to keep and should be encouraged to start a scrap-book of the loose-leaf variety (if so, make sure their papers are holed to fit the cover, to encourage each child to take good care of written class-work or printed materials).

The sense of adult importance emergent from this small formality is altogether unbelievable, unless one has observed it in pre-school children, especially when they are in a family where older siblings are in school.

King's directions for dance movement to Nordli's music are adaptable to older *beginning* students, for basic exercises in discovering relationships between meters in music and dance. When I employ this material for older children, who have mastered printing or cursive writing skills, they make their own work-books, and the dance and music work is extended into drawing and other aspects of the arts of design and color, providing a synthesis of arts program for children in elementary grades, especially when we add drama and poetry composition.

Modelling in soft clay and similiar materials, sketching and painting as well as drawing "stick figure" and making pipe-cleaner dancers, provide a class with a corporeal dimension within their dance and music studies. I have seen the most delicate and intricate mobiles, made from pipe cleaners and wafer-thin board (the latter cut to shape and painted to represent three-dimensional figures) in "showings" by elementary grade students who work in dance. Other children enjoy making and using puppets (in actual puppetry work) as extensions of their dance studies.

Such manual extensions of "the dancer" sensibly affect the psychical and physical spheres of dancing. Pragmatically, the children learn concepts for choreography for the human person, and they must comprehend the elements of choreography when they begin to create dance for themselves and others—*as the logical, spontaneous, imperative impulse intrinsic to a "creative" dance and music class*. If this impulse is lacking or does not develop, the teaching approach has failed to elicit response.

Self-analysis is also required in the basic class-work in dance and music. The child should discover and discuss in the group the quality of change, the virtue of difference, in dance and music as art. Infants and young children are very sensitive to feelings in movements that differ as *run* and *walk*, as *jump* and *gallop*, and especially perceptive of feeling in *the turn*, or *the spin*. I have described, in *The Child as a Social Person*, some preliminary work in falling and other movements; all these are within basic class-work and exercises such as those directed by King for his LP 407 recording.

And all the work emanating out of a dance and music class and its various extensions, develop comprehension and concentration, and the powers of analysis, deduction and evaluation—at their acutest intensity, because the child makes these discoveries *through experiences of the self*.

Side 2 of the Nordli-King LP 407 also has nine bands, these being for dance and song class-work. It is impossible for me to praise this recording too highly! Nordli has taken pretty, familiar nursery rhymes and arranged them, musically, to encourage and support the natural creative movements in dance of very young children, and he has succeeded in doing so within a form and style which make the music fresh and vital. The five rhymes and their airs are simple, yet dramatic. Here, again, is what Bruce King and I consider a sound example of "music for children," in that this music is of immediate value to the child, while being in every sense of this term what is referred to as "good" or "serious" music. The variations of Side 2, and the exercises of Side 1, are superior music of contemporary idiom.

Both King and I believe that the preliminary approach to this recording (Side 2) should be in song, by the teacher and the class, since after the experiences of singing the children will more happily and confidently discover those of dancing to the rhymes and rhythms. The melodies by Nordli are variations that extend the beloved nursery rhymes into dance and music forms, which the teacher accomplishes as a whole through King's directions.

He advises the teacher to say and sing the rhymes with the children. Then, discuss the dramatic action of the songs, to make certain that this is clarified for each child. My method is to invite a child or several children, depending on the size and character of the group, to describe the drama. In a single nursery rhyme such as *Jack and Jill*, four or five children may participate in this group discussion. (a-e)

After we have chanted or recited the words of the rhyme, and sung it (without accompaniment, if necessary, but, preferrably, with simple piano accompaniment) we treat *Jack and Jill* to the "parts and sum" theorizing that I advocate (and have developed for older students in opera arts appreciation, for which see *Enjoying Opera*). a) Jack and Jill *both* went up a hill—b) for a purpose (to fetch a pail of water) c) Jack fell down—d) and broke his crown (head) e) Jill came tumbling down *after* Jack fell.

Going where? and why? and what happened to each person? are the pivotal questions by which the teacher develops comprehension, and elicits articulate and meaningful response from the children.

Bruce King states to the teacher: "The children should perform the dramatic actions of the songs, after they have sung them and discussed their meaning and content, and before they listen to Nordli's music, and begin to dance the variations. *If the music is allowed to solve the problems of expression for the class, it will find no need and incentive for dancing.*"

King is here preaching the same tenets I gave the reader as my principles for making use of music, and especially of recorded and taped music. It is ruinous to the Nordli-King dance and music, as it is to Orff's *Music for Children* and all such works, for a teacher to misuse the recorded material. Listening is an actual and active aspect of the work with these materials but it is a far different kind of listening than the casual, passive listening of adults to a record spinning on a phonograph, or a tape unwinding its spool on a tape-recorder. A little of the material, at a time, used within the intimate, loving *human* approach of the teacher (or parent), are what King and I consider the arbitrary and essential principle of our approaches to the child.

King writes, on the jacket instructions for his LP 407, "*Don't use up all the music in one lesson.*" I advocate, for the pre-school child, the most judicious use of one nursery rhyme at a time, off the Nordli-King recording, this use established not by a "program" predicated by the teacher for a course, but according to the class' mastery of the basic materials, and its "discovery and experience" development of these. I have found that I usually spend at least five lessons of a nursery school week working on Band 1—*Jack and Jill*, and perhaps three times more, consecutively and in recapitulation, working on Band 2 —*Theme and Variations of Jack and Jill*, and the same or longer periods are often devoted by my classes to Bands 3–4 *Rockabye Baby*; Bands 5–6 *Mary Had A Little Lamb*, Bands 7–8 *Sing a Song of Sixpence*. But when such a class progresses to Band 9 *Oranges and Lemons*, it works with marvelous confidence and joyousness in and out of the literary theme to create works of improvisation and true composition, within Nordli's melodic development of this dear old nursery ditty.

Musical variations on nursery melodies provide excellent introduction for group dancing. The tunes are familiar (or should be) to young children, and the teacher should use them for organization of movement in relation to ideas as action, mood, and characterization in dance. Any nursery rhyme provides material for a dance and music action or dance-drama. Nursery rhymes are remarkably succinct in the literary sense, making a point clearly, quickly, and, often, with great humor.

King cautions the teacher: "The efforts of three year olds to dance will be vague and gentle. Try to be as sensitive as possible, in yourself as the adult, to what is happening within the child as he dances or attempts to create a dance. Try to understand what he feels and thinks, but refrain from any attempt to "clarify" his ideas, for fear you impress your own, adult feelings and thoughts on his. After you perceive what his idea is, help him to develop it into movement as dance form." (The child will, from the lessons on Band 1, have investigated some movements and should now, if the précis given has been followed satisfactorily, be able to identify some basic dance and music forms.)

King says: "When building a group dance, invite a different child to do each part. This establishes the action and structure of the roles, encourages recognition and appreciation of individual ideas (these are pooled as group resources), and eventually develops a realistic pattern which may be used by all the dancers, repeated by them, *and taught by them to other dancers*, when the 'work' is completed."

Young children are eager to move and they have quick-silver imaginations, founded on their experiences. Thereby, no two groups are precisely alike in intellectual and emotional development, any more than they are likely to be in physical development, and dance and music "sense." But all children, especially the pre-school groups who have not been indoctrinated into rote methods of learning, can be guided through "discoveries" of dance and music, and drama, to worthwhile experiences, some of them truly creative. The teacher making use of this book, including the description of the LP 407 dance and music materials, must know her class well enough to elicit from it the responses to pilot programs outlined in *Children and Dance and Music*.

Bruce King defines dance ideas, for Douglas Nordli's music.

Jack and Jill: the rhyme states the drama: *who, what, where, why, when*. In the melody, the teacher must lead the children to find the right time for Jack to fall down and Jill to tumble after. Actions include climbing movements, for ascending the hill; drawing water. In the action of tumbling, let the children explore means of falling, for which refer to *The Child as a Social Person*. Isolate movements and then perform them in sequence.

Band 2, the *Theme and Variations*, is music for improvising and creating a dance on the drama of *Jack and Jill*. King warns that it will take some time for a whole class to learn to change dynamics of music and movement quickly enough to be able to dance. Some will dance much sooner than others; these "natural" dancers should be encouraged to help the more laggard performers, with suggestions, and also by physical demonstration of how a movement is done—also, with the child's own description of the music's relation to the drama of that movement in the dance. Eventually, there will emerge what amounts to the ballet from the ballad of *Jack and Jill*, sometimes with obvious derivation of the literary source but, occasionally, with fresh insight and true originality predominantly as a work of dance.

Rockabye Baby has three characters and dance qualities: *baby, tree, wind*. In the melody the children find the characters and the drama: Baby-in-the-cradle rocks; the Tree has trunk, branches, leaves; the Wind moves in space.

Band 4, the *Theme and Variations*, provides music for three solos danced at the same time by the most proficient dancers, then extended and developed on more dancers, with several taking the role of plural trees, and a group assuming the character of the Wind. The role of Baby should be explored, in turn, by consecutive dancers, and some will make Baby gentle and timid, others, brave and carefree in the Wind and Tree.

Mary Had A Little Lamb is a realistic story, with characters and plot. Develop action and mood, to create a dance work in full.

The melody introduces Mary and Lamb, and the Lamb will trot and frolic with and without Mary. Mary takes a slow walk to school, the Lamb following (and chased back, perhaps once or twice); Mary arrives in school. In the schoolroom, entrance of Lamb, who plays; the children, with Mary, "laugh and play." Terrible-tempered teacher appears! Lamb banished from school, and Mary, possibly, with it, to lead it home. (Here, children often assume a mood of grief—one choreographer required the Mary in her group to become the personification of *Woe*, an occasion described in *The Child as a Social Person*.) Sometimes, the children elect that Mary return to school; at other times, they allow her to make her exit and stay out, while the day's class is completed. At the end of the school-day, Mary is seen as reunited with her frolicsome Lamb, and her friends as their play-mates. Not infrequently, Mary's teacher "drops dead, because she was really a witch in disguise."

Band 6, *Theme and Variations*, is generally the motif of a quickly developed group dance, but (I have noted in my own work) more so in a group of girls than of boys, except when the boys are allowed to alternate in the role of Lamb and to fatten this role to the "star" piece in the work. In the "play" periods between Mary and Lamb, and between Lamb and the children in school, I see very pretty patterns emerge, some of them consciously within the forms of dances such as the polka and the *Virginia Reel*, depending on the experiences and natural talents of the children in a group.

Sing a Song of Sixpence is chosen by King as the structure for a "flying" dance. Inasmuch as most young children "fly" when they begin dancing, it is a logical extension, especially of rudimentary dance such as King has described in his demonstration program for 5–6 year old children where bird roles were assumed. In *Sixpence*, the melody aids the planning (it is an old English tune, and its root is interestingly traced for older children, when dance and "social studies" are intermingled). Besides the birds (which can be of any number) there are King, Queen, Maid, each with a very clear-cut characterization. The birds should fly singly and in groups, the characters should develop movement patterns eloquent (and revelatory) of their feelings and actions. The teacher may need to help the "birds" get in and out of the pie, by inviting suggestions for these acts. Since *Sixpence* is ideal for a very large group (it has several verses and strong dramatic action) I often use it as a means of dividing the children into two corps, one as birds, one as "Pie-people." This has additional merit: it compels the children to work out methods of the birds getting in and out of the human "Pie." Usually, the problem is solved by the "Pie-people" permitting entrance and exit between their stationary forms, as they stand or sit in a circle to form the pie's edge. But sometimes a group will work to elaborate on this, as did the "Pie-people" who became a *fluted* pie-edge, and assumed that character.

Very ingenuously, they worked out a method whereby the birds went into the "pie" to march music, with a weaving movement around the "Pie-people," one by one. When the birds were in the pie, the Pie began to cook, most realistically. The "Pie-people" flexed their knees in very deep *pliés*, (hands clasped with their neighbor's to link them in a closed circle) so that the "fluted edge" rose and fell rhythmically as "it" stooped and stood upright. Then the children, on cue, half-kneeled, half-sat, and "crimped" the pie-edge by inclining first all to the right, then, all to the left, again rhythmically. After this, the birds rose and "fluttered" in the centre of the "Pie," which ("magically," I was informed) appeared to be cut into two wide wedges, opposite each other, out of which wedges the birds "flew." This "Pie" dance was gradually developed so that at one point, as the birds lay supine in the pie, the "fluted edge" dissolved and turned into diagonal patterns in between the recumbent "birds," and I was informed that this pie had a latticed top, not a whole crust, to allow the birds "to breathe while they are baking."

Sixpence has a variety of endings, when extended as a dance through the *Theme and Variations*. King suggests using Nordli's music here to get the birds into the pie with the first section, and for the birds to fly in the second section. The third section is for the royal pair, King and Queen—and most children in these roles spontaneously perform *pas de deux*. In the fourth, the Maid hangs her clothes, up comes Blackbird and pecks off her nose. It is common for the children to transform Blackbird into Prince (probably when they know the story of *Beauty and the Beast* or the fairy tale of the blackbird brothers of the dancing princesses) and to marry him off, quite tidily, to the Maid, who is likely to turn out to be the "lost" daughter of the Royal pair who previously were employers. Children cannot endure leaving the Maid without a nose and the more sentimental give her a good dowry and a husband, while the more ruthless command the Blackbird to drop dead and some benign personage to repair the Maid's face with a new nose or the replacement of her old one—"an easy thing to do, with plastic surgery," as sage infants will point out today.

All the foregoing are "realistic" dance works, with a literary basis and a dramatic theme, scene and characterization for the children to work with and on. They require other material, however, to challenge their invention, stimulate their imagination, and explore their capacity for composition in dance, and in the third they reveal their artistic intelligence as well as their inner selves.

Oranges and Lemons is the final variation on Side 2 of LP 407, and King includes it as a melodic piece by Nordli for improvisation and composition. It is in 3/4 meter, with a prelude or introduction (2 bars), four 8-bar phrases, one 12-bar phrase, and three 8-bar phrases (therefore, use it to illustrate a lesson in *measuring* music, and in the structure of music in "bars," "phrases," and meter). Offer this music to children for their use in a "pure" dance work; one without literary theme. They may simply move in it, creating "pure" dance patterns, or they may elect to compose a dramatic dance work out of it, in part or whole. They will often require extension of the music, either as repetition or as interpolation in the Nordli composition of other music. American children do not appear to know *Oranges and Lemons* as well as they know other nursery rhymes on this recording; hence, they are inclined to use its tune freely, without close relationship to any part of it except, possibly, its title.

In one use of Nordli's *Oranges and Lemons* a 7-year old girl requested the interpolation of McPhee's *Tabuh-Tabuhan*, which she had discovered in a preliminary music program with me. She was a "beautiful Mandarin Orange" that grew on a thorny bush so that no one could pick it. An intrepid deer tried to eat her up, was sorely pricked by the terrible "poisoned" thorns and fell dead— whereupon the beautiful Mandarin Orange was transformed into an angel, changed dead deer into the Boy he was, in reality, and bore him off "to Heaven."

This sequence of a whole dance work evolved, as did all other parts, out of movement patterns by the children and their inventions and *meaningful extensions of dance and music into real life* (life as they had experiences of it).

Oranges and Lemons began conventionally enough, with my stating to the class that I would play music that was composed as a variation of the song *Oranges and Lemons*. I invited them to make up solos, duets, ensemble dances (three or more children working together) as they preferred. Immediately, there was a spirited debate about oranges and lemons, with a struggle for who should be oranges between the boys and girls. "Lemon" was considered odious by these children because lemons are sour (while oranges are more often sweet) and because some of them knew the term "lemon" as indicative of a thing spoiled, gone sour, fallen flat. Besides, as the boys claimed, oranges are larger fruit.

The class was an extraordinary, not ordinary one. Although it was of 2nd Grade students, exclusively, it was evenly divided between boys and girls (I had wished to institute the gentle art of partnering), which is uncommon in the classroom. Moreover, it combined at least four categories of students, in socio-economic and intellectual classifications. This was a pilot program in a small school in a very wealthy suburb, which school was part of a large district, with great disparity of socio-economic standards. The materially privileged students of the host-school were, in this program, associated with children of their peer group from a district school whose students were from a low socio-economic standard of environment. The pilot program sought to musically enrich both groups as one, because it had been ascertained that the "rich" children of wealthy parents in the host-school were almost entirely devoid of any save a television "culture," while many of the students from the poorer class knew nursery songs, rhymes, and dance-games and folklore to an extent which made them in certain respects more cultured than their more *materially* privileged peers.

The third and fourth categories in the group were mental; some of the children from both schools were considered above average in intelligence quotients to the norm for their peers; others, in both groups, average.

There were forty students in the group, of varied capacities in singing and dancing, but (by the time we approached *Oranges and Lemons*) in general sharing the same responses to my approaches. We were all, as it were, good friends, well inclined towards dance and music, seasoned workers in our métier, for having worked together for several weeks in agreeable circumstances. All the children had by now formed pleasurable associations with dance and music, and, except for a few antipathies, with each other. Notably, regardless of the category to which they belonged socio-economically or intellectually, the boys elected to support the boys, the girls to favor their kind. The sharpest division was between the sexes.

Thus, the boys might assume all the roles that were mischievous and bois-terous when the girls showed inclination of being solemn and lyrical.

I vetoed any gender for oranges and lemons, assured them they could all be one or the other, and they turned into an orange grove (of which these California children had common experience) with just a few rampant individu-alists becoming lemon trees growing in the orange grove. When some boys tired of dancing as oranges and orange trees, they became birds nesting in the grove, bugs that ate the fruit, bees that buzzed among the blossoms and a cordon of them became a plane, which cut through the "grove," to dust the crops with insecticide. So far, all the invention had been realistic, and while I tried not to let the children fall on lazy, unimaginative decisions (boys became a plane only after I refused to accept them as birds, of which we already had a great number), I allowed them to determine what the dance would be about, and how it should be danced.

A boy proposed that he should become the owner or manager of the grove;

his proposal was turned down with the stern injunction that no grown-up characters would be admitted to the cast. Later, the children extended this ban to all human beings; thence came the deer, a boy who wished to annoy the Mandarin Orange by eating her up. He invented highly articulated finger movements for "nibbling."

The Mandarin Orange (in real life, a child named Kathy) was a talented dancer and she had by now developed her dance beautifully, with a group of other girls. They had been seeds in the earth, growing trees, buds and blossom, and were now fruit—and Kathy had established, with assistance from other children, patterns that obviously had significance and merit, since the others had learned them, and repeated these continuously, in an actual form. The intrusion of the mischievous boy brought another mood into this group, and a new pattern. When the "deer" darted in among the "thorns" and the "oranges" in search of the Mandarin, she stood still but bent her body agitatedly in all directions, but her corps indignantly converged on him, "jabbing" him, as he complained to me. The Mandarin Orange sauvely explained that he was being pricked by the terrible thorns on her very thorny tree.

The lesson period ended at that point. The next lesson began where we had stopped, with the boy "deer" caught amidst the "thorns." I asked: "How shall we continue?" We had agreed that in this dance work we should incorporate all events and always go on from whatever phase at which we reached a climax or a problem in movement and meaning. The children suggested that the "deer" should dance his way out of the thicket of thorns. When it was proved that he could not, because the "thorns" were adamant, the "deer" elected to lie down and "die," from his wounds. He lay supine and the "thorns" encircled him. It was then that the Mandarin Orange changed into an angel, the deer into a boy because, as the children explained, it had been "a test" for the deer-boy. When he was punished for eating the beautiful Orange, and was sad and sorry, then the "angel" came to save him.

This class became so absorbed in the *Oranges and Lemons* dance work, which had several other dramatic episodes besides the "deer" one, that the children decided to make the finished work into a theatrical performance, with costumes. On the proviso that they must produce it without adult help, they did so.

I did provide them with assistance of a kind, by inviting some 5th and 6th Grade students of the host-school (who were auditing this class) to work with the forty 2nd Grade students, chiefly in making costumes. The "plane" was a papier-mâché contrivance of remarkable sophistication, which the boys actually wore, by inserting their heads through holes in the wings and fuselage. Wearing this harness required them to develop the utmost coordination and precision for their gliding, swooping, and "flying" movements, which they did. Moreover, dissatisfied with available music, they composed their own from sound sources they provided, which I taped as insertion into the "score," by now considerably extended from Nordli's *Oranges and Lemons* variation, through additions of conventional and unconventional music chosen by the group.

The classroom teachers of the 2nd Grade students, at the host and guest school, found it difficult to believe that the children could and would work so hard and continuously at a project initiated in dance and music. But when the children complained that half-hour sessions were insufficient for them to "work things out" for *Oranges and Lemons*, the teachers agreed to extend the sessions to 55 minute periods.

Students from the 5th and 6th Grades (also working in a dance and music program with me) who were permitted to audit the 2nd Grade class, for analytical discussions, expressed the opinion that the 7-year old students "used their heads more," or were more resourceful, in inventing dance and solving problems for dance and music, than older students of approximately the same "beginning" status in dance and music "creative" work.

The following school-year, when the 2nd Grade students' median age was eight, allowed an extension of the program, in part into Bruce King's *Rhythmic Progressions* (HLP-4009 *Music for Modern Dance*) which is defined for use with high school and college dance students. In part, and in simplified form, this recorded music with its dance directions was the basis of a program in which the children mastered changing meter and complicated movements such as the *relevé* (*piqué*), *plié*, *passé* and *saut* of ballet (but *not* in the turn-out). Notably, the students now wanted formal patterns, conscious use of terminology, and "real dances" as part of their program in 3rd Grade, although they recapitulated what they had most enjoyed in 2nd Grade. Kathy tried to perfect her solo as "Mandarin Orange," and refused a corps; she wanted a *dancing* way of moving like an angel instead of movements imitative of flight. She was taken to the ballet and the movement as *saut de l'ange* ("fish dive"), literally: angel's jump, enchanted her although it was far beyond her capacity to perform. Aged nine she became a student in a commercial, autonomous ballet school, possibly from the interest initiated out of her orange-angel dance.

The most significant development of the first year project, when the children were in 2nd Grade, was through the "deer," a handsome, charming, troublesome boy with extraordinary energy and comparatively short concentration span. He both aggravated and fascinated the other children with his robustness and unconventionality. While not an actual disciplinary problem, his flighty ways were disruptive to class morale. Indeed, he assumed the role of the deer in the same spirit of mayhem and mischief with which (according to his 2nd Grade teacher) he disrupted work in the classroom at school. Yet this child was sensitive to approval and disapproval from his peers and obviously wished to enjoy their goodwill, and to lead them in activities. He was beautifully made, moved easily and well, and was of above average intelligence.

After the shape of the *Orange and Deer* dance emerged, as it were, from chaos, the boy's behavior altered from mischief and levity to dignity and seriousness. However, he suffered extreme frustration, anger at himself and his critical peers, despair of accomplishing what was demanded of him, shame at not being able to produce his best at the first attempt to dance as deer. When we decided to keep the deer dance within the context of the work, the boy was required to develop and refine it—or to yield the role to another boy. He refused to give up the deer role and agreed to persevere until it was accepted by the group as good enough to be included in the work. We discussed the nature and shape of deer, their habitat and behavior, in search of "deer movements."

This boy's only knowledge of deer was a casual sight of the species in a zoo. He said that he liked panthers best of all animals (and he had an almost phobic dislike of apes and monkeys) but had "never bothered much" about deer. He offered a dance as deer in a crouching position, which was rejected by the group. "He moves like a cat." The next movement was equally unsuitable. "He moves like a dog." The third provoked hilarity. "Now he moves like a crab." Pawing, neighing, prancing movements were rejected: "That's not a deer, that's a HORSE!" The child found his peers too critical to work with but, as he insisted the deer role was his because he had "made it up," I offered him a corner of the room, behind a screen, for parts of several sessions, so he could work in private. He was given a stated date by which he must produce a finished work, to meet the "production" schedule. And he met his "deadline" to the hour and the day.

He made his entrance with a delicate, almost mincing gait, with high-held head turned rigidly right and left, nostrils dilated, eyes raking blindly, obviously unseeing of the others. The group instinctively fell back against the walls and left the "deer" a large central place. The boy had retained only the "nibbling" gestures from his first improvisation, but now his mien and deportment, and his style of movement, were altogether separate from any we had discovered and experienced in the class. When he danced, he was not so much a human imitation of a deer as he was a faun, and a narcissist faun, at that. He danced without inhibitions, and with authority and control over his expression and his instrument. At one climax he asked for boys to "be trees" through which he would move; at another, he required the girls in the roles of thorns and oranges to be dancing in counterpoint. "The Mandarin Orange and the Thorns are not ready!" he complained, pre-emptorily. When the girls began their rehearsed dance he waited and, giving his own cue, began to "eat the Orange." Thereafter, all went as before: the Thorns circled him and pricked him with jabbing forefingers, he struggled vainly against the thorn-thicket, was stabbed, died, returned to life as a boy and was led away, very meekly, by the orange-angel.

The episode was worked out without music. Music had to be selected, which the deer-boy did in conference with 5th and 6th Graders who were assisting with "Musical Direction" for the production. Then the music was taped and spliced into the swelling "score," to be used for rehearsals and for the final performance.

The deer dance was the most original expression of this program. The group, making analysis and evaluation of their work, considered it the best dance but not the dance they liked best. The boys preferred the *Airplane Dance* and the girls the *Mandarin-Orange* dance. The classroom teachers of the host and guest schools concurred, because the *Airplane Dance* was "the cleverest and the most difficult to perform," and the *Mandarin-Orange Dance* was "the prettiest and best thought-out as a group dance." Neither of the teachers liked the *Deer Dance*, conceding that it was "original," they thought it "a little bit shocking."

The 7-year old "deer" had achieved a dance so raw and free, so incorrigibly honest and primitive, that it was too strong meat for conventional tastes to enjoy with comfort and pleasure.

When a teacher must work with available music rather than with music specifically composed for children's dances, she is required to use more imagination and ingenuity, not only in the choice of the music but also in the focusing of the children's efforts. In a demonstration for the National Dance Congress Bruce King showed how he approaches this task with pre-school children. He says:

"We begin, in this case, with a short but beautiful piece of music and an action idea that the children understand: picking flowers. The music is Bela Bartok's Roumanian Folk Dances, IV, *Picking Flowers.*

Set, drilled choreography for very young children is not worth the teacher's effort and has little value as dance for children. The teacher must, instead, draw on the imagination and natural grace of children, for whom good performance is relative to their personal association or connection with the material; music and theme. But the dancing has to be focused by the teacher, who must note the good ideas as they occur or are glimpsed, so that they will not be lost or negated.

In this instance, I ask the children to find a path for the dance they perform while picking flowers. I make note of the changes of speed. We decide on a beginning and an end for the dance. We study the music so as to improvise flowers. The growth and movement of the flowers re-inforce the structure and quality of the music. I ask: What do we often find in a garden of flowers? The answer is: butterflies, so there will be, as a natural extension of the flower dance, movement that relates to butterflies.

For this, we have Bartok's Roumanian Folk Dances, II, *Butterflies.* This time the butterfly movement is discovered to another piece of music, using the same teaching technique. This dance is flexible enough to be divided into two parts, in successive lessons, and put together as a whole work, proving that children can create and perform for an audience. The key to such an accomplishment is to keep the action appropriate, the communication clear, so that the children understand the structure of the music and the movement. But the timing of the dance is left free, to be developed by the dancers. It is in such a way the beauty of improvised or spontaneous dance, "creative" dance, is brought into communicative form for performance."

Appendix III

Within an arithmetic lesson, show the *values* of notes

1 semibreve	= 1 whole note
2 minims	= 2 half-notes, or
4 crochets	= 4 quarter-notes, or
8 quavers	= 8 eighth-notes, or
16 semiquavers	= 16 sixteenth-notes, or
32 semidemiquavers	= 32 thirty-second notes

A hemidemisemiquaver equals 1 sixty-fourth note:
while semihemidemisemiquavers are notes of 128 to the semibreve:

One dot following a note increases its value by half (there are exceptions to this rule but the rule suffices in a rudimentary lesson in note and rest values); a double dot after a note increases its value by one half plus a quarter and dots before a double line mean that the music is to be repeated from the double bar with dots *behind* it. D.C. is DaCapo, meaning "from the beginning. *Da capo aria* is Italian for sing a repeat, or begin again where the music commences from a double bar with dots on the right: ‖:   :‖ Music is divided
D.C.

by bars into measures; notes have certain numbers of beats.

♩ = 1 full count or

♩ ♩ ♩ ♩
1+, 2+, 3+, 4+ (plus counted as *and*)

♪ = ½ of a beat

♪♪ ♪♪ ♪♪
1,+, 2,+, 3,+ (plus called *and*)

♬ = ¼ of a beat

♬ ♬ ♬ or ♪. ♪ or ♪.♬
1 a a a   1+ a   1+ a

"Up-beat" is marked thus: ♪| ♫́ — ♪ is the smallest unit of movement in dance.

Within a language lesson, note the differences and similiarities in international musical terminology.

Pause in German, *Silence* in French and *Pausa* in Italian are the same as *Rest* in English. Slow music is *andante* (and dance that is slow is this, too, and also *adagio*) while fast music and dancing is termed *allegro*. The counts of values in notes are common to three main languages, Italian, French and German but the symbols are the same, thus making music an international language which can be understood *explicitly*. A violinist in Pittsburgh playing a composition by a man from Prague (knowing English but not Czech) has no difficulty understanding the music—but an American singer should have to learn the phonetics of the Czech verse in order to perform a Czech song.

Dance is also a universal language, with *pas* (step) taking the place of the note in music. Hence, the waltz (originating in Germany and Austria) is "waltzed" anywhere *in its form*, and could be written or notated thus: $\frac{3}{4}$ 1 2 3 ♩ ♩ ♩

(*running waltz, accent 1st of 3*) a polka (which originated in the Czech *pulka*) is recorded thus: $\frac{2}{4}$ a 1+ 2+ a (*hop, step & close, step, hop*). ♪ ♫ ♪. ♪

American musicians use a literal English translation from the German note values but British musicians do not; their usage is from the Italian, itself based on Medieval Latin. The Germans and Americans have *numerical* values:

GERMAN	AMERICAN
Doppeltakt-note	double whole-note
Ganze Taktnote	whole-note
Halbe	half-note
Viertel	quarter-note
Achtel	eighth-note
Sechzehntel	sixteenth-note
Zwieunddreissigstel	thirty-second note
Vierundsechzigstel	sixty-fourth note

Compare these spellings with the Italian and English, and with French:

ITALIAN	ENGLISH	FRENCH
Breve	Breve	Carree (square)
Semibreve	Semibreve	Ronde (round)
Minima or bianca (white)	Minim	Blanche (white)
Semiminima or nera (black)	Crochet	Noire (black)

ITALIAN	ENGLISH	FRENCH
Croma	Quaver	Croche (hook)
Semi-croma	Semi-quaver	Double-croche (double hook)
Biscroma	Demisemiquaver	Triple-croche (triple hook)
Semi-biscroma	Hemisemidemiquaver	Quadruple-croche (4 hooks)

The French are concerned not with the counts but with the appearances of the musical signs, and their terminology is vividly and *visually* expressive.

Teachers can use, also, examples of pitch; of intensity; et cetera, to familiarise students with musical terminology and notation—all within the normal curricula. Science teachers might explore the qualities of "natural" and elemental sounds; mechanical and electronic sounds; sounds of the main ranges of the human voice, male and female; sounds as produced by the conventional instruments and by unconventional ones; and in acoustics (understanding of how sound is produced through vibration) actually teach within a *musical* format.

Indeed, music's scientific aspects lend themselves easily to such use.

The *pitch* of a sound is according to the rapidity of the vibrations, rapid vibrations causing high pitch; slow vibrations, low pitch. The rate of vibration per second determines the "frequency" of a note in music.

The vibrations or *sources of musical sounds* are strings (in guitars, violins, et cetera); "reeds" of pipes (bassoon, clarinet and concertina, oboe, organ); surface as stretched skin, parchment, et cetera for drums; tubes, vibrations from air within their inner parts (when the player blows into the instrument) as for flutes. Sounds by animals (birds and human beings included) have their source in the vocal cords. (See *The Singers in Enjoying Opera*.)

Vibrations are generally compound; meaning that a string or many strings together will vibrate as a whole and also and simultaneously in parts or fractions of length, each fraction producing notes variable to the length. According to elements in such compound vibrations, greater and lesser, music achieves harmonics or "timbre." (See page 5 of *The Concise Oxford Dictionary of Music* for a relatively simple but very illuminating drawing of the vibrations of a stretched string—7 strings as one, as two equal and as three equal parts.)

It is necessary to complete musical exercises in "arithmetic," "language" and "science," with a distinctly "musical" example. For instance, by identifying the pitches or ranges of the human voice (soprano, coloratura, as in Mozart's *The Magic Flute* and so on) and the tones of conventional instruments as string, wind, percussion and keyboard. In an English literature or drama class Weber's *Oberon* overture is an example for the violin, while Tchaikovsky's *Romeo and Juliet* provides an example of viola with *cor anglais*—and the teacher with a providential means of informing students that this is neither English nor a horn, since it is an alto oboe of French, not English origin. *Tremolo* and *pizzicato* examples abound in opera and instrumental music.

The integrations of music within the common public school curricula are infinite and depend wholly on the teacher's ingenuity. Obvious inclusions for the teacher are: identifying the instruments and observing the plan of their placement in orchestras, ranging from, say, Monteverdi through Verdi and Wagner into present day—a brief discussion of the development of the opera and symphonic orchestra is contained in *Enjoying Opera*. Ballet is a dramatic, poetic, pictorial art as well as a musical art, its repertory hugely dependent on literature.

Index

Index

ACKNOWLEDGMENTS

Grateful acknowledgment is given for permission to quote the following:

From *The Essays of Oscar Wilde*, Methuen & Co., Ltd., London

From *Art and the Intellect* by Harold Taylor, The Museum of Modern Art, New York

From *The Life of Reason* by George Santayana, Charles Scribner's Sons, New York

From *The Dance of Life* by Havelock Ellis; *A Majority of One* by Sydney J. Harris, Houghton Mifflin & Co., Boston

From *Metalogue to the Magic Flute*, © copyright 1955 by W. H. Auden. Reprinted from *Homage to Clio* by W. H. Auden, by permission of Random House Inc., New York

Musical excerpt from *The Deer* by Conrad Susa, by permission of the composer

Text and musical examples from *Experiments in Musical Creativity* by permission of Grant Beglarian, Project Director of the Contemporary Music Project for Creativity in Musical Education

Material on pages 34 46 and 84–88 by permission of Sara Kreger

Material on pages 220–225, 290–300 by permission of Bruce King

Material on pages 98–101 by permission of Conrad Susa

PICTURE CREDITS

1–5: San Diego State College Department of Music; photos by San Diego State College Audio-Visual Sciences.

6–19, 21: Choreography by Bruce King; 20 Choreographed for Bruce King by Ruth St. Denis; 7, 9 photos by Hank Shulman; 10 photo by Sosenko; all other photos by Jack Mitchell.